Reading With My Eyes Open: Embracing the Critical and the Personal in Language Pedagogy

Gerdi Quist

]u[

ubiquity press
London

Published by
Ubiquity Press Ltd.
Gordon House
29 Gordon Square
London WC1H 0PP
www.ubiquitypress.com

Text © Gerdi Quist 2013

First published 2013

Cover Illustration: *After These Sheets* by Kimbal Quist Bumstead
Printed in the UK by Lightning Source Ltd.

ISBN (hardback): 978-1-909188-21-1
ISBN (EPUB): 978-1-909188-22-8
ISBN (PDF): 978-1-909188-23-5

DOI: http://dx.doi.org/10.5334/baj

Suggested citation:
Quist, G 2013 *Reading With My Eyes Open: Embracing the Critical and the
Personal in Language Pedagogy*. London: Ubiquity Press. DOI: http://
dx.doi.org/10.5334/baj

To read the online open access version of this
book, either visit http://dx.doi.org/10.5334/baj
or scan this QR code with your mobile device:

In memory of my father

Contents

Acknowledgements

I owe my thanks to many people who in various ways have contributed to the making of this book. First of all I should like to thank the students who participated in this particular study and gave me kind permission to use their words. In addition my thanks are due to the students who I have taught since, because their engagement helps me to continue to learn and develop.

I am also very grateful to many of my colleagues and friends for their encouragement and insightful comments. In particular I would like to thank Cathie Wallace, John O'Regan, Alison Phipps and Theo Hermans for reading earlier versions of the study and providing in-depth and detailed feedback, and Jane Fenoulhet, Cristina Ros i Solé and John Took for reading the manuscript. Their sharp observations and critique greatly contributed to the final version of this book.

I am especially grateful to Kimbal Bumstead for granting me permission to use one of his art pieces for the cover. His work based on personal relations, intimacy, communication, responsibility, and tracing journeys chimes with the themes in this book.

Finally a very special thanks is due to my two sons Kim and Remi for continuing to inspire me with their own life journeys, and most of all to my husband Chris for providing me with time, space and all kinds of practical and moral support. Without their encouragement and love this book would not have been written.

Introduction

This book is based on a classroom study exploring a particular intercultural approach to language teaching at university aiming to develop students into critical intercultural language users. I call my approach the 'cultuurtekst' - text as culture – approach, a term which I have borrowed from the Dutch literary critic, Maaike Meijer (1986). I had conceived of this approach as a result of reflections on my previous teaching, students' engagements and the newly developing theoretical area of intercultural communication in language and culture pedagogy.

In this book I am mapping the territory of language teaching at university and coining new concepts on the way. As the study took me over 10 years to complete – with various interruptions along the way, it represents a professional journey as a lecturer of Dutch at one of Britain's traditional universities at a time when ideas about language and culture pedagogy were developing fast. This has not been an easy professional journey; the pedagogy which I was developing at times met with resistance among the students and ran counter to language teaching approaches employed by colleagues at the institution where I worked. Moreover the data I collected, consisting of transcripts of my classes in which we discussed a particular text and interviews with students, were marred by ambiguities and if anything, seemed to point to a failure of my approach.

My initial conclusion therefore was that intercultural communication is infinitely more complex than a 'cultuurtekst' approach, or perhaps any other particular method of language teaching, can effect. Secondly, that attempting to develop students' critical awareness and language competence would need an even clearer conceptualisation coupled with a more considered pedagogical approach.

Some years later – and this is where conducting this study over a longer period of time than initially anticipated has produced unexpected benefits - I looked at the data again. This time I looked at the data from an ethnographic perspective, and not with the idea in mind of how 'successful' the approach had been. Instead, I focused on what happened in the classroom, how the students engaged with the text and one another and what the significant dialogic moments in class had been. Something interesting emerged. In the earlier interpretation I had seen students' interpretations of the text based on personal experience as a weakness; students had failed to analyse the text using the language of analysis based on concepts of culture and representation. Instead, it emerged that it was precisely the moments where students brought their personal experience and interpretation to bear upon the text that the most dialogic and intercultural moments occurred. These were the moments when students applied their 'self' to the text, where they tried to respond to the text and explain it to others - the moments when students were 'struggling for meaning'. As a result, I coined the phrase 'being a text ethnographer' to account for the way that students can engage critically and reflexively with a text from an 'inside' as well as an 'outside' perspective.

The study itself and the development of my approach was born out of dissatisfaction with existing instrumental approaches in language teaching which were – and indeed still are - prevalent in existing language materials and in many discourses surrounding language learning in general and in the field of Dutch language teaching in particular. Yet, I worked in a context - that of a Modern Language Degree at one of Britain's traditional universities, where to a large extent traditional discourses about language learning were dominant. As a result there was a general assumption at the institution where I worked, that language teaching was synonymous with the grammar-translation approach, and language classes were strictly separated from the 'content' classes addressing 'culture', which was generally conceptualised as 'literature', or – occasionally - as 'film'. The generally accepted aim of language learning was, and in some cases may still be, that of reaching 'near-native speaker' competence.

The tensions and conflicting pulls between these almost opposing forces and discourses within language learning form the background to this study. In chapter 1 I argue that neither paradigm in language education, i.e. the 'traditional' liberal humanist on the one hand and the instrumentalist on the other, can provide a satisfactory framework for language teaching in the context of a Modern Languages degree; a context, in which students are prepared linguistically, culturally and personally for the complex lives in an era of mobilities. Whilst neither paradigm is sufficient in its own right, I argue that one of the aspects of the liberal humanist paradigm, which is worth rearticulating for language learning, is its focus on criticality and intellectual engagement. However, the notion of criticality provided by that paradigm, the idea of taking critical distance to gain objectivity, provides a limited view of criticality. I point to

Pennycook's (2001) notion of 'mapping discourses' as an alternative view on critique to be taken in the language classroom.

In chapter 2 I further discuss the conflicting perspectives on the concepts of culture and of language that are often assumed in language learning at university. In discussing the relationship between these two I point to the dilemma language teachers face when wishing to emphasise complexity and transnational perspectives, whilst at the same time being charged with looking at the particularities of the language and culture being studied. I conceived of the latter as 'national articulations' in globalised discourses.

Chapter 3 focuses on the notion of intercultural communication and discusses three different approaches in language education: those of Kramsch, Byram and Guilherme. In discussing these approaches in relation to the framework of criticality and complexity set out earlier, I set out where and how I build on particular aspects within each of these approaches, including Blommaert's argument for 'boundary crossing' in intercultural communication. Following Phipps and Gonzalez's (2004) view on 'being intercultural', I explain how the notion of 'cultuurtekst' provides a way of being intercultural and being ethnographic when reading texts.

Chapter 4 forms a bridge between the theoretical chapters and the discussion of the data. Here I set out the context of my study, the conceptual framework of my 'cultuurtekst' approach based on a pedagogy of heteroglossia and multiple discourses, the syllabus of the fourth year language class in which I adopted this approach, and the methodology of my study.

Chapter 5 looks at the data from two lessons out of the yearlong language course. In these lessons we discussed a particular text from *Men's Health*, following the framework for analysis which I created based on the idea of 'cultuurtekst'. During the first lesson, we discussed the text at a 'textual' or 'product' level, looking at content and argumentation structures following a liberal humanist perspective of critique. During the second class we discussed the text at a 'cultuurtekst' level, creating a dialogic space in which the students started to engage in 'mapping discourses'. In looking at what different ways of reading the two perspectives on text yielded, it emerged that these two levels of text analysis are not easily separated. Even when looking at text at a product level, students 'went beyond' the text and engaged in critiquing the text for its ideological positioning. Equally, looking at the text as 'cultuurtekst' at times became confused with critiquing the text from the liberal humanist perspective, as not constituting a 'good argument'. The second lesson did, however, bring about much richer dialogic moments where students took on occasion an intercultural stance in engaging with the ideas in the text and with one another. The significant findings in these data were particularly how students brought their own experiences and previous knowledge to bear upon the text.

In chapter 6, the concluding chapter, I discuss the general findings of my study and I include interview data to see what approaches to text students had taken and to what extent they had used critical perspectives. I focus on two students in this chapter: Claire, who engaged readily with my 'cultuurtekst' approach and Sarah, who resisted it throughout the year. Whilst it might have been tempting to classify Claire as the 'successful' language learner, as she was reading 'with her eyes very open', as she said in one of her interviews, it was in fact Sarah who made the biggest transformation as a learner, as she had to adapt her view of communication and language as a whole. She also provided me with insights into how prior views of communication that students hold affect their learning in class. Moreover, the interviews also showed that the rich moments and understanding of discursive mapping which had occurred during the class, were not necessarily transferred in their reflections on the course as a whole.

In this final chapter I also examine the tensions brought about by working with conflicting views of text, criticality and education embodied in a pedagogy which aims to emphasise cultural complexity on the one hand and cultural particularities, through the notion of 'Dutch articulations', on the other. I conclude that these seeming incompatibilities are part of the every day realities of students anyway and I argue for positively embracing these tensions. A greater level of explicitness about the theoretical assumptions underlying language and culture will provide students with the theoretical tools needed to reflect on these tensions. I further point to the importance of engagement with personal experience in the language class. I argue for pedagogies of engagement rather than the purely rational and analytical. These are pedagogies where students can explore their own relations and sense of belongings in our globalised, complex and cosmopolitan societies.

Whilst this study looks particularly at reading texts, it is set within the context of a general language class and my proposals for future pedagogies assume reading is embedded in the interrelated network of other activities that take place in class.

It is through the self-examination aspect of my study - looking critically at my own practice - that new theoretical understandings emerged. However uncomfortable these self-examinations are, this book is implicitly also an argument for a pedagogy which not only encourages the learner to engage in self-reflexive activities, but conversely for the teacher to do the same.

CHAPTER I

Tensions Between the Old and the New: the Influence of Educational Ideologies on Language Learning

Introduction

At the start of this study, in the late 1990's, language teaching at university seemed to be flourishing. Bailey stated in 1994 (p. 41) that language teaching at our universities is thriving because of the mushrooming of language courses at universities, mainly as an extra module available to students of different degree subjects at Language Centres and Institution Wide Language Programmes, and because of the increasing number of modern foreign language degrees where the curriculum displays a greater emphasis on language learning at the expense of literature.

Now, more than a decade later, the situation is very different. Instead, language learning is said to be in crisis. There has been a decline in recent years in the number of student applications for modern languages degree courses except for school leavers from non-state schools. The concern over these falling figures, together with concerns over the funding provision for Modern Languages prompted the Higher Education Funding Council for England to commission a review of language in Higher Education in 2009 to investigate the health of modern languages (Worton, 2009). Worton attributes the decline of students studying modern foreign languages in part to the government's decision to make languages optional for pupils after the age of fourteen (Worton, 2009: 2). But, there are other reasons. Phipps explains the preference for non-language degrees by the fact that students are exposed to a utilitarian framework that makes a direct link between their decisions about education and the shape of the labour market (2007: 4). Despite marketing attempts by universities and other stakeholders to convince potential students of the pragmatic value of studying modern languages, students are still 'voting with their feet', she says. In fact, it may be precisely the emphasis on gaining instrumental skills, which is counter-productive when it comes to considerations of employability. Canning (2009: 1, 2) argues that if university language departments keep on marketing themselves mainly in terms of providing the learner with language skills, employers will offer jobs to native speakers whose skills in that language are supreme, and in addition will have other skills than just linguistic ones. Canning makes a distinction between promoting languages as 'skill' and languages as 'discipline', the latter giving learners 'humanities type skills'. He further cites Brumfit's (2005) rationale for a modern languages degree as 'giving learners the linguistic tools to behave as critical beings in 'other' cultures'. For this intercultural understanding linguistic skills are not sufficient, but language graduates 'should possess in-depth cultural insights' (ibid. p.8). Phipps (2007: 35) also argues that the field of foreign languages has made a mistake in seeing languages in purely functionalist and employability terms rather than to embrace the insights of anthropological approaches to culture.

I add here my own voice of critique to the instrumental paradigm, and argue that both the humanities with its philosophical underpinning and focus on texts, as well as embracing anthropological insights to culture, can contribute to a language learning pedagogy for engaging as critical beings with 'other' cultures. Whilst I am not aiming to analyse the 'languages in crisis' situation, I do suggest that one of the problems with language study at university is located in the lack of status the subject has had and still has at university. I will turn to this below.

The Position of Language Teaching at University

When I started this study there was a large variety of pedagogies in language teaching provision in British universities, ranging from the traditional literary-based modern languages degree, modern languages degrees with an emphasis on Area Studies and non-linguistic degrees with language as an extra module, the latter usually provided through a Language Centre. Language teaching as part of a modern languages degree, whether provided by the departments themselves or by a Language Centre, took place as a separate educational activity with a different set of aims from the rest of the degree and carrying much less prestige. This lack of prestige was borne out particularly by staffing levels, terms of employment and hours allocated to language teaching within the curriculum as a whole. In 1992 Scott et. al. pointed already to the fact that the majority of language teachers were part-time and hourly-paid, and on temporary contracts. This situation does not seem to have changed. Teachers in Language Centres are still frequently on vulnerable contracts (Worton, 2009: 31). Whilst, in comparison with a decade ago, there is a tendency in departments to employ specialised language teachers, they are not part of the 'academic staff', and as Worton says (p.26), are seen to provide 'service teaching'. Moreover, in many departments the tradition still persists of (junior) lecturers with specialisms other than language and no specific qualification or experience in language teaching, teaching language classes in order to fulfil their share in the teaching load of the department. This illustrates the view that is still common at some institutions that language teaching can be carried out by any intelligent native speaker with some sensitivity towards the language. When this is seen against the situation for other subjects, the likelihood of appointing non-specialist staff to teach for instance a literature class, would be an extremely unlikely occurrence.

Whereas the curriculum for modern language degrees as a whole is changing – with the traditional literary degrees (although they still exist) giving way to contemporary cultural studies, including contemporary literature, film studies and Area Studies (Worton, 2009: 25), language teaching still remains separated from the rest of the degree in status and content. This separation is even starker now that instrumental approaches have been adopted.

Classical Liberalism Versus Instrumentalism

Until the shake-up of the Higher Education system in Britain, which started in the sixties with the expansion of Higher Education and which culminated in the early 1990s in the transformation of the former polytechnics into universities, the educational aim at universities had been firmly rooted within a liberal philosophy of education. The key pillars of this philosophy are the pursuit of knowledge and rational autonomy; the development of the individual student towards independence of mind applied within the confines of a body of knowledge established as 'truth' in order to advance the discipline. These classical Enlightenment ideals were emancipatory - both for the individual in his striving for betterment, and for society, although this emancipation served particularly the emerging middle classes in the 19th century where the discourse of rational argument and cultural discourse were developed in the coffee-houses in England as part of an oppositional stance to the absolutism of a hierarchical society (Eagleton, 1984: 9-12).

The traditional liberal paradigm, with its notion of 'promoting the general powers of the mind' (Robbins (1963), quoted by Dearing, 1997: 71), has come under attack from several angles. One of these criticisms relates to the exclusivity of Higher Education towards certain groups in society. This is also an issue of concern addressed by Dearing (1997) in his report. This concern may now seem superfluous, since, the last 20 years or so, the university system has undergone a huge increase in the number of school leavers going to university. Whether this mass expansion was due to an instrumentalist neo-liberal response to the need for flexible labour markets or out of a liberal concern with equality is of course debatable. Nevertheless, the traditional Russell Group of universities still admit a proportional higher number of students from middle class backgrounds in comparison to the so called 'teaching universities'. Criticisms have also been directed at the philosophical underpinnings of the traditional liberal humanist paradigm. Its notion of emphasising individuality, rather than seeing individuals as being rooted in society, and its notion of pursuit of 'truth' is one which does not fit in a post-modern era. Jonathan (1995: 75-91) points out that modern liberalism has become free from the social baggage and the emancipatory idiom of its classical origins and argues for an examination of the ontological and ethical questions which are central to the development of consciousness and to the relation between the individual and the social. She points to the theoretical inadequacies of a paradigm which aims to develop maximal individual autonomy of each, for the eventual social benefit of all. The causal connection between these (individual autonomy and a socially better world) remain unexplained within liberalism, Jonathan says, and do not provide a theoretical position to reconcile the 'twin contemporary pulls of illegitimate value imposition and incoherent relativism'. She argues for reconstructing the theory of liberal education within a social theory; reconstructing the concept of autonomy as a socially located value. The key issue which Jonathan points out regarding the apparent conflict of the development of the individual within the social, is one that is also relevant for language teachers. A concern with the individual finds resonance in a new development within language teaching where pedagogies are shifting attention from a fixed authoritative curriculum to a focus on learners' identities and subjectivities (cf. Phipps, 2007; Fenhoulhet and Ros i Solé, 2010 and 2013; Quist, 2013).

As Apple (1990) points out, theories, policies and practices involved in education are inherently political in nature. Changes within the educational system thus rarely, if ever, come only from philosophical considerations, but are politically motivated. This was certainly the case in the 1980s when a huge paradigm shift occurred in education. At many universities education came to be seen in terms of a market philosophy: education as responding to economic needs. Education in the 21st century is now not solely described in terms of the development of the individual and rational autonomy. Instead, the need to fit in with the demands of a fast changing world and the importance of the global economy have started to define curricula. Dearing (1997) emphasised the need to extend the - what he saw as still relevant - liberal aim of 'training the power of the mind' to include the needs of the world at large.'

The paradigm shift from a liberal towards an instrumental view of education has been particularly pronounced within language teaching at universities. The rationale for language teaching has therefore changed from a view of increasing knowledge *about* a culture and developing one's critical and analytical ability, to one which is couched in a discourse which emulates such values as the need to regain a competitive edge, overcoming a shortage of skills, not losing business to competitors abroad and so on.

The impact of the instrumental philosophy on language teaching has been phenomenal, but not always in a beneficial way. In the next section I discuss the language teaching approaches at university within these two paradigms and evaluate their contribution to the educational aim of developing critical language users. I will look at their strengths and weaknesses and suggest that the implementation of communicative approaches - in their extreme form - have contributed to the lack of status of language teaching. I discuss the approaches in their most 'pure' form, although naturally one could expect that teachers 'borrow' from either paradigm.

The Liberal Tradition

Within the liberal tradition the aim of modern language teaching at university level was - and still is - both cultural and intellectual. Bailey (1994: 41) formulates it as instilling 'an appreciation of foreign literature and language through a scholarly analysis of their content and structure'. This is achieved through the study of 'esteemed' canonical literary texts of the past as well as a historical approach to linguistics.

Language teaching itself, within this tradition, has been modelled on the teaching of the 'dead languages', as the classics were seen as the highest expression of the liberal philosophy (Bailey, ibid.). The rationale for teaching language was to contribute to its two important aims of developing the cultural and intellectual capabilities and sensibilities of students. Whereas language learning has never been seen as an important intellectual activity in its own right (outside the subject of philology or linguistics), there was a recognised academic element in the learning of grammar. The cognitive powers of the students were challenged by exercises in sentence parsing and translation of de-contextualised sentences - even if this resulted in artificial language use - in order to apply the rules of logic and show a thorough understanding of the underlying grammatical intricacies. The emphasis was strongly on grammar and the development of written skills - an oral element to language teaching was either non-existent or incidental. This is because communication had no role to play in the traditional liberal humanistic language curriculum; its rationale for language teaching is the teaching of logical thinking skills and an 'objective' way of describing reality. Interestingly, as Cope and Kalantzis (1993: 3) point out, this traditional curriculum of prescriptive grammar has mistaken, even deceptive, pretensions to the timelessness of the classics. In ancient Greece and Rome the use of grammar was applied to the social context, forming an integral part of the teaching of dialectic or rhetoric. The classical language curriculum thus has a pragmatic communicative origin and a communicative function, which was never followed up on and which diametrically opposes the methodologies based on teaching a 'dead language'.

The second aim which informed the teaching of language was the access it provided to cultural products by exposing the student to 'good' language use and developing an aesthetic appreciation of language, through the study of a canonical body of literary work. This embodied the liberal humanist principle of language as striving for human perfection and beauty based on the Enlightenment ideas about the interpretation of the concept of culture and a wider epistemology. 'Culture' within this tradition encompasses elements of aesthetic and spiritual development (Williams, 1976, 1983: 90) which are enshrined in the valued canonical body of artistic - mainly literary - products of that society. This view pays homage to Matthew Arnold's (1869, 2006: 40) definition of culture, and its emancipatory idea of striving for betterment: 'culture is [.....] a study of perfection. It moves by the force, not merely or primarily of the scientific passion for pure knowledge, but also of the moral and social passion of doing good'. In addition, this epistemology contains within it a belief in the rational autonomous subject who can use language to control meaning. Language offers endless opportunities to describe a reality which is located outside language itself. There is a belief in the 'true' and 'real' self and the universality of language. I will discuss this further in chapter 2.

One will not find Arnold's view of culture and its moral good quoted in departmental aims and objectives at universities. Nevertheless, the tradition of literary degrees espouses the core of these values, which were up until recently widely accepted at many universities and still inform departmental courses, although this is more likely to be the case at pre-1992 Russell Group universities. At many of these institutions students studied a canonical body of works to 'sustain a moral criticism of the world' and to recognise the 'little knots of significance' in order to make sense of the world out there and to make 'distinctions of worth' (Inglis, 1992: 220). These liberal values are also reflected in the approach taken in studying canonical works, approached from a strong belief in the authority of the writer, rather than the poststructuralist emphasis on reader interpretation.

It follows that language teaching has a somewhat diminished role within this paradigm as far as language production is concerned. The aim of language teaching is to instill a sense of appreciation for the language and to recognise language as it functions and gives meaning to the 'individual' voice of the author. Language teaching is not geared around developing a language proficiency or communicative ability. Everyday language is of no academic interest. Only literary language and the voice of the author are worthy of study and so literature classes are generally taught in English and the discourse of literary criticism will take place in English rather than through the target language. Language learning and teaching achieve intellectual worth, as mentioned before, only through the study of grammar and translation, supplemented by précis and essay writing.

The traditional methodology has been heavily criticised and is seen as being thoroughly outdated, precisely because of its lack of placing language in relation to its immediate context or related to wider social and cultural forces which may influence language utterances. Students will have knowledge about the language, but will not be able to speak it. Cook (1989: 127, 128) points to the fact that the traditional approach to language learning does not take account of how meaning is created through a unified stretch of text. In short, grammar-translation approaches do not stand up to scrutiny within applied linguistic theories as the sole method of teaching language proficiency. Whilst this approach may be used at university language teaching at some of the traditional institutions, it will indeed not be used in language courses which teach at ab-initio level. Ab initio courses, and indeed increasingly language courses at all levels, generally are influenced by the instrumental paradigm.

The Instrumental Paradigm

Aims and Practice

At the other end of the spectrum to the traditional liberal language degrees are language courses which are informed by instrumental values. As with language provision in general, there is a rich variety in the practices in business and pragmatically oriented language classrooms, so any attempt to describe these is by nature doomed to be a gross generalization. Yet, there are certain characteristics which can be recognised as being fairly representative of language classes influenced by instrumental considerations. Because the aim of language classes of this kind is to provide students with the 'real-world' skills which are valuable to employers, language classes are aimed at developing a communicative competence. This would include an emphasis on speaking and interpersonal skills over writing because employers do not necessarily expect graduates to have written competence in the foreign language: "...they want people who can have everyday conversations and state of the art conversations - in other words they know the French for computer or keyboard" (quoted in Scott et. al., 1992: 18). These instrumental approaches, which at the time of starting this study may have been haphazard, have become systematically part of language teaching at universities, since the Common European Framework (CEF, 2001) has been published.

The CEF is a guideline document and does not suggest particular teaching methodologies, but instead provides an extremely detailed taxonomy of the competences, skills and knowledge that learners should possess at certain levels of study. The general aims and principles which are formulated emphasise both the functional aspect of language learning (learning to communicate in order to encourage collaboration, mobility and trade) as well as the moral aspect (respect and understanding for other cultures). However, certainly when judged by course books in Dutch which are taking account of the CEF guide-lines, the practice has developed on very instrumental lines, concentrating on transactional tasks such as buying train tickets, filling in a form, writing letters or covering conversational interests on an easy interpersonal level such as talk-ing about leisure pursuits and interests or cultural customs.

Clearly the purely instrumental view of language teaching does not fit in well with the liberal ideal of critical thinking; language as an expression of individ-ual thought and emotion. Inglis (1992: 221), for instance, takes a traditional lib-eral view when he bemoans the loss of a critical and aesthetic and value-based view towards language. He feels that 'to withdraw from the question of value making at the heart of language is [....] to hand language over to technicism and the skills-mongers whose very function is to demoralise education in the name of its orderly management.'

Within this light it is understandable that with the advent of communicative language teaching (CLT), the discipline came even more to be seen as a non-intellectual subject at the traditional departments. One can legitimately ques-tion whether the needs of employers should inform curricula in such a narrow way. Employers are not pedagogues and cannot be expected to know what the best educational route to a final aim of communicative competence is. As well as a reductive skills and information based approach to language learning at the expense of a critical approach to knowledge production, there is another problem with the instrumental approach.

It is absolutely the case that communication skills are of paramount impor-tance to our graduates. They will need to be able to function communicatively in a complex world with many different people, in many different situations, the vast majority of which will be defined by unpredictability, fluidity and changeability. Teaching standard rules and guidelines for these situations, as instrumentalist language teaching does, encourages a labelling of communica-tive partners into essentialised entities devoid or complex personal histories. But there is also a political point to make. As Fairclough said, in many profes-sional domains, power and manipulation are exercised through language in increasingly subtle and implicit ways (Fairclough, 1992: 3). Teaching set rules for communicative situations could, whether unwittingly or not, contribute to developing skills in students, which perpetuate this exercise in manipula-tion. I discuss this further in chapter 2, but it is worthwhile to note here that when offering texts from a commercial professional domain to students, the discourses of the legitimacy of self-enrichment and capitalism become natural-ised to such an extent that students might employ these uncritically themselves.

Furthermore, the uncritical submitting to employers' needs when draw-ing up syllabi may train future graduates to fit in with the economic needs of society, but it denies them the development of capabilities aimed at effecting changes in society themselves. As Hoggart (1995: 22) points to the political aspect of instrumentalism; it trains people like robots to serve the needs of industry which is 'one way of avoiding [...] 'looking seriously at injustice which runs through the educational system' and 'indicates mistrust [...] of mind and imagination'. Moreover, the focus on market forces is a safe political position: it 'provides a piece of firm dry land for many of today's politicians, barren though that land may be intellectually and imaginatively' (ibid.: 25).

Underlying Theories

Because of the instrumental aims, the immediate concerns in language classes within this paradigm are practical; developing skills and presenting learners with ready-made phrases or expressions for use in particular situations. The theoretical premises which underlie communicative language teaching (which generally informs instrumental approaches) are therefore often subsumed by practical concerns. Communicative approaches, with an emphasis on real communicative tasks, the use of authentic material in the syllabus and an emphasis on 'getting the message across', are based on pragmatic descriptions of language use derived from Hymes' notion of communicative competence (1972) and Speech Act theory (Austin, 1962).

These approaches generally start from a sociolinguistic description of how meaning is communicated in particular settings, situations and contexts and take account of a variety of parameters such as the intention to mean, the relationship between participants in the communicative act, the topic, the mode of communication and so forth. The view of language which is implicit in communicative syllabuses is thus a pragmatic one; language is seen in a functional goal-oriented sense. This contrasts with the classical liberal view which sees language on the one hand as a creative and aesthetic expression of individual thought and on the other hand as a system of formal rules. Since I started to develop my language course in the mid 1990s, communicative language teaching (CLT) has increasingly been aiming for not only developing Communicative Competence, but also for Intercultural Communicative Competence. However, these original pragmatic concerns remain the bedrock of CLT.

The two approaches I discussed here are thus almost diametrically opposed in their educational aims. The liberal tradition aims to develop autonomous critical thinking and an aesthetic appreciation whereas language learning in the instrumental or communicative approach aims at developing the competence to be able to communicate in work and social environments, including intercultural situations.

It follows then that the pedagogical theories underlying these views also differ, but in the case of the liberal tradition of language teaching, even though based on clear educational values, there is no theory of language learning which informs teaching methodology. As we have seen, the approach was based on the way that the classical languages were taught. In the instrumental approach to language learning, I want to suggest that the problem is reversed. There is no concern with personal or educational development in many instrumentally based language classes, as the main concern is to develop skills in the learner which are useful on the job market. The language teaching itself within these classes, on the other hand, is influenced by theories of language learning as an automatic process, which I briefly set out below.

Chomsky's research in mother tongue language acquisition in particular has influenced early communicative approaches in foreign language teaching: as language learning is an automatic process, the argument goes, the role of the teacher is to provide language input of the right level and tasks and situations through which the learners can practise and absorb the use of the foreign language.

Chomsky relates the idea of language acquisition specifically to the grammatical rules. However, in communicative language teaching it has become a common sense notion that the social rules of a language (the appropriateness of utterances in relation to the context in which they are expressed) are acquired along similar lines as these grammatical structures. These social rules constitute what Hymes calls 'communicative competence' (1972).

What is problematic about the view of an automatic acquisition of communicative competence, is that it might explain how certain functional phrases or vocabulary items are acquired, but it allows no role for the wider social and cultural influences which shape communication and discourses. It is possible that these are acquired automatically as well. Children certainly seem to have an uncanny ability to switch their 'social voice', without explicitly having been taught how one speaks within certain social or cultural groups. This ability to 'switch codes' is likely to have been 'picked up' from the various discourses they are exposed to in their environment, notably through television. The question for language teachers, however, is not so much whether language, which is saturated with social or cultural values, can be acquired automatically, but whether it should be.

If we want students to understand how language creates both explicit and implicit cultural and social meanings, then they need not internalise linguistic items automatically. On the contrary, they need to look at language consciously both to understand texts as a social and cultural construct, but also to be enabled to produce language utterances which are culturally and socially appropriate. This is an intellectual skill, which is not automatically achieved in a foreign language and would need to be addressed consciously.

In summary, the instrumental approach to language teaching, which views language particularly in terms of its pragmatic function is much more sophisticated than the liberal tradition in terms of learning to communicate in various settings and in terms of views on language learning. But it is lacking in other ways. Firstly, the emphasis on context as shaping language utterances tends to be interpreted only in terms of the immediate parameters that define a communicative situation and often this is interpreted in fairly reductive terms in the choice of settings, dialogues and texts. This only takes account of the immediate social context, and not the wider cultural influences and the larger social constructs, which Halliday (1989), using Malinowski (1923), defined as being of importance in language use. Secondly, while the emphasis is on intention to mean, it assumes that language use is always explicit in its functions and aims, it does not allow for the more implicit social and cultural values which are embedded in texts. I will discuss this further in chapter 2.

A Re-accentuation of Elements of the Liberal Approach

Whilst the instrumental approach to language teaching may be unsatisfactory in terms of thinking more critically about language use, the failure of the traditional liberal approach to develop communicative competence is also evident. Yet, even if the paradigm offers little towards a theory of learning, and towards creating social meaning, I do not want to dismiss the liberal tradition outright. The actual methodology of grammar and translation is not as reviled as it was during the heyday of communicative language teaching. There is increasingly a general recognition of the importance of explicit grammar teaching. Translation in particular, is also seen as a new area to increase textual and stylistic awareness, particularly from a cultural point of view. It can open up areas of cross-cultural study in examining how language mediates underlying cultural values through, for instance, its use of vocabulary and metaphor (Byram, 1997; Lantolf, 1997). Translation involves cultural negotiation. In addition, activities such as précis writing coupled with the inclusion of 'serious content' contribute to the intellectual development of the student and echoes Cummins' (1979) notion of the need to develop a cognitive academic language proficiency as well as basic interpersonal communicative skills. However, grammar and translation, even though they have a place in the language curriculum, cannot be the sole elements of language teaching.

The notions in the liberal paradigm which are worth exploring in greater depth for their possible potential in language teaching are located in three areas: a) intellectual stimulus and criticality; b) the idea of a language user speaking with an 'individual voice' to express her humanity (cf. Kramsch, 1993); and c) the notion of morality.

These elements combine easily and almost naturally in a language classroom because the content of the classes can be fluid and contain any topic from pragmatic transactions to intellectually challenging discussions on any cultural, social, political or other issue which interest the students. It is precisely the intellectual engagement which is one of the strengths of the liberal paradigm in education, and which has been almost completely lacking in instrumental approaches. This brings us to the second notion of 'expressing individual meaning'. It is through content-based discussions that an exchange of complex thought and cooperation can take place and that room can be given to students to express their unique experiences and thoughts. This will contribute to students' intellectual development as they may come to think about issues in a different light or come to realisations and ruminations, to experience perhaps the 'life-changing conversations' (Attinasi and Friedrich quoted by Kramsch, ibid. p. 29) taking place through the medium of the foreign language. However, the notion of expressing individual meaning needs to be problematised, which I will do in the next chapter.

The third notion of morality in the classical liberal paradigm can be easily translated to a modern context for language teaching through its emphasis on the emancipatory role of education and its view of a morally and socially better world. At the time that I collected the data for this study, this notion was embedded in the concept of language teaching for 'European citizenship' (Byram, Zarate, Neuner, 1997). This requires, as Byram said, more than mainly pragmatic and functional language teaching, but is rooted in a more comprehensive concept of living together. In terms of language teaching this meant emphasising attitudes of mutual tolerance and a readiness to exchange views. This idea has been developed by, amongst others, Starkey whose pedagogy of political education and human rights awareness through foreign language teaching aims for 'the development of democracy and active citizenship' (Starkey, 1999: 156). Pedagogies taking such an explicit citizenship approach tend to focus on content as knowledge in the language class. Recent developments in this area tend to move away from the original national focus of citizenship education and offer cosmopolitan perspectives (cf. Starkey, 2010), critical perspectives (cf. Guilherme, 2002) and transnational perspectives (cf. Risager, 2007). Whilst I believe the citizenship and knowledge agenda in language pedagogy are very important, I focus in this book largely on a text analytical approach, which, though less knowledge focused, incidentally also assumes a broader cosmopolitan and transnational perspective, as I will set out in greater detail in chapters 3 and 4. In my own pedagogy, the moral element is less fore-grounded than in citizenship education, although it is present through critical discussions about texts in class, and through the idea of taking responsibility for the reader. The latter, to which I refer as 'addressivity' (cf. Bakhtin, 1996 (1986)) comes into play when students do writing tasks.

Whilst all three elements of the liberal humanist paradigm which I felt warranted re-articulation, are to some extent present in my own pedagogy, it was particularly the intellectual engagement and the critical element which I focused on in the pedagogy on which this book is based. This critical engagement is emphatically not present in the instrumentalist approach. Nevertheless, it was clear to me that the liberal humanist paradigm itself was unable to provide the theoretical framework for language teaching with a critical emphasis. Its notions of objectivity and language as neutral are counter to the idea of encouraging learners to see the complexity of language and culture. My interpretation of intellectual engagement was not so much the idea of providing interesting or challenging articles in the classroom (although that too was important), but my main objective was primarily for students to engage with texts in a critical manner. My aim was for students to become critical intercultural language users. Whilst my starting point was the critical perspective taken in the liberal humanist paradigm, I also wanted students to engage with other critical perspectives. This, however, brings with it the problem of incommensurability.

Problematising Intellectual Engagement

The concept of criticality needs some explanation. I do not refer here to 'criticising' in the sense of disagreeing with or objecting to something, although that could of course be part of it. I am following Pennycook (2001: 5) in describing three different approaches to criticality in relation to applied linguistics. The first approach that Pennycook identifies is what he refers to as critical thinking, associated with the liberal educational paradigm. This is also often referred to as 'taking critical distance' – the term already suggests there is an assumed objectivity in this perspective. This approach develops 'questioning skills' in the learner and involves bringing a 'more rigorous analysis to problem solving or textual understanding' (ibid:3). Critical thinking in this paradigm assumes certain universal 'rules' of thought, which are based on rationality, logic, evidence, precision and clarity. In my context of work, it was this perspective on criticality which was dominant at the time in which this study is set. As I explain further in chapter 4, it also used to be an element in my own teaching practice, in analysing texts partly in relation to argumentation structures, and emphasising cohesion and coherence and generally the need for clarity in students' own writing. It also formed a small part of the course I taught the year I collected the data for this study, and as I describe in relation to the empirical data in chapters 5 and 6, the incommensurability of these approaches led to a certain confusion amongst students.

The second approach of criticality that Pennycook refers to, is what he calls the modernist emancipatory position. This approach is associated with the neo Marxist tradition and is based on Critical Theory. This approach sees an engagement with political critiques and social relation as the most important aspect of critical work. It aims to work towards social transformation and to tackle social inequality and injustice. In language teaching this approach is taken on by the Critical Language Awareness (CLA) movement (cf. Wallace, 2003; Fairclough, 1992; Fairclough and Wodak, 1996), where texts are analysed for the way they construct ideological positions legitimising domination and social and economic inequality. Whilst my own view was less about unmasking dominant power positions and ideologies, but more about discursive construction in general, I felt the modernist position to be a useful one for its focus on discursive constructions in texts. Also this critical paradigm offered available frameworks for text analysis, notably that of Wallace (2003), from which I borrowed for my own pedagogy.

The third approach to criticality is generally associated with the 'post' philosophies, such as feminism, poststructuralism and postcolonialism and queer theory. Pennycook refers to it as problematising practice, which consists of 'mapping discourses'. This position is also inherently political as it articulates a scepticism about truth claims made in texts (Pennycook, 2001: 42). In mapping discourses it asks questions about the social, cultural and historical locations of the speaker. It seeks a broader understanding of 'how multiple discourses may be at play at the same time' (Pennycook, 2001: 44). It is this approach to criticality which particularly underpins my own pedagogy, because of its concern with discourses in general, although the other two approaches to criticality, 'critical thinking' and critique of ideological power positions are also present. My aim was for students to be able to deconstruct the text positions and be able to respond to the 'truth claims' in a text rather than reading a text at face value as if it contained an 'existing truth'. This aspect of criticality also allows for culture to be brought into discussions around language, communication and texts as I conceive of discourses as the practice where language and culture are merging. I develop this idea further through the idea of 'cultuurtekst', which I describe in chapter 3.

I did initially conceive of these levels of criticality as pedagogical stepping stones. The first stone of 'critical thinking', I considered as a useful perspective on text to sharpen students' critical ability, to query and question what a text is about and whether its structure, presentation and argumentation will stand up to scrutiny. This, I felt was the first step towards the more sophisticated levels of critique which are embedded within the other two approaches: particularly the third level of critique, which involves the problematising of meaning and texts by acknowledging complexity.

At the time of data collection, I was aware that I applied theoretically incommensurable elements. The 'critical thinking' paradigm assumes a view of objectivity, which clashes with the 'problematising practice' of critique which asks questions, eschews simple straight forward answers and demands self reflection of the learner. Yet, I felt that this incommensurability reflects the complexity of the linguistic, social and cultural world we are introducing the learners to; this is after all fluid, messy and full of contradictions and inconsistencies that students need to deal with in their everyday life.

Conclusion

In this chapter I have traced the two paradigms which have influenced language teaching at universities in Britain. I have argued that neither of these provides the framework for language teaching that takes account of our complex society and complex needs of learners. Since this study took place, the instrumental paradigm has, as a response to the perceived crisis in language learning, grown still stronger and the liberal language classroom has become the 'dinosaur' of language learning. Clearly, instrumental aims are important, but even more important is, I feel, the developmental role of education. One of the key elements of the liberal paradigm, which is worth re-articulating, I argued, is that of the intellectual and critical aspect of language learning. However, I have also argued that the notion of criticality adhered to in the liberal paradigm itself with its assumption of objectivity, cannot solely provide the critical skills students need to engage with the complex social and cultural world. This engagement is more likely to be occasioned using a problematising approach of criticality towards texts by 'mapping' discourses; recognising the ways texts construct in culturally routinised ways the world and 'make sense of the reality to which it belongs' (O'Regan, 2006: 118).

Learning a foreign language is not just learning a useful skill; it has the potential to empower the students in enabling them to participate in a critical way in a foreign culture and to understand more about the nature and motives which lie behind communication. In order to address this question, I will look in the next chapter in greater detail at the relationship between language, meaning and culture and how these have impacted on language teaching

Some parts of this chapter were previously published in Quist, G. (2000) Language Teaching at University: A Clash of Cultures, *Language and Education* (14), 2.

CHAPTER 2

Culture Pedagogy: Some Theoretical Considerations

Introduction

In this chapter[1] I will consider some of the underlying issues of language and culture pedagogy. Whilst it is the basic tenet of this study that language and culture need to be addressed in an integrated manner in language teaching, I will nevertheless discuss language and culture separately as two interlinking pedagogic areas.

In the first part of this chapter I look at views of culture which underpin culture pedagogy as part of modern language degrees, and I describe some of the practices. I argue that teaching culture as part of language classes may be better served by a 'cultural studies' approach, rather than courses which emphasise the 'content' dimension and focus on imparting knowledge about the target language country as a coherent overview. The latter approach tends to be located in a national view of language and culture, whereas a cultural studies approach focuses on the processes and practices of culture and the construction of meaning and allows for a more complex idea of culture.

In the second part of this chapter I focus on views of language in relation to culture which have influenced language teaching approaches. In doing so I argue that a traditional structural view of language as stable still underpins some contemporary language courses, and that this view has taken on a common-sense understanding. I then describe social and cultural views of language, including those derived from linguistic relativity, critical language study and Hymes' notion of pragmatic language use.

I conclude the chapter by discussing how the two areas are interlinked in pedagogy.

Teaching Culture

Views of Culture

It is a 'truism' that the word 'culture' is problematic. Raymond Williams is purported to have said he wished he had never heard 'the damned word'. There are various common sense definitions of the word, and Williams's discussion on this is still a good place to start. As he points out, there are various overlapping categories of meaning: culture as a process, as a product and as a way of life of a particular community, but the meaning of the word shifts continuously (Williams, 1983 (1976). Stuart Hall (1997: 34-36) calls the word 'the new language of our time'; it is a catchword, used widely and frequently 'from politics to business, from life-style to media' to refer to the way people think, feel and behave. Frequently, the words 'social' and 'cultural' are used interchangeably, both in everyday use and in the literature on the subject. There are no clearly agreed definitions on what separates the social from the cultural, although the word social is more often used when we talk about structures and systems of society and relations between people or groups of people, whereas culture is often seen as encompassing anything social plus the wider notions of value and ideological systems.

In Williams' seminal book *Keywords* he lists the intricate and complex semantic transformations the term 'culture' has undergone since its early use in the 15th Century. In summary, modern usage of the term relates to three broad categories (1983 (1976): 90):

1) a general process of intellectual, spiritual and aesthetic development. This usage captures the idea of culture as a natural process of human development in a linear way, the ultimate of which resulted in the European 'civilization' and culture of the Enlightenment. Culture is then seen as a universal development of human history;

2) a particular way of life, whether of a people, a period, a group or humanity in general, in short, the anthropological view of culture. The use of the word 'culture' as 'a way of life' started in the 18th century with Herder (1782-1791) who attacked the Eurocentric view of culture encompassed in the first definition. This view contrasts with the first one, as it does not see culture as a universal process, but instead sees 'cultures' in the plural: 'the specific and variable cultures of different nations and periods but also of [...] social and economic groups within a nation' (Williams, 1983 (1976): 89). Whilst Herder is sometimes cited as being the fore-

runner of the one nation, one language view of culture, he was, according to Risager, not a National Romantic (Risager, 2006: 61). The view of culture, in terms of specific particularities associated with a particular group of people, often equated with nation or ethnicity is a dominant one in common parlance. Generally speaking, these particularities refer to behaviour, belief systems, history, language, customs, values, and so on. Within cultural anthropology itself, however, this static view of culture is seen as outdated (cf. Wright, 1998; Street, 1993; Hannerz, 1999).

3)   the works and practices of intellectual and aesthetic activities, such as music, literature, painting and sculpture, often referred to as Culture with a capital C or 'high' culture. In daily contemporary usage this view of culture now also includes products and practices from popular ('low') culture, such as film, tv and media. The use of the terms 'high' and 'low' indicate the value judgements attached to these. Hence, Eagleton represents the view of 'high' and 'low' culture as the 'culture wars' (Eagleton, 2000).

The latter definition, culture in the sense of aesthetic activities and products, is the view of culture which has been traditionally assumed in modern language degree programmes, at least in Britain. In the liberal humanist educational paradigm, culture was (and in certain institutions still is), mostly seen through the prism of the literary canon, the 'high' view of culture, which combines the aesthetic view with the hierarchical view of culture as civilisation. This concords with Matthew Arnold's (1889: 56) view of "the best knowledge and thought of the time". However, as I discussed in chapter 1, as a result of the expansion of university education in Britain and the political pressures towards instrumental aims of language learning, literature courses have been increasingly replaced by courses focusing on 'contemporary cultural studies', as Worton referred to it (2009), bringing about a change in how 'culture' is interpreted. 'Contemporary cultural studies' in Worton's report refers to courses which combine the 'high', and 'low' view of culture; literature as well as film studies. But in addition, culture is part of the curriculum in its anthropological form through 'Area Studies'. These courses tend to include the history, politics and social structures of the target country.

When it comes to the view of culture as anthropology, culture as a way of life, there is, however, a range of practice in courses taken as part of a modern language degree. At the humanities-based modern language degree programmes at the university where this study takes place, for instance, there is, for instance, no reference to the term Area Studies. Non-literature courses tend to be taught in academic disciplinary areas, such as history, film studies, and occasionally as linguistics or socio-linguistics. Increasingly courses are taught comparatively (e.g. comparing literature from different countries) or as interdisciplinary, thematic courses.

Language teaching remains strictly separate from the 'content' courses. In this book, my concern is not with separate content courses in the academic disciplines of literature or history, but with the cultural dimension of language teaching itself. For this reason I will not discuss Area Studies as an academic discipline. What I will discuss is culture pedagogy as it is practised in the language classroom.

I start with the knowledge dimension of culture pedagogy, which is often underpinned by the national dimension of culture.

Knowledge in Culture Pedagogy: Examples of Dutch Textbooks

With the knowledge dimension, I am referring to courses which are, even if implicitly, based on a view of culture pedagogy which used to be called *Landeskunde*. This term is now gradually disappearing, as Risager says, (Risager, 2007: 5) but the idea of providing an overview of knowledge of society, country and culture, an extension of the old, what Risager refers to as 'land-and-people tradition' (ibid: 27), still underpins many language courses in practice. The term *kennis van land en volk* (knowledge of land and people), is also in some cases still adhered to in the context of Dutch as a Second and as a Foreign Language. The term is gradually being replaced by *Nederland-en Vlaanderen-kunde* (knowledge about the Netherlands and Flanders), a clear indication of the national orientation of this approach to culture in language teaching. The traditional 'land-and-people' courses took a strong orientation towards typical national characteristics (ibid: 28). This emphasis has changed over the years, yet the discussion of the 'national typical', even of the national psyche, was until recently part of many language courses. I will discuss this below in relation to some Dutch textbooks which specifically address the culture dimension, either as an integrated language activity, in providing reading texts in Dutch, or as articles written in English to be used by teachers to address 'culture' in the curriculum as they see fit.

The knowledge element of culture pedagogy, particularly when it has a strong national focus, tends to be based on a view of culture in terms of its particularities. These courses are based on the idea of a defined culture or 'cultures' (Williams, 1983 (1976): 89) that can be clearly described as a cohesive unit, marked off from the cultures of other groups of people (Risager, 2006: 33). The most traditional of courses in this mode focus on the history and social structures of the target country, providing factual information on, for instance, the party political, judicial, educational and healthcare systems, economics, media and historical events. In other words, a course that describes rather than analyses. These courses tend to provide a simplified picture of society in order to create a coherent overview. An example of a book which is used (or perhaps more accurately now, used to be used, at universities abroad where Dutch is taught is *Nederland leren kennen* (Snoek, 2000, (1996)). This consists of chapters focusing on history, culture, recent social issues, economics and religion written in Dutch and functioning as reading texts in the language classroom. Another, well-respected, example is *The Netherlands in Perspective: The Dutch way of Organizing a Society and its Setting* (Shetter, 2002 (1997), an English language resource providing an in-depth historical, social and cultural 'coherent overview of the Dutch society in all its aspects' [my translation] (Beheydt, 2003). Themes running through the chapters emphasise supposed national characteristics, such as the consensual nature of Dutch society, the pragmatic approach of its citizens and institutions and, above all, the insatiable need to 'organise'.

The kind of *Landeskunde* pedagogy I referred to above, might seem a little outdated, with its broad overview and its references to national characteristics. However, the national paradigm is anything but outdated, at least in practice. Courses which aim to provide a cultural dimension are more often than not presented in a national framework, and directed towards 'the target country' and 'the target language'. Some of these courses can indeed by very informative, aiming for deeper understanding of the cultural and social complexities of the country under study. Recently, in the Netherlands a book was published with the intention to address 'culture' in a more complex context, acknowledging that Dutch national identity is fluid and apt to change as a result of globalisation and multiculturalism (Besamusca and Verheul, 2010). Their book, *Discovering the Dutch* is not primarily written for the educational market, but already it has become a key text for Dutch language and culture courses at universities in and outside the Netherlands. This book takes a more contemporary approach to 'Dutch culture' than some of its predecessors I mentioned above. Gone are the references to national characteristics of the Dutch. And there where Dutch characteristics such as pragmatism and tolerance are mentioned, this is always within the context of representations made 'through foreign eyes'. The approach to *Nederlandkunde* in this textbook is not only aimed at giving factual information, but many of the themes which are touched upon are based on research and theoretical considerations. A chapter on the multicultural society, for instance, offers a gentle critique of the 'us and them' approach adopted by the Dutch government, and sets the discussion in a complex historical context. The occasional references to the 'construction' of national identity, indicates that the idea of national identity is not necessarily taken as a given. The book clearly pushes the genre of *Nederlandkunde*, but it does not constitute a new paradigm as it remains located in a national context. This is not surprising, since the context of Dutch language and culture pedagogy, including the materials and textbooks available, is influenced by the guidelines of the European Council, which I will discuss later in the chapter. But, probably more significantly, Dutch language and culture teaching is influenced by the current political context in the Netherlands. As a response to the brand of government supporting multiculturalism, which the Netherlands pioneered in the late 1970s, the political climate has veered towards a strong national outlook, which demands cultural assimilation of immigrants. These political views also had an effect on the public discourses about 'Dutch culture' and history, and the media frequently discussed the need to reclaim the Dutch national identity. In 2006 a canon of the history of the Netherlands was commissioned by the government in order to address the fact that many native Dutch do not have a sense of their national identity and history. The canon, widely used in primary and secondary education, sets out the 'significant events in Dutch history' that all Dutch citizens should be aware of.

The national model in language learning in the Netherlands is strong. Language learning materials construct a nationality which constitute what Billig (1995) refers to as 'banal nationalism'; the representation of nationality through seemingly harmless symbols, such as the orange dress of football supporters, tulips on t-shirts, weather reports with national maps, and indeed language when it is seen as a political and national, rather than a social construct. Banal nationalism feels 'natural', because it is part of everyday life and customs.

The national outlook in culture pedagogy does then not only have its source in earlier romantic notions of nationality, but is also influenced by contemporary political contexts. Nor is it only a characteristic of Dutch foreign language and culture pedagogy. As Stougaard-Nielssen argued, the same national outlook takes place in course materials produced in Denmark (2010).

Critique of the Nationally-Based Knowledge Dimension

The national outlook is gradually being replaced, at least in theoretical discussions of language and culture pedagogy, by notions of transnationality (Risager, 2007,) super-diversity (Vertovec, 2009) and the idea of the Cosmopolitan Speaker (Ros i Solé, 2013).

The view of culture as complex, fluid, changing and indeterminate, is now dominating the pedagogical literature, as the world is becoming increasingly interconnected in an age of globalisation and mobility. Kramsch (2002: 276) refers to the invention of the personal computer as the watershed of changing views about culture. Before the 1970's culture meant national culture; 'what peoples had and held in common', whereas now she says referring to Geertz (2000) 'there is a scramble of differences in a field of connections.' As Brian Street (1993) said in an often quoted paper: culture is not a noun, but a verb. Culture is not a static object, but a dynamic process of meaning making. Holliday (2004: 132) quotes Hall to refer to the meaning making aspect of culture. 'A national culture is a discourse', Hall says, 'a way of constructing meanings which influences both our actions and our conceptions of ourselves.' (Hall, 1996: 613). These discourses of nationalities as 'imagined communities' (cf Anderson, 1983) are powerful and perpetuate the myth of national unity and national characteristics that many in a nation would share. Hannerz (1999:

393-407) argues that the seeming self-evidence of 'cultures' as entities existing 'side by side as neat packages, [as if] each of us identified with only one of them', is a time-worn anthropological concept. Most of us, he states, have more complex lives which entail various cross cultural allegiances.

Most of us come into contact on a daily basis, whether face-to-face or virtually, with people with different cultural or ethnic backgrounds, with people with different ideas. As a result we have all become global citizens, who have become part of 'a larger global tribe' as Appiah calls it, where intercultural encounters are no longer the exception but the norm for many. Appiah (2006) uses the term 'cosmopolitanism' to indicate the complexities and multifaceted nature of these daily intercultural experiences. This challenges the traditional notions of 'identity'. It challenges the notion of 'national identity' as consisting of a clearly described and delineated set of fixed characteristics shared by all within the borders of a nation-state. It also challenges the traditional notion of individual identity – the idea of individuals having a core and stable self, which remains unchanging over time.

But the notion of 'cosmopolitanism' does not assume that we all share a universal set of values. The interconnectivity of intercultural encounters that globalisation brought, is only one aspect of 'cosmopolitanism'. It does not preclude the perception of the particularities of ethnic, cultural or national identities.

Kumaravadivelu (2008) proposes that our complex cultural and subjective experiences are formed by at least 4 different 'realities' of which the global one is only one aspect. The others are formed of national, social and individual realities. It is important to note that none of these realities should be seen as fixed itself. Instead, each of these shape and reshape one another in a dynamic and constantly shifting relationship (p.157-158).

However, as I showed above, in language learning materials, the national outlook remains strong. Textbook writers and teachers of 'culture' do face a difficult choice. On the one hand teachers want to emphasise the complex social and cultural reality of 'the target culture'. On the other hand, teachers or textbook writers do not want to create a confusing message to students; after all, it would be hard to deny that there are cultural specifities. Moreover, students often want to know about what makes 'the' culture of the country or countries whose language they study different from their own. Besamusca stated that her students were disappointed when they found out that certain practices in the Netherlands were similar to those in their own country. Students had hoped the Netherlands to be more 'exotic' (2006). Similarly, Ros i Solé found in her study in learner identities that students often are attracted to the language they study because of a romanticised idea of the culture (Ros i Solé, Fenoulhet, 2013). This pull between the pedagogic desire for clarity, and the intellectual desire for acknowledging complexity, is part of what Risager (2007: 216) calls the national dilemma.

The content dimension of nationally oriented courses which focus on imparting information tends to centre on sociological and historical themes.

But there are two other areas which are also considered to be part of the cultural dimension of language teaching. Since Byram (1989) developed a model for intercultural communicative competence for what he used to call 'language-and-culture' teaching, the communication element has also become an integrated part of culture pedagogy. I will discuss this in greater detail in the next chapter. The other very significant element in culture pedagogy, apart from social, political and historical information, is the anthropological aspect of culture as everyday experienced life. This aspect has been included in the detailed taxonomy by the *Common European Framework of References for Languages* (2001).

The Common European Framework

The Common European Framework of References for Languages (CEFR for short) was commissioned by the Council of Europe and published in 2001. Even though it is to a large extent based on Byram's notion of intercultural communicative competence (see chapter 3), it cannot be completely attributed to him, as the CEFR is a consensus document between the various member states of the EU. In fact, as Risager points out, many of Byram's recommendations, particular those on intercultural competence, were not included in the final document (2007: 115). The CEFR provides guidelines for teaching, learning and assessment and does not suggest particular teaching methodologies. Instead, it consists of a taxonomy of the skills that learners should possess at certain levels of study. The CEFR arose as a consequence of the mobility schemes which were set up by the Council of Europe and which followed the removal of trade restrictions in the European market. These mobility programmes encouraged exchanges between staff in areas of governmental and non-governmental organizations in health, social care, education and other professional domains. To facilitate this movement, the CEFR was set up to encourage language learning, to provide parity in language provision across the EU to prepare people linguistically as well as mentally for the intercultural experiences that mobility would bring. It is an extremely comprehensive document which describes in detail what competences, skills and knowledges learners of a foreign language ought to possess at a particular level and in a particular domain.

The emphasis in the document is on language skills, although attention is also given to sociolinguistic aspects which stems from an instrumental rationale: one cannot be an effective 'intercultural' or 'cross-cultural communicator' without having at least a basic understanding of the social patterns and values in society as these are reflected in the way that people communicate. It relates to culture as communication. For this reason sociolinguistic information is provided to develop an awareness of prevailing communication strategies and customs (shaking hands when greeting, degrees of directness in expressing intent etc.). This is what Canale and Swain (1980: 30, 31) called 'sociolinguistic', 'strategic' and 'discourse' competence.

In addition to linguistic and sociolinguistic competences, there is a cultural dimension in the CEFR, which is referred to as 'intercultural awareness', although the emphasis is on language skills rather than on cultural aspects. An important aspect of this awareness is 'objective knowledge of the world' in respect of the country in which the language is spoken. This includes information about areas such as everyday living (e.g. food, hobbies, celebrations), living conditions (e.g. welfare arrangements), interpersonal relations (e.g. family structures, race relations, relations between genders), values, beliefs and attitudes, body language, social conventions (regarding, for instance, punctuality, gift giving, dress, and taboos), and finally ritual behaviour regarding, for instance, religious celebrations, birth and death, festivals and so on (CEFR, pp101-130).

Whilst the CEFR acknowledges that intercultural awareness should be seen in a wider sense than the context of the L1 and L2 cultures, it also emphasises that learners should be aware of 'how each community appears from the perspective of the other, often in the form of national stereotypes' (CEFR, p.103).

Even though the CEFR document does not make reference to its particular perspective on culture, the view which emerges from the CEFR seems to be partly based on a similar view of culture as underpinning *Landeskunde*: culture as knowledge. But its inclusion of attitudes and values with regards to a range of areas in daily life, suggests that Geertz's (1973) symbolic and interpretive view of culture as 'historically transmitted patterns of meaning [...] by means of which men communicate, perpetuate, and develop their knowledge about and attitudes toward life" (Geertz 1973: 89) may also have informed the CEFR.

The CEFR has undoubtedly advanced the notion of culture pedagogy as part of language teaching by introducing a considered list of the wider aspects of cultural knowledge that it considered students should possess. But in practice, at least in contemporary Dutch language courses (cf. *Contact*, 2010), the cultural dimension is limited to a few reading texts about topics such as the geographical situation of Flanders, or information about everyday habits such as customs and conventions regarding food or celebrations. The rest of the course is solidly based on a functional approach to language teaching; arguably a more considered inclusion of the cultural dimension of the CEFR would have been a step forward.

The focus on everyday life in the CEFR gives the potential to include an ethnographic element into language courses; a self-reflexive awareness of the political, cultural and social influences to which learners are subjected themselves in their everyday experiences and realities. However, this possibility is not emphasised and the CEFR's treatment of the cultural dimension of every day life is superficial. It does not encourage reflection beyond a comparing of everyday living practices with the learners' 'own' culture. A national perspective of culture is taken, which links the foreign language to an essentialised idea of 'the' target culture and does not allow for a critical understanding of the complexities of cultural realities such as power inequalities, differences in role or status and the 'lived experience' occasioned by the complex and fluid cultural identities and subjectivities of people. It tends to represent culture as homogenous and stable and reduces culture to facts and information. This can provide students with pragmatic and useful information, but it also brings with it the danger of reinforcing, or even creating, unchallenged stereotypical images.

Despite the influence it has on language teaching in Europe, Risager only mentions the CEFR in passing in her overview of language and culture pedagogy (2007: 143); 'its conception of the relationship between language and culture, and that between language teaching and culture teaching [in the CEFR], is unclear and without theoretical foundation', she states. Yet, the CEFR informs many language courses in Britain and seems a force to stay.

Whilst I think an element of knowledge about the target country needs to be addressed in language pedagogy, it should not present culture in a bounded, stable and one-dimensional way, as that will not provide the enabling of an intellectual critical development in the students. This brings us again to the issue of criticality.

Criticality and Culture: My Own Considerations

When I initially started to develop the Dutch language course on which this study is based in the mid 1990s, one of my prime motivations was to introduce an intellectual and critical element to the course. I discussed the motivations for this in the introduction. At the time, criticisms against a national approach had not yet arisen in the pedagogical literature, except as a rejection of the ultimate aim of language learning to emulate 'the native speaker'. The cultural content element of language teaching courses was largely limited to the national. My own discomfort with the national approach, honesty demands me to say, was at the time not theoretically motivated, but was the result of practical considerations. Wanting to introduce a critical element into language and culture teaching based on the practice of asking students to discuss intellectually stimulating topics, rather than only providing information, I found, unsurprisingly, that most topics relating to culture and society had international relevance. In discussing environmental issues, for instance, students would automatically introduce perspectives, angles and examples which were related to their own experiences, and to discourses with which they were familiarised through their own varied contexts of living. But rather than taking a comparative perspective, it soon appeared through these discussions that the discourses on which students, or the articles I presented them with, drew, were not limited to national situations or view points, but rather to global ones. The differences between perspectives were not informed by nationality, but by ideological and general worldviews which crossed borders.

So from starting out to address critical skills at the level of 'critical thinking', or questioning skills, which is located in a humanist educational perspective, I arrived through pragmatic considerations at, what Risager calls, the transnational perspective. I conceptualised this as 'global discourses', but since national political situations impact on global debates, I also conceived of the notion of 'national articulations' within these discourses. I will develop this idea further below.

What I had conceptualised at the time, was that culture, language and communication were infinitely more complex and fluid than most language and culture courses allowed, and that the criticality for which I aimed needed to go beyond the questioning skills of 'critical thinking'. The criticality that was needed to understand how meaning is created, which discourses come into being, why and how, and generally to understand the processes of meaning making, demanded a different ontological view of culture pedagogy.

An information-based approach would not suffice. A better option for the language and culture teacher would be to address culture in terms of its wider definition, and see cultural products and practices in relation to the meaning making processes that inform them. I found this in the Cultural Studies approach.

Cultural Studies: Context

The term cultural studies needs explaining as it is used in different ways in different contexts. In modern language degrees the term is often used to refer to academic subject courses with 'cultural content', such as literature, film studies or area studies. In language pedagogy literature the term has also been used. In his 1989 book Byram called the language and culture pedagogy for which he started to develop a theoretical basis 'Cultural Studies'. However, his use of the term is not the same as that of the Cultural Studies movement which I discuss below. Byram has since dropped the term, as his overriding concept came to be the 'Intercultural Speaker', which I discuss in chapter 3.

I use the term cultural studies here in line with Turner (1992: 9) to refer to an interdisciplinary area of study - rather than one particular approach - where various concerns and methods converge which have 'enabled us to understand phenomena and relationships that were not accessible through existing disciplines'. Its interest encompasses a very broad field of contemporary cultural practices, products and processes, although its main focus tends to be on 'popular' culture, as it rejects the notion of the 'canon'. Whereas a *Landeskunde* approach focuses on providing information and knowledge, a cultural studies approach allows students to engage with texts, to 'discover' information about cultural practices, values or processes through reading and interpreting texts.

In chapters 3 and 4 I set out my particular take on how to include a cultural studies approach in a language class, but below I provide a short overview of some of the main ideas and concepts associated with cultural studies as an approach to culture pedagogy.

Overview of Ideas of Cultural Studies in Culture Pedagogy

Cultural Studies developed initially in Britain. The Centre for Contemporary Cultural Study (CCCS), the first of its kind, was established in 1964 at the University of Birmingham. The birth of cultural studies marked a movement which took a very different view of culture than the traditional one, which is based on the literary canon, and regarded culture as a socially informed construct rather than purely the expression of an individual great mind. The distinction between high and low culture became irrelevant. Raymond Williams, generally considered to be the godfather of this movement, has been seminal in seeing culture as a process as well as 'concrete lived experience', and in analysing cultural products in relation to the institutions and social structures which produced them (Williams, 1961).

British Cultural Studies changed the way that people think about, study and teach culture, but as the approach developed beyond Britain, different interpretations underpinned by different theories, emerged. Much of British Cultural Studies was initially informed by a Marxist agenda, centring around issues such as power relations, particularly those determined by social class. Later academics, such as Stuart Hall extended the notion of inequality in society to incorporate areas of ethnicity and gender. An important moment in cultural studies was the adoption of Gramsci's (1971) notion of 'hegemony', which views the cultural domination of a particular group as being achieved through persuasion or consent. Submission to the dominant ideas is then partly a consensual undertaking. People submit to dominant views because these views have developed a taken-for-granted perspective. Power is then exercised not so much by a dominant group or ruling class imposing its will on other groups or people, but instead power is the legitimisation of certain ideas in becoming the norm. As Van Dijk (1993) states, we speak of hegemony when subtle forms of 'dominance' seem to be so persistent that it seems natural and it is accepted that those that are dominated act in the interest of the powerful. Behind this principle of hegemony, as Wallace points out (2003: 30), is the view that people in general are not aware of the operation of power, especially as embedded in language. The idea that language practices and conventions are invested with power relations of which people are unaware, is also the focus of a strand of language pedagogy, Critical Language Awareness, which I will discuss later on in this chapter.

The issues in cultural studies are wide and varied but a consensus concerns the extent to which, and the processes through which, cultural meanings are made and accepted, and are imposed upon or resisted by us. The central questions are therefore to do with ideology and power. The notion of ideology which is used in cultural studies is a complex one. The concept of 'ideology' is often traced back to a Marxist view which pertains to ideas of economic and cultural domination of the ruling class over the working class. As Wetherell (2001: 286) says, 'Marxist work on ideology was concerned with testing ideas and statements for their truth value, or their accordance with reality'. However, this early view of ideology has become superseded in cultural studies by other views which are based on notions of reality which are more complex and subtle.

Stuart Hall (1983) uses the term 'ideology' to refer to a framework of ideas and concepts to make sense of the world. This view of ideology as a belief system is the one which is used most frequently in the 'common sense' understanding of the term. The notion of 'ideas' as encompassing a belief system is, I think, given more subtlety through the concept of 'discourses' as used by Foucault, which explains how ways of thinking about a particular topic or slice of the cultural or social world can become so dominant that it 'infiltrates' people's mind and takes on the aura of 'truth'.

What thus becomes relevant for study is not just what products or practices are part of a particular way of life, but rather the meanings attributed to them. Quite how we interpret cultural products and practices, whether we see them as forms of self-expression or socially enforced meanings, as acts of resistance or incorporation, depends on the theoretical paradigm and underlying epistemology from which we approach the texts we study.

Interpreting texts then, is not just a matter of seeing how meaning is encoded, but it is a process of *constructing* the meaning of signs which must take account of the wider context in which the texts are produced and in which they are read and received, or how they are 'articulated' (Stuart Hall, 1985). Meaning is thus not fixed, as different meanings can be ascribed dependent on the position from which we approach the sign. Different people, in different contexts, with different ideological backgrounds and different individual histories, will interpret texts in different ways. The importance of looking at signs not merely from the viewpoint of text production but also of text reception is central to many contemporary cultural studies practices. One of the key issues in this respect is the notion of intertextuality. As Maaike Meijer (1996) argues, this goes beyond traceable references to other texts and should be interpreted in its widest sense as the whole of the social and cultural climate and conventions. The reader constructs the meaning of the texts through his/her knowledge of and experience with other texts and a whole network of conventions and discourses. In this way a text becomes what Meijer calls a 'cultuurtekst', a network of accepted ways of talking about a particular theme. Seeing a text as 'cultuurtekst' necessitates looking at the cultural and social environment in which the text is produced. The intertexts also provide a wider context through the other cultural phenomena and practices to which the text refers and the discourses on which it draws. Intertexts provide the cohesive structure through which text and context can be studied in relation to one another.

Culture in Cultural Studies is not an aesthetic view of culture, but an anthropological one. This, as Risager (2006: 49) says, is an extension of Geertz' interpretative view of culture as a system of meanings. Whereas for Geertz, she explains, an already existing meaning needs to be 'unearthed' from texts or practices, in a Cultural Studies approach the emphasis is on the creation, recreation and the attribution of meaning as part of a process of people in interaction or 'dialogue'. This, as well as the notion of 'cultuurtekst' are key aspects in my own pedagogy which I will discuss further in chapters 3 and 4.

Language in Relation to Culture

Orientations Towards Language

In this section of this chapter I want to address some of the theoretical positions from which language is seen in relation to culture and how these theories have been reflected in language teaching. Looking at this relationship assumes that there is an intrinsic link between language and culture. This view of an automatic link between language and culture needs to be problematised, and I will do so at the end of this chapter. Indeed, this link is now almost commonly accepted in the theoretical literature on language and culture pedagogy, even if, in practice, certainly in the case of Dutch language teaching, the inclusion of culture in course books is very haphazard, and the pedagogic activities frequently display a view of language as stable and autonomous.

I will first discuss this approach to language as being stable and autonomous. I discuss this here as part of a traditional approach to language learning, before looking at social and cultural views of language.

Traditional and Linguistic-Oriented Approaches

I will start by briefly backtracking to the traditional approach to language teaching in university language degrees. This pertained to an Arnoldian concept of culture (part of which survives in traditional universities) and incorporated two views of language concurrently. On the one hand, language had a central role to play in the conceptualisation of 'high' culture, so that language was valued for its historical, literary and aesthetic dimensions. On the other hand, language teaching was divorced from these ideals and instead emphasised the structural properties of language, in accordance with methodologies derived from teaching Latin (Cope and Kalantzis, 1993: 41-45).

As a result, language, as it was conceptualised in language teaching, became separate from its original anchoring in those traditional philological degrees. This split between an aesthetic and a formal view of language was occasioned, I believe, by the two conflicting trends of thought about language which were current at the time and which Vološinov[2] (1996 (1973): 53) describes as 'individualistic subjectivism', rooted in historical views and concerned with human consciousness, and 'abstract objectivism', which considers language as 'completely independent of individual creative acts, intentions or motives'. The first trend emphasises the individual and creative aspects of speech. Vossler, as quoted by Vološinov (ibid. p. 51), formulates it like this: 'linguistic thought is essentially poetic thought; linguistic truth is artistic truth, is meaningful beauty'. The link with an Arnoldian view of culture is easy to recognise. The second trend, known especially for its Saussurean interpretations, looks at language as a system, and, as Vološinov (ibid. pp. 67, 68) says, ignores the social function of language and fails to do justice to its changeable and adaptable nature.

These two opposing trends in linguistic thought remained separate within foreign language degree courses and offered a two-tier view of language within one and the same degree; on the one hand language as literature; on the other, language as grammar. Neither 'individual subjectivism', nor 'abstract objectivism' is easily married with the idea of a relationship between language and culture, if culture is interpreted as a meaning making process as part of the wider social environment and its value systems. Whilst a Saussurean view of language allows both for an individual as well as a social side of language, Saussure sees these two elements as separate. His view is complex, but I feel relevant to the language teacher as many of these concepts have taken on the aura of 'common-sense' assumptions (Kress, 1994: 170, 171), and have influenced views on foreign language teaching. Saussure's notion of *langue* as a system of forms represents the social aspect of language in the sense that the linguistic rules have been agreed upon by a speech community. *Parole* (the utterance) on the other hand, as the execution of speech, represents the individual choices the language user makes. In separating these two elements, Saussure (1973: 11) says we can at the same time 'separate 1) what is social from what is individual; and 2) what is essential from what is accessory and more or less accidental.' What is essential to Saussure is *langue*, the system passively internalised by the individual speaker. In this trend, as Vološinov (ibid. pp. 52-54) explains, 'the individual acquires the system of language completely ready-made'. There is no room for individual creativity, because the linguistic system is fixed. A Saussurean view has no time for social values as reflected in texts or utterances, and is not interested in language as constructing social reality. Structuralism sees language in terms of its formal properties and not its use. This approach remained *de rigueur* in language teaching until the 1960s when it was gradually replaced by methodologies informed by contextual and communicative concerns.

However, a Saussurean-based view of language has influenced language teaching in more than its view of grammatical correctness as a major criterion in teaching. Saussure's notion of language as a system of signs encoding meaning also continued to inform language teaching approaches. For Saussure, the *sign* consists of the *signifier* (the outward stimulus) and the *signified* (the mental construct which the signifier conjures up). The problem with applying these notions directly to language teaching lies in the two assumptions embedded in this conceptualisation of the signifier and signified. One assumption is that the relationship between signifier and signified is arbitrary, that there is no inherent link between form and meaning, but that this relationship is established by convention alone. The other assumption is that language as a system is stable, fixed and bounded; meaning is tied to form and exists independently of context (Kress, 1994: 171). In other words, language is seen as an autonomous system without any relationship to culture.

The point I would like to make – and to which Kress refers - is that if we do not think there is a motivated relation between words and meaning, then language users merely engage in recycling pre-existing meanings. Applying this notion to language teaching would lead to the conclusion that it is sufficient to teach these pre-existing meanings, whether as grammar, vocabulary or functional phrases, as has indeed been the case in functional approaches. Language teaching becomes then in effect a mere re-labelling, sticking a different label to the same concept. How can we then express individual meaning? Or, looking at it from the pedagogic perspective of reading, the consequence of this view is that the text entails a definite meaning which the reader needs to extract.

The implication of a Saussurean view for language teaching is that semantics is restricted to surface meaning and does not extend to underlying meanings, or using Halliday's term, its 'potential to mean' (cf Halliday, 1978). Much of language teaching reflects this stable view in the tendency to look at texts and use them as exercises in testing comprehension of the explicit meaning presented. Yet it is by looking at implied meanings and at what texts do *not* say, the significant absences in texts, the reading between the lines, that students can access the social and cultural as well as individual meanings, which are constructed in a text.

In short, the views of language, which were, and in some cases still are, in operation in traditional language degrees, i.e. on the one hand language as expression of individual and creative thought and on the other hand language as a system of formal rules, would not form a good basis from which to derive principles for language teaching. I will now turn to cultural and social views of language and argue that these do not necessarily negate the potential to express individual meaning.

Social and Cultural Views of Language

Hymes' Theory of Communicative Competence

Hymes' view of communicative competence (cf. 1967; 1972) brought an anthropological understanding to language, as it provides a model for analysing a communicative event in its socio-cultural context. His model indicates the various parameters that govern communication in terms of what to say, when, to whom and how to say it, and with what intention. This set of parameters in its pragmatic, goal-oriented and functional aspects has served as a guide for language teaching since the 1980s. It formed the basis of the functional approach to language teaching (cf Wilkinson, 1976), which was developed further in the Threshold Levels (Van Ek, 1991) of the Council of Europe, the precursor to the Common European Framework, which I discussed earlier in the chapter.

This approach focused on language functions in a few specific domains of language use such as shopping, travel, house and home, food and drink. Language teaching for communicative competence reduced Hymes' notion of communication to a limited and fixed set of situational topics, through which the learner would encounter and practice communicative acts such as giving a warning, inviting someone or asking for help, within set domains using set phrases. Its focus became a goal-oriented view of language where limited features of the situational context were the principal determinants of the linguistic choices to be made.

Reducing language teaching predominantly to the context of situation limits the learners' understanding of the role that our social and cultural environment has to play in our language use. Considering the context according to set parameters assumes that the rules for social communication used in one situation are the same in all situations of that kind. Like the Saussurean tradition, it assumes stability of meaning. It ignores the unpredictability of communicative events and the individual choices we might make in our utterances to respond to the context. It could be argued that learners would at least need to learn the conventions used in certain communicative settings, but even in situations governed largely by conventions we have the freedom to act in accordance with those conventions or not. As Kress (1994: 176) argues, even a decision to conform is an act of choice, and as such involves a 'new production of the meaning of conformity'.

However, it is not only the limited interpretation of Hymes' (1967; 1972) formulation of communicative competence view of language which is the problem. I believe that his model, whilst helping us to understand the very important role of the immediate context, or the context of situation, does not fully address the idea of the complexity of culture. Even though cultural conventions are addressed through the parameters of 'norm' (social rules) and 'genre' (arguably a social view of text), it does not question or consider the wider view of 'context of culture', which consists of wider societal influences and ideological forces and discourses (Halliday, 1985). Hymes did consider ideology in his later work, which I will refer to in the next chapter, but that work did not have an impact on language teaching.

The two notions of context come from the anthropologist Malinowski (1884-1942). Kramsch glosses Malinowski's idea of 'context of situation' as the 'immediate physical, spatial, temporal and social environment in which verbal exchange takes place' (1998: 126). Indeed, this is similar to Hymes' parameters governing communicative competence. But in order to understand meaning more fully, one also had to take account of the context of culture, Malinowski argued, which, as Kramsch quotes Malinowski, means taking account of 'tribal economics, social organisation, kinship patterns, fertility rites, seasonal rhythms, concepts of time and space' (ibid. p. 26). Whilst this relates to a traditional anthropological and static view of culture, the idea of context of culture can include a poststructuralist view of culture. The aim of achieving communicative competence in language learning has now been replaced by the notion of Intercultural Communicative Competence (Byram, 1997). I discuss this in chapter 3.

Sapir-Whorf

A strong culture-bound view which stems from a cultural anthropological perspective of language, is the Sapir-Whorf hypothesis, first formulated by Whorf in 1940 (Whorf, 1956) which holds that language and culture are completely interwoven. The Whorfian hypothesis posits that language determines the way we think; the possibilities and limitations of our language structure our thought, so people see the world differently because of their language. This view borrows from the romantic idea of culture that there is a direct link between a particular language and the particular culture where the language is spoken. In the literature of Dutch language teaching, this close relationship is often stated. In her monograph, aimed at teachers of Dutch as a second language, Van der Toorn-Schutte (1997: 9) suggests that the reason that foreign language learners of Dutch struggle with learning the language is because, not having grown up in the Netherlands, they perceive the world in a different way. Referring to etymology, as well as to pragmatics, she gives examples or words, expressions, linguistic as well as functional aspects of language, which are 'culturally determined'. Whilst van der Toorn-Schutte seems to hold on to a strong notion of the Whorfian hypothesis, Van Baalen (2003) and Van Kalsbeek (2003) who also both refer to Whorf, agree that language is culturally determined, although they see this in a weaker form; of language reflecting rather than determining culture. Nevertheless, they both hold on to the one language, one culture view. Van Kalsbeek particularly focuses on miscommunication to which she refers

as 'culture bumps', whereas Van Baalen uses Wierzbicka's cross-cultural semantics to encourage students to look at the 'culturally determined norms and values embedded in words' [my translation] (ibid. p. 107). Examples of these are
words such as *vriend* (friend), *tolerant*, and the supposedly untranslatable word
gezellig which refers to 'cosiness' as well as to 'having a good time in company'.

The problem with using the Sapir-Whorf hypothesis to inform pedagogy
and the assumption of a direct relationship between one particular language and one particular culture is that it does not acknowledge the complex social, linguistic and cultural realities of people's lives. Roger Andersen
(1988: 83) suggests that an influence of language on thought is indisputable.
I agree that language has an influence on our perception of the world. However, I see this relationship not as being between 'a' language and 'a' culture,
but rather in the way we construct our world through discourses which are
part of culture and which we encounter in our daily lives. I come back to this
later in this chapter.

Whilst Andersen (ibid. p. 88) also critiques linguistic relativity because it
ignores the fact that people have different experiences, both in social terms
and in their relation to the natural world, he adds a critical angle. These different experiences of people are not necessarily haphazard, he says, but based on
inequality, because social and material knowledge are not distributed equally.
For this reason, he suggests, issues of power relations need to come into the
equation when looking at questions of language and thought. Interpreted this
way, the issue becomes an ideological one and bears on similar concerns to
the questions asked by cultural studies - to what degree are we free to create
our own meaning, and can we resist the dominant 'taken-for-granted' interpretations of text? These questions reflect a critical approach to language and
culture, in critiquing how power is reproduced through language. I will discuss
this view of language below.

Critical Language Awareness

Critical Language Awaress (CLA) is not a view of language as such, but a pedagogic approach. I include it nevertheless in my discussion of social views of
language, because its critical approach, derived from influences such as Critical Linguistics (cf. Kress and Hodge, 1979), Critical Pedagogy (Freire, 1970),
and Critical Discourse Analysis (CDA) (cf. Fairclough, 1989; Fairclough and
Wodak, 1996) is part of a shift moving away from viewing language as autonomous, to a more "ideological' model with connections to media studies and a
more grounded understanding of social processes' (Pennycook, 2001: 9). Its
aim is emancipatory: to encourage social transformation through denaturalis-
ing ideologies that have become naturalised (ibid. p. 81). CDA studies focuses
particularly on unequal relations as produced through conversations, e.g. doc-

tor and patient interviews, such as who gets to speak about what and for how long (Fairclough, 1989: 43-47).

CLA, as the pedagogic wing of CDA, aims to promote an awareness in learners of how power relations and inequalities are produced and reproduced through language. There are various practices of CLA, although there is usually a strong focus on the use of text and reading (cf. Wallace, 2003). CLA pedagogies encourage students to look at the way that power is reflected in the use of particular conventions, what the conditions and motivations were of the producers of a given text and how texts positions readers or listeners in terms of their role or identity. It raises awareness of how through the use of language people can maintain or change power relationships.

This pedagogy was developed in Britain and is used in some English Language Teaching contexts, but does not seem to have made much impact on foreign language teaching. One reason for this might be that a pedagogy of critical language awareness does not fit in easily with the now dominant skills-based traditional approaches to foreign language teaching.

However, Critical Language Awareness approaches are also used to develop productive language skills, particularly writing. Romy Clark (1992: 134-137) argues that in the case of academic writing, for instance, students should be aware of the prevailing conventions within the academic community and should be able to apply them. But equally important is, as she states, a critical attitude towards these conventions; by challenging dominant practices, students can learn to produce alternative discourses and inscribe their own meaning.

This last point has potential for further development as a pedagogy in the foreign language classroom. It hinges on the dual aims of empowering the learner to recognise social meanings and to be able to employ these if needed, but also to allow for human agency to create individual articulations within established discourses. I describe elsewhere (Quist, 2013) how in an oral presentation, one of my students employed both formal conventions and consciously departed from these. She did so by adopting generally an informal tone, in order to ensure her 'audience', who she had imagined to consist of a range of different people representing hierarchical relations, felt all equally respected and included.

I borrow from CLA in my own pedagogy in the sense that I ask learners to look at how people in texts are positioned and represented. However, my pedagogy deviates from CLA in the sense that its primary aim is not to 'unmask power', but instead to recognize the complexities of discourses in texts. In doing so, I am more in line with O'Regan (2006) who critiques CDA (the theoretical precursor to CLA) for its 'unintended privileging of a final reading of the text'. O'Regan locates this predilection of CDA in its attachment to humanist values of reason and truth (2006: 21). His concern with criticality is to query the 'truth certainties' and the 'truth claims' in texts (ibid: 17). Whilst his motivation is political, in the sense that it is critiquing the naturalising of discourses of power inequalities, it is also moral in its concern with tolerance, and social justice. His take on criticality is not located in the ideology critique of 'emancipatory modernism' (Pennycook, 2001), but in the poststructuralist critique which Pennycook refers to as 'problematising practice', which finds its practical application in 'discursive mapping'. This brings us to a discursive view of language.

Discourse and Power

The term 'discourse' is central to many social sciences studies and takes on a range of meanings. Foucault offered a 'three dimensional' definition, as Kumaravadivelu (2007: 218) states. The first of these definitions relates to all language in use; i.e. all texts or utterances. The second one relates to 'specific formations of fields' such as the 'discourse of racism', or the 'discourse of feminism'. The third definition, Kumaravadivelu says, extends beyond language to the 'sociopolitical structures that create the conditions governing particular utterances or texts'. Discourse, then, relates to the entire conceptual world in which knowledge is produced and reproduced. From this perspective language is only one of the entities that construct discourse. Texts are generated by *discursive formations* or *discursive fields* of power and knowledge. These fields construct certain ways of understanding the world (within particular domains) which then take on the status of common sense assumptions. A discourse then provides a limited set of possibilities and structures of what can be said and how it can be said within certain domains.

The field of education may provide an example. Discourses prevalent when talking about Higher Education, for instance, are those located in the discursive field of liberal humanism or that of vocationalism. The former provides a way of thinking about education as well as a general shared understanding of society which prioritises the individual over the social, which focuses on the individual's development of rational and rigorous thinking, and which is seen as leading to a general improvement of a 'moral' society. We could also add that this constitutes an understanding of education from a largely western perspective. The discursive field of vocationalism on the other hand, constructs the value of education as helping students on the career ladder. To do so students do not need critical thinking, but practical skills. The implicit values relate to prosperity, ambition, business, booming economies and financial security rather than an individual's development of the 'mind'. These discourses are reflected in prospectuses of HE institutions.

However, it is also clear that prospectuses would not be written using only one of these discursive fields. As Kress points out (1985: 7, 8), discourses do not exist in isolation, but in larger systems of sometimes opposing and contradictory, or just different, discourses. As discourses tend to, what Kress calls, 'colonise' areas, i.e. to account for increasingly wider areas outside the initial domain, texts attempt to reconcile these 'contradictions, mismatches, disjunctions and discontinuities' to seamlessly interweave these different strands (ibid.:10). A university prospectus may therefore reflect both discourses of liberal humanism and vocationalism in a seamless fabric, interwoven with other strands such as those emphasising the discourse of 'community of the university', as well as those referring to comfort and pleasure. Indeed, I draw on a range of discourses in the field of education myself in this thesis, and not always explicitly so. It is difficult for an individual to think outside these *discursive formations* which determine to a large extent what we can think and say in particular domains.

Discourses then seem to be deterministic: to reduce the role of human agency and to limit the autonomous free-willed subject's ability to step outside these discourses. After all, according to Foucault, discourse produces knowledge and meaning. As Stuart Hall explains: 'physical things and actions exist, but they only take on meaning and become objects of knowledge within discourse' (Hall, in Wetherell et. al. 2001: 73). In other words, it would be difficult to see a particular situation or action from a different perspective or attach a different meaning to it, then the meaning which is, as it were, provided through discourse. Discourse then, guides how 'reality' is interpreted. Knowledge, as Hall (Hall, in Wetherell et. al. 2001: 75) explains, is 'always inextricably enmeshed in relations of power because it was always being applied to the regulation of social conduct in practice.' In this sense 'discourse' comes close to ideology, but I prefer the notion of discourse, like Foucault, to make it clear I reject the Marxist position which focuses mainly on class.

Instead of 'ideology', Foucault put forward the notion of 'regimes of truth', discursive formations which seem to become 'true' because 'knowledge, once applied to the real world has real effects, and in that sense at least, 'becomes true' (Hall, in Wetherell et. al. 2001: 76). Hall gives the example of single parenting. If everyone believes that single parenting inevitably leads to delinquency and crime, and single parents are being punished accordingly, 'this will have real consequences for both parents and children, and will become 'true' in terms of its real effects [...].'

However, I believe the individual is not trapped within discourses, because in living complex and mobile lives, we are exposed to a multitude of discourses on which we draw at any one time, and sometimes these are ambiguous, conflicting or overlapping. Moreover, as an educational approach, we can step outside a particular discourse, when engaging in what Pennycook (2001) calls 'discursive mapping' or 'problematising practice'. Through discursive mapping, students can become aware of how discourses operate in texts to produce this configuration of power and knowledge. This discursive mapping can consist of relating the text to one's own experiences, both in terms of other reading as well as in terms of one's own lived experience. Using this approach allows students to see culture not as a one to one relationship with language, but in relation to the cultural complexity of our contemporary globalised society.

Relationship Language and Culture: Generic and Differential

To conclude the discussion on the different views of how language relates to culture, I have argued there is a close relationship between language and culture; not as a direct link between a national language and a national culture, but rather through the ideas, values, knowledge and power structures of discursive formations which are expressed through language. Risager has theorised this distinction (2006: 2-5) as the *generic* and *differential* levels at which language and culture relate. Language and culture in the generic sense are 'phenomena shared by all humanity'; phenomena which are part of social life. In this sense, language and culture cannot be separated. At the differential level, on the other hand, we talk about different 'languages', whether national, e.g. Dutch, French, German, or language varieties. At the generic level, language and culture are inseparable, Risager argues; at the differential level, however, they can be seen as separate, as 'a' culture does not necessarily conform to 'a' language.

This duality helps to conceptualise the complexity of the language and culture relationship. Pedagogically, I believe, the language class should address both these levels. On the one hand, we should address the critical understanding of discursive formations in culture and society as reflected in and constructed through discourses – this is the generic level. On the other hand the main task of the modern language class is still to teach students to speak, write and understand 'a' language – in other words to teach, in my case, Dutch at the differential level. Whilst this would include teaching the standard variety of grammar, it should also include different language varieties, genres and voices. Teaching at the differential level does not necessarily mean teaching a stylised, standardised and sterile form of the language. But the complexity lies at the generic level, where I interpret the pedagogic activities to involve more awareness raising exercises and critiquing rather than actually teaching 'discourses', although, as I will discuss in chapter 4, part of my pedagogy is to get students to write for different purposes drawing on different discourses.

Discourses transcend the differential and national levels. In the contemporary world, many discourses are global, or at least extend across wide geographical areas. Examples are the discourses of 'terrorism', or 'environmentalism', or 'multiculturalism'. But, sometimes these discourses have a national accentuation. With this I mean that due to social or cultural histories and experiences of nations, as part of their nationhood, discourses may be 'articulated' differently in different places and contexts. One of these contexts is a national one. With this I do not suggest the existence of essentialised national discourse, but instead I argue there may be, in my case, a Dutch, articulation in texts, as one of the layers of meaning.

Dutch Articulation

Discourses reflect largely meaning making practices which cross borders and are not limited to particular nations. This is the generic level where language and culture relate. However, due to historical processes and structures in society, which are formed along national lines, such as governments and educational systems, globalised discourses may take on a national 'articulation'. This has nothing to do with how people behave and think as a group and what characteristics they have, but it relates to accentuations of discourses which are deemed to be more common or more acceptable in certain social and cultural environments, including national ones. Similar articulations could just as easily exist in other countries or cultural groups, but if these accentuations are validated through the media in one country and not, or less so, in another, maybe we can talk about a 'national' articulation. The idea of a 'Dutch articulation' then became part of my idea of 'cultuurtekst'; as a nationally articulated 'flavour' or 'taste' of a particular globalised discourse. I use this as one aspect of my approach to analysing texts in the classroom (see chapter 4).

An example of Dutch articulation, as I saw it, is found in the *Men's Health* text, which I used for the data collection lessons; it drew on a discourse of gender roles and domesticity which, in my view, would not have been acceptable in Britain, nor indeed now, 10 years later, in the Netherlands itself. This discourse, exaggerated as it was in places, was made acceptable through the way it was interwoven with other discourses into a 'seamless fabric' (cf. Kress, 1985).

I know, I am treading on dangerous ground, as, keen as I am to emphasise complexities of culture, the idea of a Dutch articulation could be perceived to be an essentialist view. However, I do not see this notion as directly linked to 'a' national culture, but merely as shifting tendencies. This articulation is in itself continuously changing, shifting and contested. In chapter 4 I describe my interpretation of the Dutch articulation of the text which I used for my classroom data.

Summary and Conclusion

Central to this chapter is the concept of 'culture'. I argued that knowledge based language courses with a national bias do not provide insight into the complexity of culture, although when taught at an academic level, it can develop a critical understanding of the target country in terms of querying information given and understanding changing events in relation to the wider global and cultural situation. A cultural studies approach to culture in language teaching allows for acknowledging the cultural complexity and indeterminacies of contemporary life.

I discussed various views of language and argued that the view of language as being stable and autonomous, as it is in the structuralist paradigm, leaves no role for cultural or social context. This view, whilst widely considered to be outdated in modern language teaching, still, unwittingly, underpins language courses.

Social views of language include the determinist Whorfian hypothesis, which is frequently quoted in the field of Dutch language teaching, to theorise the unrefuted relationship between language and culture. Whilst I believe there is indeed a strong relationship between the two, this is not at the level of 'a' particular language in relation to 'a' particular culture, which the Whorfian hypothesis supposes. Instead, this relationship is occurring at the generic level.

A more complex view of language and the social world underpins Critical Language Awareness approaches, which provide a critical stance and deepen learners' understanding of the processes of producing texts, and the ideological forces that have a bearing on this. CLA particularly focuses on how power is produced and reproduced through language. These approaches could be applied to modern language teaching, but the critical understanding, which is occasioned through CLA approaches, should be supplemented with an understanding of other cultural parameters, in addition to power.

Hymes' view of communicative competence provides such a view in considering a range of parameters, including time, place and social conventions. However, this view focuses primarily on the context of situation and does not allow enough space for the wider cultural ideas provided through the context of culture. Finally I argued that looking at language as discourse, and its meaning making potential, can help students to develop a deeper understanding of the complexities of the cultural world in which the language under study is spoken.

Risager's concepts of a generic and a differential level of language and culture help in considering how the notion of discourses can be conceptualised in relation to language teaching. I argued that both levels, the generic and the differential are part of language teaching, and the generic level avoids the narrow one-to-one relationship of the one language, one culture view.

Looking at language as discourse, Pennycook points us to pedagogies of 'mapping discourses' (2001), which helps to understand the multiplicity of discourses, how discourses cross borders, and develops students' critical awareness of how texts construct truth claims. Despite my focus on the global aspect of discourses, I also argued, that we cannot deny particular national 'accentuations', even if these articulations themselves need to be understood in the context of the complexity of culture in an age of mobility.

Finally, through discursive mapping students are invited to think about the relations and interrelations which are part of the process of communicating in different cultural situations and realities, and ultimately practise them.

It is this aspect of intercultural communication, which has been implicit in this chapter, which I will discuss explicitly in chapter 3.

Notes

[1] Some parts of this chapter were previously published in Quist, G. (2000) Culture in the University Language Curriculum. *Dutch Crossing* (24), 1.

[2] The book is widely believed to have been written by Mikhael Bakhtin, using Volosinov's name.

Being Intercultural Through Texts:
The Student as Text Ethnographer

Introduction

In the previous chapter I looked at views of the nature of language and the nature of culture, particularly as applied to the context of language education. In this chapter I focus on the intercultural aspect of language pedagogy and develop the idea of being intercultural through text. I argued in chapter 2 that the relationship between language and culture is very close on a generic level, but not at a differential level, i.e. there is not a direct and straightforward link between a particular language and a particular culture. At the generic level, language and culture come together through discourses. I use discourses in the way that Foucault uses these; discourses as discursive formations giving rise to certain routinised ways of talking and thinking about specific topics or areas of social life. I argued for an approach to language teaching which is akin to cultural studies, taking account of the notion that language is to a large extent a social construct which is influenced by its context of use. The complexity of the interrelationship between language and its context of use is reflected in discourses, voices and genres; language as 'styles for certain spheres of human communication' (Bakhtin, 1986: 64).

For that reason, I want to extend the notion of context as used in language teaching beyond that of merely situational and immediate concerns, to include a 'context of culture' (Kramsch, 1993), as the area where meaning is constructed. Context is then not just formed by the situation in which the communicative event takes place, but also by what the broader views, ideas, and taken-for-granted assumptions and meanings are in particular contexts of use.

Cultural studies as a discipline itself can be approached from at least two different angles, Turner (1992) says: a text-based or a context-based approach. With the former he refers to the study of texts from literature, film or popular media. With the latter he refers to Area Studies: courses which cover historical, social and political aspects. Arguably, the same applies to language teaching. I will refer to Kramsch's 1993 book, *Context and Culture in Language Teaching* and to Byram's notion of *Intercultural Communicative Competence* as the two dominant examples of respectively a text-based and a context-based approach, at the time when I started this study. Both Byram and Kramsch have slightly rearticulated their positions, but many of their basic tenets are still relevant, and indeed often referred to in the pedagogic literature.

Both approaches have taken language teaching out of the mere functional concerns of communicative language teaching and have advanced language and culture pedagogy. Both challenge the myth of 'the native speaker', and both use the model of the Intercultural Speaker. I build on both Kramsch's and Byram's approaches for my own pedagogy. However, I believe we need to further problematise the nature of intercultural communication, and acknowledge its complexity, particularly in multicultural and global societies, without denying the existence of cultural patterns.

To do so I will look at Blommaert who, although not a language pedagogue, puts forward a view of intercultural communication which can be usefully applied to the debates about language and culture pedagogy. I make use of Blommaert's insights and relate these to various emerging views in the last few years of a new conceptualisation of intercultural communication in language teaching. But, whilst intercultural communication and the inclusion of culture in the language curriculum is a much-debated issue at a theoretical level (cf Risager, 2007; Phipps and Guilherme, 2004; Starkey, 1999; Sercu, 2005; Fenoulhet and Ros i Solé, 2010, to name but a few) in practice, this is still haphazard in many course books, certainly in Dutch, and is even ignored in influential language exams.

My challenge then is to find a model of language teaching as part of a general language course that contributes to the development of the learner as a *critical intercultural language user*. In this chapter I build on the concepts discussed in the previous chapters which underpin such a pedagogy, and in chapters 5 and 6 I look at how students engaged with this pedagogy.

Intercultural Communication in Language Teaching

Ideas and Practices

The notion of a pedagogy of intercultural communication as part of language and culture teaching was not formally theorised until the 1990s. Michael Byram in Britain (c.f. *Teaching and Assessing Intercultural Communicative Competence*,

1997) and Claire Kramsch in the US (*Context and Culture in Language Teaching*, 1993) have been the main reference points in this area. In the last few years particularly, the idea of intercultural communication as the area where language and culture meet in the classroom, has gained momentum and different strands and views are being developed. My intention here is not to give an overview of these developments; Risager (2007) offers a comprehensive overview and discussion of this field. Here I will set out to what extent Kramsch and Byram, as well as others, have influenced my perspective on language and culture teaching and to what extent I deviate from them.

As I said earlier, I suggest that a cultural studies-oriented language and culture pedagogy can be approached from two different practical starting points: a text-based or a context-based approach. Kramsch uses the former, Byram the latter.

Both approaches rely on text as well as context in their pedagogy, but the differences lie in the main focus of the pedagogical tool; a text-based approach aims to develop an understanding of culture and language through analyzing texts, whereas a context-based approach focuses on the cultural situations in which language is used, as well as on a body of knowledge that is taught, discussed or 'discovered'. In a text-based approach the role of cultural knowledge is less fore grounded; knowledge is conceived of as the contextual knowledge needed in order to interpret the text. But knowledge is then also conceived of as meta-knowledge; knowledge of the interpretation process itself and the concepts needed to talk about the texts. Kramsch uses texts as the starting point of her pedagogy. Byram on the other hand, represents a socially oriented, especially an ethnographic, approach through making cultural knowledge an important part of his pedagogy, following on from the idea of Area Studies which I discussed in the previous chapter.

A Text-based Bakhtinian Approach: Kramsch

It may seem paradoxical to locate Kramsch in a text-based rather than a context-based pedagogy when her great contribution to language and culture pedagogy is her conceptualisation of context as a complex structure. But here I refer to the pedagogical tools which Kramsch uses, which involve looking at texts, in her case, specifically literary texts. This is not to say that she does not use other classroom activities: on the contrary, her follow up activities after reading a text could, for instance, include a role play trying to emulate the 'voices' in a text.

Kramsch's pedagogy has roots in the European liberal humanist philosophy of education, with a text-based analytical approach and concerns for developing the intellectual and critical ability of students. In contrast, Byram aligns himself more with instrumental and pragmatic goals of language and culture learning, as we will see later, although he takes a much less reductive approach than the strong instrumentalist paradigm which I criticised in chapter one.

Working in the American context, Kramsch criticises the instrumentally-oriented action pedagogy, rather than a reflection-oriented one. Its sole concern to get students to talk and write as well and as fluently as possible has, she argues, trivialised language teaching. In such a syllabus the teaching of culture has become a controversial issue, as the argument is that depth and breadth of thought belong to other subjects (1993: 4).

This instrumental approach is also very dominant in teaching Dutch as a foreign language, as evidenced by course books and the examination which is taken worldwide by adult learners of Dutch as a foreign language, *Certificaat Nederlands als Vreemde Taal* (CNaVT). As I set out in chapter 1, the instrumental approach is also becoming more dominant in language teaching at universities in Britain, particularly since language teaching in the context of language degrees is increasingly taught through special provision in places such as Language Centres. This means language classes are separated from the so-called 'content' classes which are perceived to be intellectually superior.

I align myself with Kramsch's educational aims. As I argued in chapter 1, although the main aim of the general language class is to be able to *use* the foreign language, there is a developmental and intellectual aspect to language learning, over and above learning a *skill.*

Kramsch's pedagogy of language learning provides the critical and intellectual demands in terms of students needing to reflect on the interrelationship between text and context. Her pedagogy focuses on the interaction between linguistics and social structures: teachers should not teach either form or meaning but the interaction between the two, she emphasises. Her approach to language and culture pedagogy was new in 1993, and still holds valuable insights. Kramsch's contribution, I feel, is that she provides a more fully conceptualised notion of context than that previously offered in the Threshold levels which saw context only in relation to set phrases tied to certain set situations which occur in typical everyday pragmatic exchanges of shopping, getting a coffee and so forth. But also, crucially, she considers a range of theoretical models from linguistics, ethnography of communication, and language philosophy to provide a view of context, not as a natural given, but as a social construct.

Context, she suggests, consists of linguistic, situational, cultural, interactional and intertextual dimensions. In describing context as being 'shaped by people in dialogue with one another in a variety of roles and statuses' (p. 67), she marries Hymes's model of communicative competence, Halliday's notions of context (1989), and Bakhtin's notion of dialogue. Context is then created by situations, including the classroom situation itself, previous 'cultural' knowledge, as well as the ongoing dialogue or interaction between people and their socio-cultural environment. Crucially, she adds the dimension of intertextual context; the relation a text has to other texts, assumptions, and expectations. The notion of intertext comprises not just the other texts, assumptions and expectations a 'text' may refer to, but also the assumptions, expectations and previous experiences of texts that readers themselves are imbued with.

Kramsch suggests that in an intercultural communicative event, the engagement between the language user's own cultural context and that of the cultural context of the interlocutor (or the text) creates a new or 'third culture' where the perceptions and knowledges of the interlocutors about their own and the 'other's' culture intermingle. This also happens, she suggests, in a classroom context, particularly in a multicultural one, where complex relationships take place between the students, the teacher, the foreign language, the 'target' culture and the culture of the learners themselves (ibid. p. 13). In this 'third culture' or 'third place' students can express their own meanings and discover their own identities in a foreign language without being bound by either their own, or the target speech community's identity (ibid. p. 256). It is a place where hybridity and plurality flourish. For my initial pedagogy, I interpreted the metaphor of 'third place' as a space for learning and dialoguing in the classroom, where a 'dialogue' can take place between students themselves, between students and the teacher and between students and the text under discussion. Reading the text becomes a 'dialogue' with the text, as the text will be rewritten, reinterpreted and re-accentuated several times during the classroom discussions. However, the notion of hybridity, which is encompassed in the idea of 'the third place', is one which is also problematic. Whilst the notion of the third space allows the classroom to be perceived as a place where cultures intermingle, meet and clash, and where students can become 'border crossers', it also assumes students identify strongly with their 'native culture', and that their intercultural encounters will be with people who identify strongly with 'the target culture'. Kramsch has now distanced herself from the idea of the 'third place', as being too static and not capturing the relations and operations between multilingual learners (2009: 200). For my own pedagogy, I interpreted the dialogic space in the classroom as 'being intercultural', which means, as Phipps and Gonzalez say, it is 'beyond the captivities of culture' (2004: 168), where students engage with language and culture in a process which Phipps and Gonzalez call 'languaging'.

For the purpose of this chapter I will remain with Kramsch's 1993 book, even though it does not encompass the idea of 'being intercultural' as the messy, indeterminate and fluid struggles with which her later work is concerned. Her pedagogy described in *Context and Culture in Language Teaching*, influenced my own approach, particularly since it is largely based on the use of texts. Her approach, partly rooted in the liberal paradigm, is geared to giving access to a range of speech communities, which then opens up areas for reflection and discussion and introduces the idea of multivoicedness in texts (1993: 27).

Kramsch's contribution to language and culture pedagogy, as I said earlier, has been inspiring because of the conceptualisation of context as a complex social construct. Moreover, she distances herself from a strong national paradigm in language teaching. She criticises the link made in many language textbooks by which any speaker of the language is automatically representative of any national (e.g. German) speech community. It is rarely acknowledged in language teaching, she says, that even if learners share a common native language, 'they partake of a multiplicity of 'cultures' (1993: 93).

Risager criticises Kramsch for not systematically analysing the relationship between linguistic practice (as cultural practice) and cultural context. Risager's criticism focuses particularly on Kramsch's radical social-constructivist position and the fact that Kramsch does not sufficiently distinguish between the relationship of language and culture at a *generic* or at a *differential* level (2007: 108). Risager and I (see my argument in chapter 2) agree with Kramsch that language and culture relate at a generic level; the cultural meanings and connotations of language utterances which are reflected and refracted by participants in contexts of use. But, Risager suggests, Kramsch is close to suggesting that language as text, and cultural context are identical. Risager suggests instead to make a distinction between the 'aspects of the context that are directly created via the linguistic interaction, e.g. the immediate social relations, and the aspects of the context that exist in advance as objective facts and that constitute the historically specific setting' (2007: 109). This reflects Risager's particular point of view regarding the relationship between language and culture as well as the inclusion of cultural knowledge in the curriculum.

My own criticism with regard to Kramsch's 1993 book is slightly different from Risager's. For Kramsch, cultural knowledge (which Risager refers to as 'objective facts that constitute the historically specific setting') relates to both the shared cultural knowledge in the context of production as well as in the context of reception. Kramsch does not see it as necessary that students need a coherent body of knowledge of the cultural context, i.e. the national context. Instead students will need to have the cultural knowledge needed to interpret the text at hand and to be able to relate the text to both the context of production as well as the context of reception in the target speech communities. I agree with Kramsch on this. I also like the fact she uses text in her pedagogy, as her concern, like my own, is with meaning making. However, the texts that Kramsch uses in the classroom tend to be from the literary genre only, whereas I provide another angle by including mass media texts which are rich in discursive constructions. The latter is not one of Kramsch's concerns. Her aim is not to critique power and knowledge constructions in text, and her focus tends to be at the differential level, with particular languages and particularities of culture, rather than with 'discursive formations'. Whilst I feel that the Bakhtinian text-based approach of Kramsch goes a long way in helping students to understand the complexity of communication and the complexity of context, it does not address the discourses and power as they are used in everyday language events.

A Social and Context-based Approach: Intercultural Communicative Competence

It is precisely the text-based approach that has attracted criticisms from other scholars in the field of language and culture teaching. Byram particularly takes issue with the text-based approach and its focus on literary texts. He positions himself against the literary tradition in language teaching, because it does not deal with the real every day world in the target language countries. This view of culture, as I discussed in chapter 2, is the anthropological one (cf. Byram, 1989). In this context-based approach the 'real world' is the starting point for the pedagogy, whether in terms of factual knowledge, or communicative events. Whilst Kramsch and Byram agree on the need for reflection on the 'other'; as well as the learner's 'own' culture, for Kramsch this reflection takes place through thinking and talking about texts, particularly in relation to how learners interpret the contexts of production and reception. For Byram this reflection takes place through focusing on and comparing information about 'the' culture, especially relating to everyday life. For Byram then, cultural *knowledge* is a very important part of the syllabus, whereas cultural knowledge for Kramsch is incidental; it is part and parcel of discussing the context of production. As mentioned above, for Kramsch it is not desirable that students learn a body of coherent cultural knowledge related to 'the' foreign or 'target' culture, whilst Byram feels there is a certain body of knowledge that students learning a foreign language need to possess.

Byram's work in theorising language and culture pedagogy became enormously influential in Europe as a whole. In fact, culture pedagogy, as Risager (2007: 92) points out, did not get under way until Byram's work in the 1980s. He formulated the notion of *Intercultural Communicative Competence* (ICC for short) as a model for language teaching and assessment of language learners which focuses on acquiring linguistic *as well as* socio-cultural knowledge and discourse competence (1997: 73). Byram builds on Van Ek's notion of communicative competence which is focused on language rather than culture. To understand people of other national groups, Byram notes, we cannot only depend on 'communicative competence'; learners also 'need to acquire the ability to comprehend cultural differences and cultural relativity' (1992: 165). Byram sees language and culture learning as clearly consisting of a language and a culture element, but these generally remain, unlike with Kramsch, separate.

One of the important new aspects of Intercultural Communicative Competence is that learners not only need to learn *about* the foreign culture, but that they also need to relate this to their own cultural experiences. Byram based the idea of Intercultural Communicative Competence on the concept of the *Intercultural Speaker* which he developed with Zarate as part of the work they undertook for the Council of Europe with the project *Language Learning for European Citizenship* (1997). The aim of language teaching is not for language learners to try and emulate 'the' native speaker, but to become 'intercultural speakers'. The notion of the Intercultural Speaker has become a widely accepted goal of language teaching and has replaced the previously used target aim of 'near-native competence' at most (except for the most traditional) Higher Education Institutions. The intercultural speaker is 'someone who has an ability to interact with 'others', to accept other perspectives and perceptions of the world, to mediate between different perspectives, to be conscious of their evaluations of difference.' (Byram et. al. 2001: 5).

Intercultural communicative competence (ICC) is to a large extent formulated as a set of competences. These are a range of skills and knowledges that can be taught as well as assessed, which Byram called the 5 *savoirs*. The *savoirs* present a complex picture of the skills needed to be a competent intercultural speaker, including (socio-)linguistic skills, cultural knowledge and a focus on intercultural attitudes, and being prepared to relativise one's own values, beliefs and behaviour.

Promisingly, the savoirs also include what Byram calls, 'critical cultural awareness' (*savoir s'engager*). With this Byram means that learners can turn their attention to their own beliefs and belongings, and in doing so become aware of their own (often unconscious) cultural assumptions. He also introduces a political and critical element to language teaching. The learners, Byram (1997: 20) says 'can also be encouraged to identify the ways in which particular cultural practices and beliefs maintain the social positions and power of particular groups. The analysis can become critical.'

I agree with Byram's emphasis on the context of everyday culture and reflecting upon one's own preconceptions in cultural exchanges. This has developed into the inclusion of self-reflection activities and ethnography in language teaching (cf. Byram and Fleming, 1998) and preparing students for residencies abroad, such as the 'The Intercultural Project' at Lancaster University (http://www.lancs.ac.uk/users/interculture/subproj4.htm) and the Ealing Ethnography Research Project developed at Thames Valley University (Roberts et.al. 2001). It is particularly the development of critical awareness and ethnography, which I feel is very beneficial for language learners, because the methodology of ethnography helps learners to become intercultural.

Byram's notion of Intercultural Communicative Competence then is very helpful in addressing learners' engagement with the complexities of everyday cultural contexts. The model provides a clear method for developing a range of competences. However, this approach is not sufficient on its own to fully address areas of criticality and super-complexity. Its emphasis is on encounters *between* cultures by reflecting on comparisons between 'the target culture' and the learners' own, and which, despite Byram's emphasis on differences within cultures, can easily lead to assuming relatively fixed notions of these 'cultures'. And whilst the Intercultural Speaker has an open attitude towards the cultural other, she, as Ros i Solé (2013) points out, does not move in and out of, and in between different cultures. Nevertheless, it is particularly Byram's fifth *savoir*, 'critical cultural awareness', which provides most insights for culture pedagogy based on views of culture as complex. Guilherme developed the idea of critical cultural awareness to focus on just that.

Guilherme's Citizenship Agenda: The Critical Intercultural Speaker

Guilherme developed a pedagogical and philosophical framework as a possible formulation of a critical approach to intercultural language learning which is a more complex and theoretical extension of Byram's notion of critical cultural awareness. She locates this pedagogy, like Starkey (cf. 1999, 2010) within the area of citizenship education. Being critical in this approach means 'questioning dominant cultural patterns and seeking the reasons which lead to these patterns being blindly accepted and unquestioned' (2002: 19). Guilherme borrows from Giroux's (1992) notion of 'border pedagogy' in which critical reflection is an important element. Referring to Barnett (1997), who saw reflection as 'meta-critique', she explains that in order to question dominant patterns one has to take a critical perspective towards one's own knowledge and social context, as well as being critical in trying to inhabit someone else's cognitive perspective. Critical reflection is then a vital element in developing cultural awareness as, when reflecting on cultural differences, it will help to make explicit how one justifies one's own beliefs and actions, as well as how these beliefs and actions might be perceived by the other, Guilherme states (2002: 40). She continues: 'From this perspective, reflection-in-action allows for the coming into consciousness of factors that interact in a cross-cultural event such as the unconscious concepts and rules or routine responses that are taken for granted by each side as well as the emotional impetus that drives the intercultural encounter (ibid).' In her critical approach to intercultural language learning, Guilherme attempts to respond to the contemporary complex realities of border crossings, of multiculturalism and hybridity. Her 'border pedagogy' rejects a Eurocentric approach towards any culture and favours the inclusion of non-European cultures in curriculum content. It perceives the cultural subject as multifaceted, ever-changing, and in relation to a complex, also evolving society (Guilherme, 2002: 43). Border pedagogy then does not only involve the acknowledgement of facts, that is, the input of geographical, historical, social or political information. 'It should focus on the complexity of hidden meanings, of underlying values, and how these articulate with the micro- and macro-contexts they integrate (ibid:45).' Guilherme takes a transnational perspective in formulating the notion of the '*critical* intercultural speaker' (her emphasis). The *critical* intercultural speaker, she states (ibid: 126, 127) has to problematise the concepts of nationality and ethnicity, both in terms of their origin and their present developments. She must be aware that the development of identities involves a 'constant negotiation between remembering and forgetting, idiosyncrasies and common interests'. Guilherme looks towards Giroux again who states that the pedagogical goal is not to have students exercise rigorous analytical skills in order to arrive at the right answer but to have a better understanding of what the codes are that organise different meanings and interests in particular configurations of knowledge and power (Guilherme quoting Giroux, 2002: 46). By reflecting on these configurations, students studying a foreign culture should be able to translate them into their own contexts. 'The meanings and interests of the Other will echo their own thoughts and feelings and, by becoming critically aware of them, students will identify and clarify their own struggles, points of view, predisposition which are likely to help them make more enlightened choices' (ibid).

Guilherme's framework offers a multi-perspective approach as she borrows from modernist theories, such as Critical Theory and Critical Pedagogy, and from postmodernist approaches. In this, there are similarities with my own pedagogy that I describe in chapter 4, as being located in different paradigms of modernist and postmodernist critique, although as I have mentioned before, there was an incommensurable element to my own multi-perspective approach. Risager (2007: 151) critiques Guilherme precisely for this. On the one hand she seems to refer to a language-nation derived concept of culture, and on the other hand, she formulates a language independent conception based on 'border-crossing', 'hybridity' and 'diversity'. My own feeling is that Guilherme's thoroughly theorised model has much to offer for considering practical pedagogies for the critical intercultural language user. Her focus is on citizenship, rather than on actual language and texts, and thus functions more as a theoretical consideration than a practical example. However, Guilherme's theoretical considerations in relation to problematising the national view and the idea of stable identities resonates with my own pedagogy.

I now want to make a slight detour from the discussion about how language and culture pedagogy can do justice to the complexity of this relationship and develop learners as critical intercultural speakers, and look at how intercultural communication has been conceptualised in the discipline of intercultural communication itself. I shall then draw on this for an application to language pedagogy.

Three Views of the Study of Intercultural Communication

The study of intercultural communication (ICC) as a disciplinary study in its own right does not seem to have had a strong influence on language teaching. As I have set out in chapter 2, other theories have been brought to bear upon language teaching. However, I believe that it is worthwhile to take a brief look at different views in use in the discipline of 'intercultural communication', because this disciplinary area is focused on actual communication – 'what happens when people engage in an exchange of meaningful semiotic symbols' (Blommaert, 1998: 1). There are various historical overviews of this area of study, but I will use a talk given by Blommaert (1998) which charts three views of intercultural communication with different ideological underpinnings. Whilst Blommaert charts these views, by his own admission, in a sketchy manner, it is relevant for my purpose, precisely because he takes an approach which concentrates on how 'culture' affects, or is seen to affect, speech styles. And, whilst my research is not about speech styles as such, it is about language and culture connecting in everyday speech in everyday communicative events.

Culture and Difference

The first model which Blommaert highlights is a strongly essentialist one. He points to a large body of work which shares the theoretical premise that modern nations have dominant national character traits which can be revealed by measurable data. Cultures in this model are described as essential values and practices and are therefore seen in terms of their difference from one another. This model is particularly dominant in the area of ICC studies (intercultural communication) for business purposes (cf. Pinto, 1990; Hofstede, 1994). Culture in this model is seen only in terms of behaviour or as a set of fixed values and beliefs. Culture is then viewed as a problem that can lead to misunderstandings: culture as a problem to be overcome. As Hofstede said on his website in 2010, 'cultural differences are a nuisance at best and often a disaster', although this statement has now disappeared from the website in question.

It is undoubtedly the case that in order to make sense of the multitude of ideas, impressions, and information that we experience in our everyday life, humans need to order these impressions into categories. To be fair to the body of work produced in the business related field, this work is not produced in the context of *education* with its developmental and intellectual aims that I argued for in chapter 1, but in the context of *training* with its instrumental aims. The aim is not to understand the complexities of the world, or to be critical but to understand behaviour which would otherwise be 'puzzling or unacceptable' (Verluyten, 2000: 340) or lead to 'misunderstanding, miscommunication and mismanagement, of which damage to business and personal interest can be the result' (Pinto quoted by Blommaert, (1998: 2)). And with the increasing emphasis on instrumentalism in language teaching in Higher Education, it is prudent to be alert to these argumentations which are borne out of commercial self-interest. The problem with the difference view of ICC is precisely the simplification of a complex social and cultural world to a coherent, manageable set of fixed ideas. As I argued in my previous chapter, language teaching should help students to recognise the complexity of the world and not focus on ideas that lead to stereotyping.

Blommaert strongly criticises the essentialised 'difference' model, not only because this model posits a simplified notion of culture, but more problematically still, because this model draws a direct and simplified link between 'culture' and communication. Kumaravadivelu (2007: 213) quotes Hall, who developed the first courses in 'intercultural communication' for American diplomats, as having declared unequivocally that 'culture is communication and communication is culture' (Hall, 1959: 186). The model assumes that the way that people communicate is related to 'their' culture, frequently interpreted as a national culture, rather than to a range of other social, political or individual factors. As referred to in chapter 2, seeing a national culture in terms of shared values and norms begs the question: are these values shared by everyone all the time? It also assumes that nationality and identity are natural givens, rather than constructions which are perpetuated through everyday conceptualizations of the nation, such as in weather reports, what Billig (1995) called 'banal nationalism'. Nationality does not dictate a particular communicative style. At the very most, people's nationality or ethnic identity may suggest tendencies; the '*possibility* of ethnic or cultural marking in communicative behaviour [...], but it in no way imposes ethnic or cultural characteristics onto the communicative behaviour a priori.' (my emphasis). Moreover, presenting intercultural communication as dealing with the 'other' who has his/her own set of different values and behavioral styles that follow on from that, leads to a 'massive overestimation of the degree of and the nature of difference in speech styles' (Blommaert, 1998: 5).

Whilst he criticises the essentialised model of difference as represented by intercultural consultants such as Pinto and Hofstede and numerous others, Blommaert also criticizes the cultural relativist idea of what he calls horizontal stratification. Differences in terms of differentials such as age, nationality, ethnicity, gender, class, are seen as just existing on an equal par with one another. We might like to think, Blommaert says, that all languages, cultures, all groups, in fact all people are equal, but in reality they are not. And it makes no sense to talk about cultural differences as if they are all equivalent. Vertical models of differences which look at power differentials, he argues, are more in line with reality. An approach to ICC which has the potential to take account of the relevance of power differences in roles and status is that of ethnography.

Ethnographic Approaches to Communication

To illustrate this particular model of intercultural communication, Blommaert refers to work by Gumperz and Hymes. The importance of this model, he says, is 1) that it recognizes the complexity of the relationship between culture and communication, and that 2) differences in communication in this model are not marked by national culture, but, critically, by differences in the *context* in which communications take place. Nationality is only one of the factors in that context of situation. Gumperz' contribution to the study of intercultural communication, Blommaert says, is on the one hand that he highlights that it is not so much 'culture' in the sense of values and norms which has an effect on communication, but instead 'communicative repertoires', such as conventions, speech styles and narrative patterns. These repertoires are formed by 'traditions' such as those of class and ethnicity which have become part of the language; 'we don't just use 'a' national language, like Dutch or German, but instead we always use a variety of 'a' language; 'a genre, a speech style, a type of interaction'. People identify themselves on the basis of such speech styles, which often relate to social traditions of class, gender, ethnicity etc. An important aspect of this is that these traditions and identities cannot be separated from issues of power. It makes a huge difference, Blommaert indicates, who the dominant party is in a particular interaction, whether, for instance, the interlocutor is the immigration officer or the asylum seeker for instance.

The all important role of a wider context means we cannot predict what will happen in an intercultural exchange purely based on someone's 'culture', whether national or otherwise, as the horizontal difference view holds. There are too many factors in different contexts at play. Moreover, we cannot predict what will happen in such an exchange; people might mutually adapt to one another's speech styles, both or either participant may sacrifice or exaggerate cultural conventions. In fact, more often than not, Blommaert says, 'ethnically' or 'culturally' marked aspects of communication are influenced by emotional factors such as feelings of frustration, anger or powerlessness. In other words, there is no fixed link between certain speech conventions and certain cultural groups; the reality of communication is too complex.

Paradoxically, the model of ethnography of communication was the main inspiration for communicative language teaching, but it was interpreted in a reductive manner, as I discussed in previous chapters, so that the principles of this model, which Blommaert describes as allowing for nuanced analyses of communicative events, were almost completely lost.

Incidentally, even though Gumperz carried out important work in this context by showing that a range of social factors influence communicative styles, including the power difference between interlocutors, when Gumperz applied his work pedagogically in a *training* context in 'Crosstalk' (1979), he largely ignored the notion of power. In Crosstalk Gumperz does exactly what Blommaert criticizes; he makes the trainees aware of the direct link between particular cultures and particular speech conventions. This highlights the issue of the training context, where pedagogy is more neatly organised and focuses on a limited, clearly defined area, where there generally is no room for reflection and complexity.

Whilst Gumperz, as Blommaert said, noted the role of power between participants in a communicative exchange, Hymes (1996) showed another aspect of power in intercultural relations; language varieties themselves are not neutrally valued, as some of these varieties are seen to be 'better' than others. Particular language varieties or even languages tend to be associated with certain attributes, particularly status, which immediately imposes a power structure on the interaction. But, apart from different hierarchical relations, what is important in relation to intercultural communication, is that power legitimises certain views over others, it legitimises certain languages and certain language varieties over others. And as language or language variety tend to be associated with a particular social group, the question becomes as Blommaert states, 'whose culture is being used in intercultural communication?', which we could paraphrase as 'whose version of reality counts'? The differences which occur between participants from different cultural backgrounds are not neutral. The many intercultural communication courses in a business context convey a very specific global form of intercultural communication where the language of interaction is almost always English and the participants are generally highly educated. But where intercultural communication involves a meeting of people who are members of different social groups such as in immigration contexts, these meetings take place in contexts where one interlocutor has more status and power than the other. Another factor then is the larger context of interethnic relations in that area or at that historical point of time and, I would suggest, the discourses which are in operation around otherness which would inform the assumptions and stereotypes which are held. When these discourses become dominant, such as 'the Clash of Civilisations' (Huntington, 1998), they become powerful as supposed 'truths'.

What is relevant to the foreign language teacher in this work is the notion that in intercultural communication we do not just deal with a national language, but that if we want to prepare our students for real intercultural exchanges we must make our students aware of language varieties, discourses, register, genre which, as Bakhtin showed, reference socially charged contexts. Or to use Risager's terms (2007), we should not just think about language and culture at the differential, but also at the generic level. And as Blommaert shows, it is not just being aware of the existence of these varieties, but also the value or status which they are afforded in certain contexts and in relation to other language varieties or genres. But intercultural communication is still more complex than that and, as Blommaert points out, 'difference is not always there, can appear in one context one time and not another time, and is also 'caught in patterns of social evaluation' (1998: 11).

Crossing Ethno-linguistic Boundaries

The third view that Blommaert identifies in the study of intercultural communication allows for difference and complexity in a much greater sense. Intercultural communication cannot be seen *without* taking account of the social dynamics amongst people within communicative events. Blommaert uses Rampton's (1995) study as the prime example of this view and argues that this could be a way forward to studying examples of intercultural communication. Rampton showed how young adolescents in urban areas in Britain did not stick to clear ethnic boundaries when using language associated with a particular ethnic descent. Instead they performed regular 'language crossing', switching in and out of ethnically marked varieties of English when communicating with friends from different ethnic groups or in different social settings. Ethnic identities were being manipulated and negotiated; the study showed 'how identities can be picked up, dropped, altered, combined and so on, in ways that defeat any form of simplism or singularity'. Rampton also concluded that the different speech varieties were not associated with one specific context of use, but were sometimes used for even conflicting purposes, whether as a sign of resistance, an expression of solidarity, or showing a recognition of prestige. Culture for these adolescents then, Blommaert says, serves as a set of resources which partly operates automatically, but can also be strategically activated in different circumstances and for different purposes.

This view of intercultural communication which Blommaert suggests here as a step forward in thinking about interculturality, is a marked change from the 'difference' view; not only does it not primarily focus on a national culture, it also emphasises that people move in and out of various forms of cultural symbolic behaviour, in terms of using different language varieties or genres, and indeed by feeling different allegiances. Moreover, it also shows that the same behaviour or language can be utilised for completely different purposes. The idea of context is made much more complex precisely because it allows for the use of conflicting discourses and indeterminacies.

There is a parallel in the boundary crossing model with thinking about identity and cultural complexity. Our sense of 'belongings' is formed by the affiliations to the various roles, relationships and memberships of 'communities of practice' people feel they are part of, as Kumaravadivelu (2008) says. None of these communities are fixed and stable entities in themselves. Instead they are complex mixtures of 'pleasure and pain', of 'trust and suspicion', of 'friendship and hatred' as Kumaravadivelu says, quoting Wenger. How these complexities of the different realities can overlap, was illustrated by Baumann in an ethnographic study of Southall, a very diverse and multicultural area in London. 'The vast majority of all adult Southallians saw themselves as members of several communities', each shifting and potentially conflicting with one another. 'The same person could speak and act as a member of the Muslim community in one context, in another take sides against other Muslims as a member of a Pakistani community, and in a third count himself part of the Punjabi community that excluded other Muslims, but included Hindus, Sikhs and even Christians' (Baumann, 1996).

Significance of the Boundary Crossing Model for Language Teaching

The strength of Blommaert's model, or view on intercultural communication, is that it acknowledges that context is complex and there is not a straightforward link between one particular context, especially not a national one, and particular speech styles. The model is a useful way of thinking about intercultural communication in the context of language teaching. Even though I will not use the concept of code switching in a linguistic sense for this study, the idea of culture as a set of resources (linguistic and otherwise) that people can pick and choose from to utilise, resist and create new meanings, I think is very relevant for critical intercultural communication in language teaching. Blommaert's model does not give us the answers we need in terms of pedagogy and whether we should opt for a context or text-based approach, or what to include in a language teaching syllabus. Moreover, Blommaert seems to refer specifically to speech. We cannot, in short, apply his views directly to language teaching, but his models provide a way of thinking about intercultural communication which is important for us as teachers. His view of culture as 'resources' to draw upon bears similarities with Holliday's view (2004: 12).

The fact that choosing from these resources operates, not just on an unconscious, but also on a strategic level, is an important point. If people use these resources partly strategically on an everyday basis, they become more easily available for conscious reflection, which can be used in the language class.

The notion of switching and mixing language styles and varieties depending on a range of complex factors with regard to the social context, as well as factors outside the social arena such as emotions, can be made central to language and culture pedagogy. Such a pedagogy would focus on difference in terms of styles and discourses and look at the embedded ideologies and values, see context as influenced by a complex set of factors, focus on making learners take account of who they address and direct their communications specifically to their audience. This addressivity - 'the quality of turning to someone', as Bakhtin (1996 (1986): 99) so aptly calls it, comes into play particularly in writing, as students have more time for reflection on their language output. But an awareness of varieties of styles and discourses, and indeed how the reader is addressed, also helps students to delve deeper into text and go beyond the content of the text.

Cultural meanings are then created through discourses; structures of meaning which also hold in Bakhtin's words a 'stylistic aura' which reflect the ideology pertaining to that discourse. But these cultural meanings are often global. Areas of human activity are after all not limited to a particular national culture. For the language teacher who frequently is expected to teach the national paradigm, this provides a dilemma.

Dilemmas of Intercultural Communication in the Language Classroom

One of the dilemmas of intercultural communication for the language teacher is that on the one hand we want to emphasise the complexity and diversity of cultural environments that we are looking at in the classroom, and at the same time we cannot deny that certain tendencies and cultural patterns exist. Conceptualising culture within a pluriform society, with different sets of values, lifestyles, genders, political views and so on, can also easily fall prey to a similar essentialising of, what Holliday calls, 'small cultures' (2004: 63); describing such subcultures as consisting of people sharing a set of collective characteristics. This could still lead to learners thinking of culture or subculture as a fixed and bounded entity. It would be futile to think there are no differences between the way people live or make sense of their world, whether between different countries or groups within a country. But the most important thing is to recognise these patterns as tendencies which may be hard to pin down; with vague and fluid boundaries. As Blommaert said: the world is indeed full of differences, but these differences are not always there, or are not always the same, and they are partly determined by unequal power relations (1998: 11).

As I set out in the previous chapter, foreign language teaching has had a take on culture (and on language) using somewhat stereotypical and stable notions of a national culture. This is understandable to a degree, because, despite the fact we have all become part of a 'larger global tribe' (Appiah, 2006), national, and indeed sub-national realities, even as *imagined communities*' (Anderson, 1983), remain important in how people describe their complex cultural identities and subjectivities, as Holliday (2011) showed. In his study on this topic, he noted that nation is an 'undeniable powerful source of identity, security and belonging, but it is an external one which may be in conflict with more personal cultural realities'. We can also see this in books which take a comical look at a national culture and focus on stable notions of a culture, e.g 'The Undutchables' (White and Boucke, 2006). These books are so popular and seductive precisely because the information they contain is so easily recognisable; we tend to recognise what we already know as it slots so easily into our existing mental schema. Coleman (1996) pointed out that students of German who spent time in Germany as part of their Residence Abroad scheme came back with all their ideas and stereotypes of Germany and the Germans confirmed.

In a recent survey of Dutch language teachers at Institutions for Higher Education worldwide, it was found that many teachers recognised the dilemma of not wanting to stereotype, yet felt that cultural information as part of language teaching is frequently about behaviour as part of a national culture. Teachers opted for giving cultural information accompanied with the warning: this is a generalisation, but nevertheless there is a core of truth in it (Rossum and Vismans, 2006).

I would like to suggest that the 'kernal of truth' view can be just as limiting as the stereotypical view, as it pretends to recognise complexity, but still focuses on essential meanings. We need knowledge about another culture, but that knowledge must be looked at critically and must be placed in context. The kernal of truth view is dangerous because it perpetuates the idea of fixed cultures.

I will now turn to the implications for the classroom.

Towards a New Conceptualisation of Interculturality in the Language Classroom

A more useful way of conceiving of interculturality in the classroom, which allows for complexity, a level of fluidity, individual agency is the notion of *being intercultural*, put forward by Phipps and Gonzalez (2004), where 'being' is emphasised over 'knowledge'. They argue that the central activity of modern languages degrees should be 'languaging', 'being intercultural', and 'living with supercomplexity' (p 8). The key element in the process of being intercultural is that of 'languaging'. In 'languaging' the emphasis is on 'real' communication and dialogue in the classroom rather than on artificial language tasks; it is 'living in and through the language' (p.111). 'Being intercultural' means understanding another world, which takes place through the process of dialoguing with others and being part of another cultural group. Crucially, this process can only take place from a position where students challenge their world and 'let it be enriched by others' (p. 27). The notion of 'intercultural being', as conceptualised by Phipps and Gonzalez, focuses on engaging with the other, on processes and on critical reflection. Being intercultural is more than an attitude of how you feel towards other countries as Byram's notion of ICC holds. 'It is more profoundly about how one lives with and responds to difference and diversity. [....] It is about living out the network of diverse human relationships – not just abroad, but down the road as well' (p.115).

'Being intercultural' is not about getting information *about* the other culture, but it is about engaging *with* it, both from 'within' to get a sense of what the other thinks, feels and does, and from a position of real critical understanding. Phipps and Gonzalez argue for not just the insertion of *critical reflection* as part of the language curriculum (p. 92), but the active engagement which they call 'critical being'. Learning is about 'testing and exploring ideas in and against reality, and then reflecting upon the process' (p. 124). This combination of the experiential and intellectual is found in the practice of ethnography as a way of understanding the cultural and social practices of a (cultural) group. But, Phipps and Gonzalez argue, ethnography is more than a tool to enable learners to develop into intercultural beings. It is about 'people meeting in human encounters and in ways which may change the way they see the world' (p.125).

I interpret the notion of 'being intercultural' as taking the learner conceptually out of the classroom, and into the real world. It is an intellectual engagement with the real world. It may consist of 'real' dialogues with fellow students, or even other speakers of the language, but the notion can also be extended to engaging with written texts as if in 'dialogue'; relating what is read explicitly to one's own experiences and understandings and to keep on querying these. Indeed in chapter 5 I explore how students, when testing their ideas against their experienced 'realities', made them realise the positioning of the text we discussed.

Ethnography as a Method of Being Intercultural

Ethnography for language learners, even though it hasn't yet made its way into many syllabi at university language departments, has nevertheless attracted increasing interest in the last few years as an exciting way to combine the intellectual and experiential aspects of engaging with the other culture. The aim of ethnography is twofold: on the one hand it encourages the learner to recognise the cultural in his/her everyday life and ideas by 'making the familiar strange'. On the other hand the learner is encouraged to try and understand the 'strange' from within its own perspective. The learner will then start to recognise that what previously seemed natural, was actually culturally constructed. Of course, it is impossible ever to see things from the perspective of the other. We will always see the world through the filter of our own experiences. An important aspect of ethnography is to realise that what you see and observe, is coloured through your own experiences, your own cultural and social background, and ideas and assumptions, your own ethnocentricity. But, even with that knowledge, we can never truly know what phenomena, ideas, objects, customs, behaviour, everyday life events actually 'mean' for the 'other'. We cannot observe neutrally. Every observation will always have what Hermans (2007: 147) calls a 'blind spot', because every observation can be interpreted only from the context of those that do the observation.

The main technique of ethnography is creating 'thick descriptions': by giving extremely detailed accounts of what can be observed, students discover things which might otherwise have escaped their attention or would have been taken for granted. But thick descriptions involve reflection on one's own observation and response to what is observed at the same time. Doing ethnography then is to question the sources of evidence presented and thereby challenge assumptions and stereotypes (Barro et.al., 1998: 76-97).

Probably the first ethnographic project of its kind for language learners was the Ealing Project, in which students first made the familiar strange through writing 'home ethnographies' before applying this to a closely observed ethnographic project during their year abroad (Roberts, et.al., 2001). This project, though undertaken by language learners in the context of their modern languages degree and as preparation for their residency abroad, is not an actual language class, but more a cultural studies class.

Because its focus is on 'lived experience' and 'culture as practice' ethnography is very suitable for study abroad. Indeed, I adopted and adapted the Ealing Project in a similar way and incorporated it in a cultural studies course, which prepares student for doing their ethnographic year abroad project. But, ethnographic projects have also been used in the language classroom itself. Morgan and Cain (2000), for example, undertook a collaborative project between two schools; a French class at a school in England and an English class at a school in France. The aim of the project was to let pupils think about their own culture as well as that of the other group, seen from the 'other's' perspective. To this aim pupils were asked to represent aspects of their 'own culture' around the theme of 'Law and Order'. Students from each class worked in small groups to create cultural material for the partner class. In doing so they had to be aware of what was specifically English or French about the topic, but more importantly, they had to think about the communicative needs of the partner class, both in content and language use. By looking at the material the partner class produced, pupils could discuss and compare the similarities and differences. Whilst it may be said that this approach still did not encourage a non-essentialist attitude to the other culture, and was still located within a national paradigm, pupils were encouraged to think about the perspective of the other; to imagine how others might feel and how they might engage with information given to them.

Phipps and Gonzalez take integrating ethnography in the classroom probably furthest. One of the projects that Phipps worked on with her students was a project about 'rubbish' (Phipps and Gonzalez, 2004: 126). Students collected data and interviewed Germans living in Glasgow about environmentalism. This integrated project work outside, in the 'real world', with language work inside the classroom. This is an exciting initiative which includes project work as part of classroom work and makes a direct, experiential link between everyday experienced culture. Moreover, by interviewing Germans living in Scotland, a narrow national focus is avoided. I feel that projects such as these point the way forward to more ethnographic real world experiences, and should be explored further in language teaching. However, in my own pedagogy I adopted not a project approach, but I aimed to include ethnography as part of the general pedagogic activities in the classroom. This became a text-based approach using principles of ethnography. I will set this out below.

Text Ethnography

Ethnography is well suited to an intercultural approach to language teaching because of the opportunities it affords for being reflexive about one's own cultural environments and the focus on querying the 'taken for granted', as well as 'stepping into the shoes of others', although care needs to be taken not to see these cultural environments as fixed. But ethnography can be integrated further in the language classroom, I believe, than by just being the focus of separate projects, as in the Morgan and Cain study. Ethnography could also be usefully applied to looking at texts, thereby integrating text and context. Texts are after all a natural focus for the language and culture classroom. Moreover language always happens as text (Kress, 1985), and texts reflect and reconstruct specific instances of culture.

An ethnographic approach to text helps students to recognise how culture underpins texts, to query the taken-for-granted and to see how language and culture interrelate. This is a process of discursive mapping. However, an ethnographic approach also looks at the role students have to play in their interpretation. Looking in an ethnographic way at texts then, allows us to make the 'familiar strange', and the strange familiar. Being intercultural through text then can be a pedagogy of an integrated look at language and culture which takes account of the complexity of context, interculturality and criticality. But, before we can discuss what it means to be intercultural through texts, we first need to look at what we mean by 'text', which I will do below. These views of text are similar, but not the same, as the views of language which I discussed in the previous chapter: views of the liberal humanist perspective; of a structuralist perspective; and text as a semiotic encounter where text and reader 'meet' to create meaning.

Texts

Ways That Text Has Been Conceptualised

For the purposes of this study, I am looking at texts as 'written' texts. Whereas my pedagogy sees text in a wider range as 'transmitters of meaning' which could also be visual and/or aural texts, I focus particularly on written text in the empirical part of this study. During the lessons which form the empirical part of this study (see chapter 5), I tried to alert the class, when discussing a particular text, to the extra layer of meaning added by the illustrations and page layout. However, this discussion did not generate illuminating data, and I do not include the multimodality of text in my discussion below.

Historically, the concept of text has been conceived in different ways within language teaching. I will briefly set out traditional views of text, before focusing on the conceptualisation of text which is the core of my pedagogy, i.e. that of 'cultuurtekst'.

In the liberal humanist educational tradition, which I discussed in chapter 1, text itself was not an issue for theorizing. Text is a written *product*, and not a *process* of communication. A product, moreover, which was the result of intellectual thought and ideas. The most important attribute of a text is the content which, in 'a good text' is generated through solid thinking and expressed in good writing. The quality of these thoughts is reflected in the actual quality of the language, the structure of the text and the strength of the argumentation. As the 19th century educationalist Blair, cited by Emig, said, the aim was for writers to produce products of moral superiority and rationality: 'embarrassed, obscure and feeble sentences are generally, if not always, the result of embarrassed, obscure and feeble thought' (Emig, 1983: 7).

Texts in this traditional view are wholly the responsibility of the individual writer, regardless of whether anyone else, such as an editor could have had a role to play in the writing. The writer is thus unproblematised. The reader on the other hand has no role to play in the interpretation of the text, except, perhaps, to appreciate (and imitate in the case of learning to write) the quality of the text. The assumption then is that quality is not subjective, but objective, there is an agreed notion of 'the good text'. Moreover, it is a product which contains a stable meaning.

This view of text is now generally no longer held in the academic world, but it survives as a 'common sense' assumption amongst many people, as evidenced by newspaper discussions bemoaning the declining quality of writing of school pupils in the subject of English. As a result the notion of a 'good text' has an enduring appeal with (some) students, as I found out when analysing my data (see chapter 6).

The second view of text which I discuss here, is the structuralist view of text. This view, whilst less concerned with the idea of 'the good text', does also emphasise the autonomy of the text. But in contrast with a liberal humanist educational view, the emphasis shifts towards a more prominent role for the reader in 'extracting' meaning from texts (Wallace, 2003: 15). This view correlates with the view of communication put forward by de Saussure, the 'speech-circuit', which as Daniel Chandler says (2002: 176) can be seen as an early form of the transmission model of communication; the Shannon-Weaver model (1949). The latter sees communication as sending a message from person A (the sender) to person B (the addressee) as if it were a package. I would suggest that, again, this is the common sense idea of communication that most people, including our students would hold. This idea of communication as 'sending a message' is subsumed in much of (Dutch) language teaching practice, both in reading and writing tasks. Reading in foreign language classes then frequently consists mainly of comprehension tasks and activities, which typically include multiple choice tasks, or comprehension questions regarding writer intention or the meaning contained in the text as if these were unproblematic constructs.

Later versions of the structuralist model allow for a more complex idea of communication and crucially include the notion of context. This model also allows for a view of text beyond the written product alone. The text can thus be anything that 'sends a message', whether a conversation, a visual image or even a form of behaviour of dress. As such this model allows not only for a much broader view of text, but also the emphasis in communication has shifted from the producer of text to the text itself.

A more interactional version of the structuralist encoding and decoding view of communication, is that espoused by Widdowson (and others) in relation to language teaching, which grants a greater role to the reader and to the role of context than the traditional views based on the Shannon-Weaver model. For Widdowson reading is not just a matter of transferring information from the author to the reader, but is instead a process of communication; the reader is active in the decoding process, engaging his or her prior knowledge, experiences and ideas. Encoding, or writing, is not just a formulation of messages, says Widdowson (1979: 175), but also giving pointers to the reader to help him or her along in the process of decoding. The responsibility of the text still lies with the writer in the sense that he needs to take account of the reader in writing a text. A writer must therefore see writing as a cooperative activity. The writer provides directions to the reader and anticipates the questions an imaginary and critical reader might ask; questions such as: Oh yes? How do you know? In that sense Widdowson's view of text may also seem to be reminiscent of the liberal view of 'the good text', because the text needs to adhere to certain criteria. But these criteria are not necessarily located in the clarity of thought of the writer, but in the way the writer directs him/herself to the audience.

This is the same addressivity that Kramsch emphasises in her approach, where she borrows the term from Bakhtin. However, Kramsch (and Bakhtin) see this reader-oriented writing as a social aspect; the writer imagines the reader and what his/her previous knowledge, interests, objections to the text and so on, can be. Widdowson's structuralist position towards writing, on the other hand, is not dissimilar, I would suggest, from the maxims that guide the conversational Cooperative Principle put forward by Grice - communication is understood as being guided by the 'rules' of 'being truthful', 'being clear', 'being informative', (i.e. not being too wordy for the purpose) and 'being relevant'.

Widdowson's view allows for a stronger role for the reader than either liberal or structural views generally take on board, as the writer relies on the active participation of the reader in order to comprehend the text by understanding the pointers the writer gives, but it also sees communication more as something taking place between individuals, rather than as a social process.

The third view of texts which takes the interactional element much further still is that explicated by Halliday, who sees texts as *both* product and process. The text is a product in the sense that it is an artefact, it is there in the physical sense and we can read it. But at the same time, text is also an interactive process, 'a semiotic encounter' where participants (the writer and reader) meet to create meaning in a particular situational context. Wallace uses Halliday's conceptual framework of text as a starting point in her critical pedagogy of reading where she sees reading and writing as closely interrelated (2003: 12). Wallace locates her work in CLA (Critical Language Awareness), which as I discussed in chapter 2, as a pedagogy encourages learners to deconstruct texts to critique the ideology embedded in them; analyzing linguistic features in the text raises students' awareness of how the discourses privilege those with power. Wallace takes a view of reading where text interpretation is partly guided through analyzing the social interaction between the participants, the social situation and the language used. This is not a completely fluid and open interpretation of the text where it is up to the individual reader to recreate his or her meaning. Following Eco she says that texts do carry meaning in and for themselves 'apart from writer intention (and indeed apart from reader interpretation) at a number of levels signaled, in complex ways, by the nature and combining of the formal features selected' (ibid. p.13).

My own view is to some degree in line with Wallace, in the sense that in text interpretation, at least in the context of language education, we can look for 'preferred readings' (ibid. p. 16) which students can access by considering specific linguistic features and contexts. These apparent intended meanings of a text, refer to, as O'Regan (2006: 113) says, how, 'from the perspective of a reader, the text seems to want to be read'. Preferred readings then are the apparent arguments, perspectives and orientations, as they appear to the reader, and, O'Regan states, 'it is the text itself [that] seems to indicate this preference' (ibid.). But, in my own pedagogy, and indeed the framework for analyses of texts, which I used with my students, I also deviate from Wallace, in the sense that, when looking at texts, my concern is not so much with ideology, but rather with discourses as meaning making practices and how these produce knowledge and make claims to truth. Looking at discursive formations in texts also gives the student reader a window on the context in which these texts are produced. And even though I assume that text interpretation does not allow unlimited readings, as I argued earlier, I also take into account that students rewrite the text; they imbue it with their own meaning, derived from their experiences and discourses to which they have been exposed, and the intertextual knowledge they gained through these.

I have argued earlier that in my own pedagogy I encourage students to employ various critical strategies to interpret texts by referring to the linguistic choices made. I am partly borrowing from Wallace (2003) in this. But, as my concern in the foreign language classroom is not only with critique of how power is sustained and constructed in texts, but also with culture, I am using a different view of text which allows for both elements. For this reason, I am focusing on models of text which are more suited to 'being intercultural' through text.

Bakhtin offers a good starting point.

Being Intercultural Through Texts: Dialogism and Addressivity

Text, or utterance, according to Bakhtin, is about a dialogue with an other. Text then, does not exist in its own context, but is always directed to someone else, and as such his model of text can function also as a model of communication. Text can therefore be seen not just as a product in its own right, but it is always produced *for* someone else: a reader, interpreter, listener, which makes it relevant for intercultural learning, both in reading and writing.

This 'addressivity' goes further than just helping the reader or listener along through using structural markers in the text or writing in a reader-friendly manner, such as writing with the use of discourse questions in mind, as I discussed above in relation to Widdowson's view of texts. Instead, Bakhtin's notion of addressivity or 'dialogism' means taking account of the reader or listener in a more substantial way and considering what the possible reader or listener's previous knowledge and expectations and possible responses to the text might be. A reader's responses to a text are based on his/her cultural and social experience and history, particularly in relation to previous reading experiences, but also in relation to the addressee's conceptual world, which is made up partly of conventions of communication in certain areas of life (e.g. genres such as academic articles, law reports etc.), as well as his or her own ideological positions, or at least the discursive fields the addressee is familiar with.

But text and communication are not just addressed towards a (future) reader who has a past and cultural baggage; texts (utterances) are also addressed to past language or communication. Language, Bakhtin says, is always a response to a greater or lesser extent to other utterances (1996 (1986): 91, 92). This applies to communication in real time, e.g. a response to a previous utterance in a conversation, or a text which has been written in response to another text or any other intertextual references.

If we apply this notion of engaging with the other to 'being intercultural', the intercultural learner is not just responding or engaging with the other culture, but also with another past. Words, like texts, are not neutral. There may be neutral dictionary meanings of words which ensure that speakers of a given language understand one another, Bakhtin says, but in live speech communication words are always contextual (1996 (1986): 88). Language in use is not neutral because the context of the whole utterance gives the word 'colour' or 'sense'. Furthermore, as speakers we are not the first people to use words. What we say is not just addressed to the object, the topic we speak about, but to what others have said about it. A text is a 'link in the chain of speech communication' (ibid. p. 94) and it cannot be seen separate from this chain. A text, or an utterance, carries echoes with the past, or as the playwright Dennis Potter says it more succinctly: the problem with words is that you don't know whose mouths they have been in (quoted by Maybin, 2001: 68).

This is of particular relevance to the foreign language learner, who has not been socialised in the foreign language discourse communities and indeed might not be able to relate any discourses to particular people, events or cultural and ideological views, at least not in the foreign language context. To understand a text, you can never only take the thematic content into account, because the text also responds to what others have said about the same topic. A text is then not just about its content, but it is a representation of something in relation to the other texts to whom it (perhaps unwittingly) refers: texts are filled with 'dialogic overtones' (Bakhtin, ibid., p. 92).

But texts do not just exist as 'echoes of the past', texts themselves are not just written within one voice or discourse. As Kress showed, frequently there are various, even conflicting, discourses in a text, and it is these clashing discourses which give rise to the text itself (1985: 82). This heteroglossia consists of the seemingly endless voices and discourses in which social and ideological positions are embedded.

It is the notion of dialogism - being in dialogue with past, present, future and the other, which, I believe, constitutes the *inter* in intercultural. The *inter* in this interpretation is not a direct relationship between two cultures. As I argued earlier, intercultural relations are a complex set of cross cutting allegiances in which speakers act their complex multifaceted identities, or different 'belongings'. In the next section I explain what the *cultural* in intercultural is when we adopt a Bakhtinian version of texts, as a way of communicating with the other.

Cultuurtekst as Discourse and Representation

In the previous chapter I already pointed to the notion of 'cultuurtekst', text as culture, coined by Maaike Meijer, a Dutch feminist literary theorist. She developed this notion of text into a theory of text interpretation or reading, mainly for literary analysis purposes. She focuses particularly (following Kristeva, 1966) on the notion of intertextuality contained in Bakhtin's view of language being 'echoes of the past', but, in literary analysis, she maintains, recognising intertextuality is a limitless task. Often it cannot even be determined exactly how or where a text is borrowing from other texts. In order to create a framework for literary interpretations outside the notion of literary intertextuality, it makes more sense, she suggests, to recognise the *discourses* (in a Foucauldian sense) in a text. Texts are not created as fresh and new meanings, but are a reworking of old notions and ideas and conventionalised historically accepted ways of talking about certain things. This 'culturally routinised way of talking', Meijer calls 'cultuurtekst'.

Culture then, in 'cultuurtekst' is the 'conglomerate of accepted and recurrent motifs and ways of representation around a theme, which is organising itself again and again in new texts, whether literary, journalistic scientific or otherwise' (my translation) (Meijer, 1996: 33). It is meaning-making in relation to the whole cultural space; 'the scenarios' which are provided by the surrounding culture. Each individual text is a retake of those scenarios, she says. 'Cultuurtekst' encourages us to look at how a text rewrites and reproduces the available scenario. Or, in other words, how a text re-articulates the commonly accepted meanings, values and attitudes.

Meijer's view of 'cultuurtekst' is not a completely open-ended framework. It is not about a text having a single meaning, but about not having infinite meanings either. Groups of readers who have been socialised in similar ways, will 'smell', as Meijer calls it, similar discourses. They recognise the underpinning ideologies and values without being able to quite 'put their finger on it', as students have explained this sense of vague recognition to me.

Meijer's notion of 'cultuurtekst' is close to Foucault's notion of *discourse*, but it differs from it in that her notion encompasses both that of the individual concrete text itself, as well as that of the 'invisible' or implicit discursive fields which are operating within those texts. (1996: 33-35). This notion is useful for language teaching, as we are not just dealing with discourses, but also with text itself at a 'textual level'.

Mapping Discourses

Using the notion of 'cultuurtekst' also gives us the advantage of seeing culture in more pluriform terms: not a formulation of features specific to a national culture, but as a mapping and critiquing of discourses. I derived at the term 'discursive mapping' from Pennycook (2001), and see it, as he does, as a 'problematisation' of texts. I conceptualised discursive mapping as part of discussing with students how meanings in the text are created through discourses. This allows us, as Pennycook says, to map out different formations of meaning and to see how these are constructed through intertextual relations: a search for how social reality itself is produced and reproduced in language (ibid: 111). In this, the discursive mapping approach is a critical undertaking. O'Regan (2006) developed a model for reading texts in the classroom, in which he uses the idea of discursive mapping, an approach which he calls TACO, the 'text as critical object'. His model incorporates a number of stages from looking at the 'preferred readings' of texts, 'how the text seems to want to be read' (ibid: 24), through to a 'representative', a 'social', and a 'deconstructive' interpretation. I did not use O'Regan's model for my own 'cultuurtekst' approach to reading texts in the classroom, since his study was not available then, but I will come back to the TACO approach again in the next chapter when I discuss my own framework for text analysis.

Seeing text as 'cultuurtekst' then also brings to the fore the multiple discourses, to which Kress refers (1985: 7) and which are current in any context. Bakhtin calls this 'polyphony' (multivoicedness). Any context, except the most stable one, contains a range of 'voices'. I take 'voice' here to be similar to discourse. Bakhtin refers to different ideologies and discursive forces being inherent in all words and forms: 'Each word tastes of the context and contexts in which it has lived its socially charged life: all words and forms are populated by intentions.' (1981: 293).

The idea of 'cultuurtekst' then gives us access to the idea of culture as a complex, fluid and dialogic construct, which whilst containing patterns of meaning and behaviour, also recognises that these patterns change and merge and submerge in (sometimes unpredictable) ways.

An added advantage of applying the model of 'cultuurtekst' to language teaching, is that it gives language classes more intellectual content, even if discussing trivial texts, i.e. texts with a popular appeal, or everyday topics. It helps learners to think about language at a more theoretical level, as well as touching on the notion of addressivity, and the processes of meaning making, which is an inherently critical task.

Finally, the idea of 'cultuurtekst' works not only as a mode for interpreting texts, but, when combined with the notion of 'addressivity' is also very useful as an awareness tool for writing texts. I have incorporated this into the syllabus of my general language class (see chapter 4 for an overview). My emphasis in the fourth year language class under study was particularly, but not exclusively, on reading and writing, as an intellectual dialogue.

Implications for Teaching

The need to conceptualise text in social ways in terms of the context of production and reception is fairly widely accepted these days. However, as indicated before, in the practice of language teaching an uncomplicated view of text is still prevalent. Texts are frequently used as vehicles for grammar and vocabulary work, for translation, or for comprehension exercises on the content level only. Questions of text generally are aimed to 'check' whether the learner has passively understood the surface messages contained in the text. In language teaching, text is still frequently seen as a written product; a carefully constructed framework with a clearly demarcated beginning and end which constitutes an intelligible, cohesive piece of writing, and any language work relating to texts frequently separates the activities of reading and writing. Students also frequently hold similar assumptions about text. As I show in chapters 5 and 6 students can struggle to recognise the complexity of texts as a result of these assumptions.

Yet on the other hand, students also engage with texts as social and cultural beings themselves; their responses to texts are based on their own experiences, ideas and assumptions. This is what I turn to next.

Personal Lived Experience

Traditional psychological schema theory (cf. Bartlett, 1932) holds that readers relate the incoming data they receive from the text to existing mental representations of situations or events. These are, as Widdowson (1983: 34) points out, primarily cognitive constructs which aid the organisation of information.

However, information is always located within a social context (Wallace, 2003: 22). This is the context of reception, the context in which the information is received, which is located within the wider context of culture, i.e. the views, ideas, knowledges and discourses which the reader is surrounded with or has encountered.

The previous knowledges and experiences which readers use to interpret the text relate to areas of academic as well as social experience; what they have read, learnt or heard about the topic, whether in formal education or through the media or everyday life. Moreover, readers also relate the text they read to their 'lived experience' of their relationships and encounters with other people which include power relationships. In short, we interpret texts by relating them, frequently unconsciously, to the discourses we have been exposed to ourselves. These unconscious understandings take on a taken-for-granted assumption of the world.

The resonances people hear are relevant and indeed give meaning to the text, but interpretations are never complete. They are dependent on the frameworks people use, the situation they are in, their experiences and interests, their life-world knowledge (cf. Habermas, 1984). In short we see texts from our own ethnocentricity. We also have, as said before, our own 'blindspots'. In order to deal with these and to try and take a position 'outside' the text, readers need to be reflexive about their own position.

Asking students to 'map' the discourses in a text, as I do in my 'cultuurtekst' pedagogy, brings to the fore two things: firstly, you need to take a position outside its discourses in order to critique a text, otherwise the discourses will seem 'natural'. Discourses are, after all, resistant to internal criticism, as Gee has said (2009 (1990): 161). Conversely, students may not be familiar with the discursive fields that gave rise to the text, as they would not share the knowledge inherent to which the text implicitly refers, in which case it may also be hard for them to 'problematise' the text or they may be half conscious of the discursive fields, but cannot quite 'put their finger on it'. To access the cultural meanings through discourses on which the texts draws then, we can, I suggest take the position of an ethnographer; an ethnographer of text, which includes the notion of reflexivity. I will turn to this next.

Being Intercultural Through Text: Reading as a Text Ethnographer

An ethnographer looks at cultural difference from both an inside and an outside perspective. Taking an inside (emic) perspective is trying to see the world as the 'other' experiences it, i.e. 'trying to stand in the shoes of the other' through being as much part of the experience as possible, by talking to people and being a participant observer. Of course an ethnographer can never completely understand the inside perspective; it can only ever be an interpretation. At the same time ethnographers try and take an outside (etic) perspective by trying to be aware of their own assumptions which influence their interpretation of what they see. This is the outside perspective, 'making the familiar strange' through creating 'thick descriptions'.

I consider the text ethnographer to go through similar processes in reading a text. An inside perspective of text cannot be the same raw everyday experience of the ethnographic observation or interview. The text is itself already a mediated artefact of the social and cultural world. However, by reading a text from an inside perspective, the text ethnographer is not so much trying to understand the writer of the text, but the environment the writer is describing in real life. This means the reader tries to understand the content of the text in relation to the wider cultural environment to which the writer wittingly or unwittingly refers. But, importantly, the reader can only understand the content and context in relation to her own experiences. So trying to understand the text from an inside perspective, i.e. trying to understand what the text might mean for the audience for whom it is intended, the reader will have to make use of her own experiences. These experiences could be those of empathy with the ideas or participants in the text, or these experiences could be brought to bear in relating and exploring the ideas and descriptions in the text against the reader's own reality. This is an 'engaging with'. It is not quite the same as the 'languaging' concept from Phipps and Gonzalez, because it does not involve 'real' face-to-face engagement in the language, but taking an emic perspective as a text ethnographer, can, I believe, be an engagement with otherness and relating it to oneself. Even if it is not a 'raw' ethnography in its experiential form, it is an intellectual engagement through relating the text to one's own experience and ideas and making it 'real'. In the classes which I used for data collection, there were some almost 'raw' experiences as students emotions became part of the very personal responses to that text, as I will show in chapter 5 in relation to a particular instance.

But the inside perspective needs to be accompanied by an outside perspective, i.e. reflecting on the taken-for-granted interpretations the reader makes herself. By being reflexive about his or her own interpretation, the reader engages in a process which queries the taken for granted realities and interpretations which reflect his or her own assumptions which are part and parcel of his/her ethnocentricity.

Again, the outside perspective I am describing is not quite the same as an etic perspective, as it does not involve making 'thick descriptions', but it can be a way of 'making the familiar strange'.

Summary and Conclusion

This chapter set out more specifically the underpinning ideas of my pedagogy. I drew on Byram and on Kramsch's early work, and on Guilherme's critical pedagogy. I aligned myself with the latter's critical emphasis, with Byram's focus on 'the everyday' aspects of culture, and with Kramsch's notion of context as complex and multilayered, her focus on text and on the notion of dialogue in class. I interpret this dialogue as taking place between students themselves as well as in relation to the teacher and the text under discussion, including the multiple discourses which occupy the cultural spaces which exist and open up in such dialogues.

Whereas language and culture in language teaching has been frequently seen as relating to information about the target country, and what to say in what situation, intercultural communication as a discipline, developed initially for diplomacy and applied to business contexts, focuses exclusively on interpersonal relations, seeing a direct link between 'a' communicative style and 'a' culture. I argued, drawing on Blommaert, that language and culture teaching should not focus on this perceived link, because even though there are patterns of communication in specific, including national, groups, language teaching should take account of linguistic and cultural complexity.

One way of conceptualizing a new way of thinking about intercultural communication is that put forward by Phipps and Gonzalez of 'being intercultural'; an actual engagement with 'the other' in and through language. Ethnography is an excellent tool to encourage interculturality, as it encourages students to observe, participate in, engage with, and reflect about the 'other' in relation to themselves and their own complex cultural environment. Even though ethnography is about engaging with 'real' situations, I argue that the idea can be applied to looking at text as well.

I set out different views of text which have prevailed in education, but the view of text which allows for a critical, an ethnographic, and a dialogic reading is that of 'cultuurtekst', as this view of text combines the idea of text as a product, and text in relation to the context of culture as shifting, complex and reflecting multiple discourses. The idea of 'cultuurtekst' then underpins my pedagogy. The advantage of this model, I argued, is that it lends itself to 'discursive mapping', which I see as both a critical practice and as an engagement with the cultural contexts of the texts.

In the next chapter, I set out the context in which this study took place, discuss the text I used for this study and I will introduce the framework for analysis which I used with the students.

CHAPTER 4

Context of Teaching and Research

Introduction

In this chapter I set out both the methodological concerns of this study, as well as its context; a space where the tensions between expectations, mine and students', and the normative processes of traditional liberal humanist educational perspectives and instrumental ones were constantly felt.

The aim of this classroom study was to find out how students engaged with my pedagogy of intercultural language education which I had been developing over the previous years: a cultuurtekst approach. The process of this study was not a neat and linear one. As I let the data 'rest' for a few years after I initially collected these, the underpinning ideas to this pedagogy kept evolving. This was as a result of reflection on the analysis on my data, the everyday experience of teaching this particular language course and a range of other courses, and through further theoretical reflection. The first three theoretical chapters of this book, then, do not just set out the theory underpinning the data chapters, conversely the data chapters also underpin the theoretical chapters, as my notion of the cultuurtekst approach, and its accompanying idea of becoming a 'text ethnographer', and how this contributes to learners' cultural and intercultural awareness became more refined.

Background to the Study

When I started this study in the late 1990s, the theoretical field of intercultural communication as part of language teaching had only just started to develop. The idea that the notion of the Intercultural Speaker should replace that of the 'native speaker' as the aim of language learning was only posed in 1997 by Byram and Zarate. At the university where I worked, language teaching was at many language departments still largely grammar and translation based with an assumption that students should achieve the level of 'near-native speaker' competence upon graduation. The underlying educational principles in language departments were rooted in the liberal Arts and Humanities with their emphasis on critical and rigorous thinking, objectivity and the notion of 'high' culture. The texts which were used for reading and translation in language teaching were challenging in their intellectual content, but the actual pedagogy did not emphasise communication in the foreign language in real life situations.

As I set out in chapter 1, outside the institutions adhering to liberal education, the grammar-translation approach was, justifiably in my opinion, recognised as outdated. A contrasting approach, that of Communicative Language Teaching (CLT), was favoured at universities with less traditional language departments or at Language Centres attached to universities. The content of these latter courses was originally developed with exchanges in typical tourist situations in mind, but this was soon incorporated into the new educational paradigm of instrumentalism which was gaining significance in HE.

Contemporary published language teaching materials for Dutch, such as *Code Nederlands* (1992, 1996) strictly followed the principles of the functional-notional syllabus with its bite-size approach to memorising phrases to perform language functions such as asking for directions, or ordering in a restaurant. Unlike the grammar translation approach, the pedagogy of CLT was informed by general theories of language acquisition and learning. The strength of this approach was clearly that students learned to communicate in every day situations and were familiar with appropriate phrases in a range of contexts. Students would be more likely to use 'authentic' language expressions within these set contexts. However, as a language teacher, I felt equally dissatisfied with this approach because of its lack of structure and linguistic underpinning on the one hand, and the reductive content focusing on pragmatic language exchanges only, on the other.

It would seem an obvious solution to integrate the positive aspects of each of these approaches into one syllabus, i.e. integrating the learning of grammatical structures in relation to communicative language functions, and, in addition, adding more interesting 'cultural' content. Indeed before embarking on the study for this book, in the mid to late 1990s, I had developed the second and fourth year language courses at the department where I taught. My brief had been to 'improve the language skills' of students. The principles that influenced my courses at that time were informed by, amongst others, Wilkins' notion of the semantico-grammatical category[1] (1976), Hawkin's (1984) notion of language awareness as a meta-linguistic construct, and views of language as 'discourse' in the sense of the units of language which contribute to coherent texts, i.e. the 'traditional' applied linguistics view of discourse. I wanted students to develop their language competence and skills both at the level of social inter-personal communication as well as at the level of academic and cognitive language use; the areas that Cummins (1979) refers to as BICS (basic interpersonal communicative skills) and CALP (cognitive academic language proficiency).

In practice this meant that in my courses I focused on the integration of form, function, text structure, text coherence and cohesion. But in addition, I also introduced an element of critical thinking in the courses, particularly in the fourth year language course. At that time I had not conceptualised criticality either as ideology critique, or as 'discursive mapping' (see chapter 3), but instead conceptualised critical thinking to mean scrutinising argumentation for its logical interplay of ideas in texts and being able to write logical and cogent arguments. In the initial syllabus for the fourth year language course then, I included a range of language activities focusing on 'heavyweight' topics such as the political and ethical principles of the various Dutch media or the political ideals and historical influences which were embedded in the current arts policy of the Dutch government.

The initial results of this course (developed in the mid-1990s) suggested that students' language and writing skills improved in the sense that they showed a greater competence in writing cohesive and coherent texts than was previously the case. They also showed an awareness of the reader (albeit a universal one) in writing reader-friendly prose[2]. Yet, I was still not satisfied with the course and its learning outcomes; the students' writing lacked authenticity and engagement. I realised that this was due to the fact that they were not able to understand, and certainly not produce, the subtle and connotative cultural meanings in language use. Students were quite capable of comprehending the surface meaning of texts and recognising stylistic points such as the degree of formality or informality of a text, but they tended not to respond to more subtle or specific cultural meanings. Nor were they able to produce language themselves incorporating these subtle or cultural meanings. Moreover, the texts that I exposed students to covered - due to the nature of the topics, mainly one register: that of the 'quality newspaper' or popular academic article. I realised that in my desire to provide a high standard university course encompassing critical thinking, I had unwittingly interpreted the notion of content and culture as couched in the liberal humanist ideology: culture as the 'better' products of intellectual thinking. And in having done so, students received a one-sided and value-based view of language and text as needing to adhere to certain standards.

Research Challenge

The challenge for me became to develop principles for language teaching and learning for a general language course in the context of a language degree, which would conceptualise communication as not only taking place in a *context of situation*, but also in a *context of culture*. I followed Kramsch in using these two parameters. The course would need to develop students' general communicative and critical language skills and relate these to the immediate context (which I had focused on in my original course), as well as relate it to the wider cultural context of 'ideas and values'. As I came to understand later, the notion of 'cultural values' carries with it the assumption of stability and clearly delineated 'cultures' which are distinct from others. As I started to conceptualise the idea of cultuurtekst, I soon came to use the notion of 'discourses' and 'discursive formations' (see chapter 2) in my own conceptualisation, although I used these terms only occasionally to students themselves, since they showed a resistance to these concepts. As a result of this study my own conceptualisation of criticality also changed. My intention was initially to develop students' critical language skills in both the 'critical thinking' paradigm I set out above and in addition in terms of CLA, which I saw as a way of alerting students to the fact that texts invite us to take up certain reading positions, particularly in relation to dominance of particular ideologies. Later in the study, I came to think of this as 'discursive mapping' as that afforded texts to be looked at in relation to complexities, contradictions and tensions in real life as well as the 'text producing environment'.

My intention was to develop these principles through re-designing my fourth year language course, and to reflect on my pedagogy and the students' responses to see how the course 'worked' in practice. This course is taken by students when they return from their Residency Abroad - a period of a year or half a year, spent at a university in the Netherlands or Flanders.

My initial intention with this study was to develop principles for good practice in language and culture teaching. As my study progressed along dialogic lines, i.e. a continuous reflection on practice in relation to theory, new concepts started to emerge. The research focus changed as part of this reflective process. Early on in the study, I articulated the initial aim further as 'developing principles for a pedagogy that would enable students to see text as cultuurtekst within a general language course'. Later on my research focus shifted from *developing* principles of good pedagogy, to *understanding* what happens in the classroom, and how students engaged with the concept of cultuurtekst, which had become the focus of my pedagogy.

It was the juggling and problematising of the initial and emerging concepts which posed the challenge of this study. In the process I followed various angles and themes, later abandoned them, resurrected some, picked up new ones, only to abandon some again. I will describe below which concepts in the end informed the thesis and how they changed over time. However, first I will set out the nature of the enquiry and the particular methodological features of this study.

Methodology and Messiness

The data for this study consist of two recorded and fully transcribed lessons out of the fourth year language course and two sets of fully transcribed student interviews. In collecting and analysing these data I engaged in a few different research orientations. As my study was aimed in part at improving my own pedagogy, it can be said to be a form of action research. However, this study aims to be more than a 'procedure designed to deal with a concrete problem' (Cohen and Manion, 1985: 223), as it seeks to understand how students responded to my approach and to see what would emerge from my classes in terms of student learning and engagement. In that sense my methodology is ethnographic in nature in trying to understand the 'richness, complexity, connectedness, conjunctions and disjunctions' (Cohen et. al., 2007: 167) of the classroom environment. I used the 'traditional' ethnographic methods of participant observation, although there was a tension between my dual roles of teacher and researcher. I also carried out in-depth ethnographic style interviews. My study reflected to some extent the tension which exists in ethnography between traditional naturalistic perspectives which sees the ethnographic product of field notes as a closed, completed and final text, and a postmodern orientation influenced by the linguistic, or interpretative *turn*. The latter orientation looks upon the discipline as characterised by difference and diversity and a series of tensions ethnographers and the people they study both engage in.

As I indicated earlier, my data seemed messy and contradictory. The realities of the classroom and the students' experiences seemed at times ambigious, elusive and slippery. However, it is in reflection that I can conclude that this indistinctiveness is an inherent part of research which seeks not to reduce or simplify the complexity of social reality. As Blommaert (2010: 11) states, social activities are 'not linear and coherent, but multiple, layered, checquered and unstable.' By refusing to impose ordered methods to complicated and kaleidoscopic realities, ethnography becomes critique, Blommaert suggests (ibid).

It can be said that in my own study I used the standard social science approaches of observations and interviewing. Similarly, in the initial stages of the data analysis I followed the 'mechanical' approach which is inherent in that standard methodology. Nevertheless, my intellectual engagement with the data, as well as with the 'project' as a whole, has embraced ways of thinking about method which sees messiness not as an unavoidable disadvantage, but as a 'way of working' and a 'way of being' (Law, 2004: 10).

In my reflection on the data, this study also borrows from grounded theory (cf. Glaser and Strauss, 1967). Rather than having a clear hypothesis at the start of the study to explain certain phenomena, research using a grounded theory approach aims to understand these phenomena through the data. Concepts and categories of explanation are 'discovered' through careful analysis of the data, as well as through reference to and reflection on theoretical literature. The tentative categories and concepts which emerge can be tested over and over again, against new data in a continuous cycle. In relating the data to concepts and to make links with existing theories and categories, I developed and rearticulated the concepts which I discussed in the previous chapters. This process of developing categories and concepts took place through 'coding': reading and re-reading the data and going through these to see what categories emerge, whilst acknowledging the multiple voices and what Denzin and Lincoln call the 'breaks, ruptures, crises of legitimation and representation [and] self-critique' (quoted in Atkinson et. l. 2007 (2001): 3).

The Concepts which Informed the Study

In developing my approach to language and culture teaching, I conceived of context of situation and context of culture as consisting at two levels: context of situation as the basic level that students would need to understand, and the context of culture as the level which would allow students to become inter-cultural – to understand where the text or the speakers were 'coming from' at an ideological level. Both levels are necessary to discuss and understand text, and indeed to become a competent language user and intercultural speaker. The second level, the context of culture, addressed the relationship between language and culture at the *generic* level; how values and ways of thinking are articulated and refracted in language through discourses. Following a range of other concepts, such as a Foucauldian notion of discourse, Bakthin's notion of multivoicedness and dialogue, Kress's notion of conflicting discourses and Maaike Meijer's idea of cultuurtekst, I applied these ideas to my language teaching courses, in what I came to call the cultuurtekst principle of language teaching. As I set out in previous chapters, this principle holds that seeing text as cultuurtekst helps students to become aware of the discourses and values which underpin our everyday communications and which are often taken for granted. I wanted to make students aware of this through reading texts, and also to apply, or at least be aware of it in their own communications.

The notion of cultuurtekst also helped me to address the tension that exists in the relationship between language and culture at the *differential* level, i.e. 'a' language related to 'a' specific culture. As I set out in chapter 3, we cannot hold to a view of a direct relationship between a language and 'the' culture with which it is associated. Yet, at the same time we cannot ignore that there are cultural patterns which relate to or, at least, are experienced by people as a national or localised entity (cf. Holliday, 2011). Many of the discourses that learners come across, however, are global and cross many different national borders, e.g. the discourses of 'terrorism' or 'environmentalism', but these 'global' discourses can be articulated differently in different contexts, includ-ing national ones. I have called this in relation to the text we discussed in class a 'Dutch articulation'.

In the process of conducting my study and analysing data, making tentative inferences and recognising categories, new concepts emerged. Whereas earlier on in the study I had worked with the notions of context of situation, context of culture, and different views of criticality, which then led me to the idea of cultuur tekst, the analysis of the data brought new categories to the fore. One of these new categories was particularly the importance of students' previous personal experiences, their emotions, their lifeworld knowledge as ways of making sense of the world in interpreting texts. Also, I realised that the view that students had of 'text' became an important part of their response to the text. The 'partial' or 'half' understandings (as I saw them), I recognised later to be an important part of the 'struggle to mean' and to gain a deeper understanding of these complex issues. As I realised, the 'rich' learning moments in the lessons had been where students engaged with and related the text to their own experiences.

Students did not just approach the text in an intellectual way, but also in an experiential way. That is to say, they read text in relation to their own experiences. I came to think of this way of intellectually and experientially engaging with text as 'seeing text as a text ethnographer', which I describe in chapter 3.

It was only retrospectively, after the process of analysing, further reflection and further theorising on the course that I came to see how reading text as an ethnographer is a way of engaging with the other, and being intercultural through texts, so it was not part of my pedagogy at the time of data collection.

This study analyses two lessons in the fourth year language course. In order for the reader to understand where these lessons fitted in, I will give a short overview of the course, its aims and the distinctiveness of my approach.

Distinctiveness of the Course

The course which I am using as the basis for this study, is a fourth year Dutch language class. The reason for focusing on this year group was partly pragmatic, in that this was the only language year group I was teaching at that point. However, more importantly, I felt that for researching the understanding of the cultural locatedness of texts, the fourth year class would be the best starting point as the students had just returned from the Netherlands or Flanders on their Year Abroad, and would therefore have already experienced various cultural practices; in other words they have already participated and have been socialised in the 'shared cultural knowledge' that the Dutch readership for the texts we are using would have. The fourth year students would therefore be more likely to recognise the discourses in the texts in relation to the context of production, and be able to discuss texts at a critical level because their language competence would be that much greater than in the first or second years.

Whilst the course takes a cultuurtekst approach, which borrows concepts from cultural studies, it is important to emphasise that this study took place as part of a general language class and not a cultural studies class per se. This means that students were not just engaged in reading, discussion and interpretation, but also in other practical language tasks which included all the four traditional language skills. However, as the students on this course have just spent a substantial time in a Dutch-speaking environment, they are confident communicators at the interpersonal social skills level (cf. Cummins), and are confident intercultural speakers. For that reason, the course focuses more on cognitive language skills. It is largely centred around texts (including oral and visual ones, although the latter were only touched upon), discussed in class and with a range of follow up writing activities.

At the time of data collection I had articulated the overall aim of the course at a practical level as enabling students to function and communicate at a professional, social and academic level in a Dutch-speaking environment within a wide range of social and cultural contexts. Apart from advancing students' actual language skills, this functioning particularly requires the students to develop an awareness of how language, communication and culture relate to one another. As I mentioned earlier the students need to be able to engage with communicative instances at the level of context of situation as well as context of culture. Both levels would demand a particular level of criticality. Looking at texts in relation to the context of situation requires students to engage with texts as products and encourages them to think critically about the text in terms of its interplay of ideas, its coherence and clarity. Looking at the context of culture requires students to engage with text as a process and encourage criticality in terms of 'discursive mapping': looking at texts for the way they draw on discourses and produce 'truth claims' and maintain assumptions about the world and power differentials. Students need to be 'critical intercultural language users', not only in their ability to read and talk about texts, but also in being able to write and address readers themselves, taking into account the communicative demands set by both levels of contexts.

As set out in previous chapters, the course differed from other Dutch language courses in its focus on awareness raising of 'culture in language'. In my previous chapters I criticised the instrumental approaches to language learning which are informed by the guidelines of the Council of Europe. Particularly in the Netherlands there is a strong instrumental focus in language teaching. My criticism of instrumentalism is directed at its limited and reductive approach to the social and cultural world. Frequently in instrumentally oriented textbooks, examples of 'language in use' are presented as if the language users all share the same context and speak with the same voice; as if there is a universal (native) speaker.

That does not mean that I believe preparing students for the world of work is irrelevant, but I believe that the 'world of work' is part of the complex wider cultural context. We cannot predict what particular linguistic and cultural contexts our graduates will encounter. What we can predict, however, is that these situations will be complex and differ each time, will be challenging, consist of many indeterminacies and will be intercultural.

As well as linguistic skills, students should develop intellectual skills which go over and beyond the cognitive academic language proficiency of writing cogent arguments in order to understand and become aware of language and its uses in the cultural world. These are not just skills for functional and pragmatic purposes, but also for ideological purposes: recognising on the one hand how ideas and values are reflected and constructed in texts, how power relations are reproduced and how the reader is positioned in certain texts.

With these factors in mind, I designed the course so that students were gradually made aware of the wider cultural context of the text and how this is reflected and constructed in the language used. I had 'packaged' this approach to students in the more pragmatically formulated notion of 'style'. After all students' expectations and their own objectives for this course would have been primarily to improve their language skills, not to learn how to analyse texts. The importance of looking at cultural values in texts, I explained, was partly to recognise as a reader where a text is 'coming from', but also, it would help them in their practical writing skills by being able to write stylistically appropriately for different aims and purposes.

Overview of the syllabus

The course of 20 weeks is split into two parts. In practice the material that I wanted to cover in the first part took approximately 12 weeks, with 8 weeks left for the remaining part of the course. The table below shows a schematic overview of the course. However, the course did not progress as neatly as the overview suggests. As well as discussing texts and doing writing activities, we also did grammatical exercises where appropriate. In addition a number of lessons were spent on translating texts as this offers a way to discuss cultural aspects of a text.

The first 12 weeks of the course consisted of two blocks. The first block, introduces the notion of 'style' in relation to the aim and audience of a text before looking at how language in its stylistic choice of structures and lexis can reflect particular ideological positions in texts. In order to help students to query the seemingly natural positions in texts, I introduced most texts in 'pairings' so that students could see how else the topic could be talked about. I also structured the ideas in a gradual way, moving from ideas of situational context to context of culture. Paired texts covered the same topic, but were either written for different purposes, for different audiences, or consisted of different genres or draw on different discourses.

The second block of this first part of the course applied these conceptual ideas to a more 'traditional' area of advanced language teaching; that of argumentation and text structure. In looking at structure and argumentation we initially focused on the 'textual' and 'product' level of the text, I introduced students first to the academic, rhetorical and linguistic aspects of these areas, e.g. how arguments and texts are constructed, and cohesion and coherence in texts. Then we looked at these texts in their situational and cultural contexts. It is in this block that I introduce the notion of cultuurtekst using the *Men's*

Health text which is the focus of this study. I will discuss these lessons in more detail below.

The second part of the course aimed to put the framework and the new understandings of cultuurtekst into practice in more practically and professionally oriented situations and contexts, such as report and letter writing and giving oral presentations. I ask students to look at addressivity and at positioning of the texts, as well as to write for different contexts, and drawing on different discourses. My main aim in this second part of the course with moving from cultuurtekst to instrumental and goal oriented areas of language teaching was to encourage students to apply their critical awareness of discourses to communicative events which may seem even more natural than those of popular media texts, but are equally filled with different voices, discourses and ideologies. In their writing I want students to be responsible towards their readers and audience – to take account of 'addressivity'.

Course overview

TERM 1 Language and Culture Block 1	**Aim:** to introduce the concepts in progressive fashion
Topics: • Representations of Dutch (and English) culture and society in the Dutch media • Comparing discourses • The multi-cultural society • A current debate, e.g. euthanasia • Gender roles and representations	
Texts used include: • Two newspaper reports from different newspapers reporting on an attempted prisoner break-out'. Newspapers: *Telegraaf* and *Volkskrant*. • Two interviews conducted by a female journalist in a series of interviews with 'experts' about their views on Dutch identity. One was an ex-diplomat, the other a young female parliamentarian of Turkish descent. Newspaper: *Volkskrant*.	• Texts from same genre, but different audiences and orientations are compared for different representation of the same event in terms of information focused on or left out; grammar, lexis and their effect. • Texts from same genre are looked at critically and used for discussion of content and are compared for different positioning from journalist and interviewee and the other way round, through language used.

• Two informative texts about Dutch identity: 1) textbook for social studies at secondary school; 2) the first two pages of an article from a popular academic monograph *Het nut van Nederland*.	• Text from text book is looked at critically for essentialist representation of an aspect of Dutch culture, and scrutinised for how the language used and its 'breezy style' help to 'convince'. Text from academic monograph is used to compare its style: its structure and stylistic strategies (e.g. repetition and contrast) also help to 'convince'.
• Three texts representing regional identities: 1) article from Dutch newspaper, *Volkskrant*, about the Cotswolds; 2) column in newspaper, *Trouw*, by Dutch novelist about his experiences of and views on London. 3) a texts from popular media, *One*, a magazine aimed at young women, 'exoticification' and essentialising particular travel destinations.	• The travel texts are used to further talk about representation of identity, and how the language and style used aids respectively 1) its nostalgic impression of the Cotswolds through romantic literary language, 2) discussing students' personal responses to the novelist's views, and 3) its exoticising and directing at audience by fitting in with expectations of genre, using techniques of rhyming and repetition and focusing on senses.
	• We analysed the texts for genre, purpose, audience and style. This led to talking about different values about work and personal development which were reflected in some of the texts.
• A set of texts to make the differences clear between aim, audience, style and genre of text. Topic: self development courses. Texts: 1) PR material from personal development/vocational training company; 2) a section from a popular weekly publication for young women (*Viva*) giving 'vignettes' of people talking about courses they have taken and how this helped them to develop personal skills; 3) course description from the website of a publication aimed at professional staff, *Intermediair Loopbaantrainingen*.	**Tasks and assessment:** Activities included discussion about and analysis of the texts. Writing tasks are in preparation for the assessment task which is to write two contrasting pieces: a fairly essentialised description of a country or region or town in a 'closed' style as well as a more nuanced version about the same place in a popular academic style.
Block 2 Argumentation	**Aim:** to apply the concepts to a larger range of genres relating to arguments, debates and discussions. Introduce the concept of cultuurtekst more explicitly.

Texts and materials used include:	Focus:

• Text book for native speakers about argumentation structures
• *Ons drugsbeleid mag er zijn.* Rationale for drug policy written by Dutch Health Secretary (published in *NRC* newspaper.)
• Three texts about a new euthanasia law in the Netherlands: 1 and 2) two newspaper editorials from *Trouw* and *Volkskrant* respectively. 3) An emotive interview with a mother whose child died through euthanasia.
• Three texts: 1) *Het multiculturele debat,* Paul Scheffer, NRC. This text later became a key text in the discussion surrounding multiculturalism in the Netherlands. 2) A criticism on this article and 3) Scheffer's response to that.
• Three texts about gender roles and representation: 1) a polemical text: 'De man als dinosaurus', Liesbeth Wytzes, *Volkskrant.* 2) An argued response to this text; 3) *Men's Health text:* 'Pas op. Er word op je gejaagd'.
	• **Text in context of situation:**
	  - Text purpose
	
	  - Audience
	
	• **Text as product:**
	  - Argumentation structures
	
	  - Argumentation types/genres
	
	  - Cohesion and coherence
	
	• **Text as context of culture**
	  - Genre
	
	  - Intertexts
	
	  - Implicit argumentation/discourses
	
	  - Cultuurtekst

NB The discussion of this particular text forms the focus of and is the entry point of my study.	
	Tasks and assessment: Activities included discussion about and analysis of the texts. Writing tasks were in preparation for the Assessment task which was to write an argument about the same topic and more or less the same viewpoint, but for different audiences and purposes and hence drawing on different discourses.
TERM 2 Practical skills	**Aim**: Apply the concepts introduced in the first half to communicative situations often encountered in work-related contexts

Oral presentations	Authentic contexts
Materials used: Textbook on communication Presentations from a symposium about the topic whether Dutch language is in danger of disappearing	We look critically at text book examples. It is useful to gain new language expressions, but we critique its lack of authenticity. We talk about different styles and audience needs and contexts. Addressivity and audience. We listen to two presentations held at a symposium in the Netherlands to see how they are structured and what techniques the speakers use, such as repetition. **Tasks and assessment** Students work on sample presentations for different contexts. These are recorded on film and discussed individually with students for pointers on style and manner etc. Oral presentation: students use the same topic as their year abroad research project and choose an appropriate and authentic context, and determine what role they themselves and the audience need to play. Students are assessed on relevance and appropriacy of content and style within the chosen context.
Report writing	**Identity**
Materials used: Authentic reports of institutions and companies	We look at these reports partly in terms of product, the kind of conventions within report writing and expressions and representations of statistical information, but we particularly look at these in terms of context of culture: what corporate or public identity the institution/company is representing through language and the information focused on (i.e. traditional and trustworthy, or dynamic, market leader, environmentally aware, successful, etc.). **Tasks and assessment:** Activities include discussion about and analysis of the texts. Writing tasks are in preparation for the Assessment task

	which was to conduct a simple study, i.e. in local swimming club or amongst students regarding eating habits, and to write two reports using more or less the same information but for different audiences and purposes.
Letter writing Text book on communication for a few examples. Many authentic letters: e.g. asking for donations, newsletter, letters from school to parents, invitation to a leaving party of a colleague at work, invitation to project meeting and so on.	**Addressivity** We look at text book examples critically. It is useful for some language expressions, but we critique its lack of authenticity. Talk about different styles and audience needs and contexts. Addressivity and audience. We used a framework I made for analysing letters and focus on interpersonal relations and positioning and power relations and how these are embedded in language. **Tasks and assessments**: Tasks included writing a range of letters for different purposes and audiences and 'relationships' including power roles This task is assessed during the exam where students have to write two letters about the same topic using different roles and purposes and positioning, e.g. provost sending letter to students advising not to go on strike, union sending letter to students urging them to go on strike.
Summary	**Context** In the last couple of lessons we focus on the importance of context in writing a summary. Depending on why you want to write a summary and for whom, you will focus on different aspects and formulate it differently.

The Lessons

The two lessons I focus on in this study represent the point in the course where I introduce the notion of cultuurtekst explicitly to the students. Even though we have looked at discourses in texts at earlier points in the course, I had masked that as looking at 'style'.

These two particular lessons fitted into a series of lessons within the block on argumentation, which had as its starting point gender roles and representations. Prior to discussing the *Men's Health* text, the class discussed a feminist polemical article, '*De man als dinosaurus*', ('The male as dinosaur'), by a female journalist, and a critical response to that. The students looked at this text particularly to see how the linguistic representation through grammar and style enhances the impression of the strong successful female and the weak disempowered male. I then introduced the text which forms the focus of this study, the text from *Men's Health* (see appendix).

The reason for discussing the *Men's Health* text was that it provided a range of different and contrasting discourses with the previous texts. Whereas the first two texts, respectively the feminist text and a critical response to it, came from a 'quality' newspaper (*de Volkskrant*), the *Men's Health* text is a different genre text from a popular lifestyle 'glossy' for men.

The rationale for using a text from the popular media is that discourses tend to be more exaggerated and easily recognisable. Moreover, as Wallace citing Luke et. al. (2001: 113) states, these texts may seem innocuous, neutral and requiring just a simple response, 'cumulatively they document and shape social and cultural life' (Wallace, (2003: 1). This particular *Men's Health* text, I felt, would easily yield a discussion around discourses and values in texts. The topic crossed national boundaries and the article drew on various conflicting discourses familiar in the western world. Moreover, I thought there was a Dutch articulation in the text, as I will explain below.

Framework and How it Relates to the Two Classes

The framework I have developed (see below) borrows to some degree from Wallace (2003: 39), in the sense that her concern with critical language awareness (CLA) is both with critiquing the logic, arguments and sentiments expressed in texts, as well as the ideological assumptions underpinning these (ibid: 42). As the basis of my framework I adapted Wallace's orienting questions which she based on Kress (1989): 1) why has the text been written?; 2) To whom is the text addressed?; 3) What is the topic?; 4) How is the topic being written about?; 5) What other ways of writing about the topic are there? However, I am not following Wallace's Hallidayan methodology, based on Halliday's Systemic Functional Linguistics (1994), partly because of its high level of abstraction which would demand much more specialist in-depth analysis and the use of metalanguage. My theoretical concerns are less with in-depth analysis according to clearly delineated linguistic categories. Instead, I saw my framework partly as a tool for looking at texts, at both levels of 'text as product', and 'text as cultuurtekst', each encompassing a particular perspective on criticality. As I set out before, one of my concerns with reading texts in class is also with the cultural. I saw cultuurtekst not only as a tool for analysis, but also as a guideline to facilitate the dialogue in class, to provide the 'fuel' in the process of collaborating in making sense of the text. Moreover, cultuurtekst also embodies the cultural aspect of language learning, as by looking at discourses in texts, students can access social, historical and political meanings.

I intended for the discussion around texts to move from a focus on text at a textual level, to text at a cultuurtekst level, which I saw in relation to respectively the context of situation and the context of culture. I based the level of context of situation on Hymes' model of communication, even though strictly speaking this model also encompasses cultural and social contexts as part of some of the speech categories such as norm and genre, but, these, I would say, are distinct from the context of culture, as they do not explicitly consider values embedded in language use. For my framework then I conceptualised the context of situation in a slightly more 'pared' down manner than Hymes' model, focusing particularly on the where, to whom, when, why and how. Or as I have phrased it in my framework, the text audience, the text function, the text structure.

English translation of framework

Framework for analysing and understanding texts

1 – Content: what (or who) is the text about?

- what is the main point?
- maybe also: what are the subsidiary points?
- what is exactly said about those points?
- **Relating to your own expectations and knowledge**
- to what extent do you recognise the theme of the text?
- in what kind of situations have you come across this before (having read or heard about it?
- and in what way?

2 – Immediate context:

- **aim/function**
- what does the text 'do'? (what does the text want to achieve?) examples of functions are: *to inform, to analyse a problem, to suggest a solution for a problem, to amuse, to give an opinion, to convince the reader of a particular argument, to explain something, to try and convince the reader to change his/her behaviour, etc.*
- Describe the function in relation to the content of the text. For example: *this text provides an overview of the different saving accounts available at this bank.* Or: *this text tries to convince the readers that the product of this company is the best on the market.*
- Which (strategic) means are used to achieve that aim?
  For example: *Engage the reader by appealing to making the theme recognisable, or engage the reader through grammatical structures, e.g. use of imperfect tense.* Or: *Convince the reader by referring to sources of authority, or by making comparisons, or by referring to a generally accepted 'rule' or convention, etc.*
- **target audience: who is the text aimed at?**

- is the text written for a certain situation or a certain publication?
- and what do you know about that situation?
- if you don't know that situation or publication, are there clues in the text which could help you to find out what kind of audience the text is aimed at? (for example: *is the reader expected to have certain prior knowledge, the way the reader is addressed (or not), the kind of arguments which are used, kind of sources which are used, complexity, liveliness, formality, and use of grammar: use of passives, complex sentence structures, use of verbs, nouns, adjectives etc.*)

3 – genre

- What kind of text is it? (for example: *a business letter, a personal letter, an invitation for a party, a news report, an opinion article in a newspaper, an essay, a report, an academic article, a conversation, a joke, an informative article in a women's glossy, dietary advice etc.*)

4 – text as text

- **structure**
- How is the text structured?
- What is the effect?
- **cohesion**
- How are the sentences and sentence parts connected? (for example: *formal markers, use of ellipsis, repetitions, through word order, synonyms, bridging sentences which indicate links explicitly etc.*)
- What is the effect?

5 – text as cultuurtekst

- How does the text talk about the topic and the 'participants'? Show this by referring to specific words and expressions. (For example: *written from perspective of the 'participants'; distant; critical; ambiguous; knowledgeable; angry; sympathetically; with empathy; with disdain; from a power position; as truth; cautiously etc.*)
- How is the reader addressed? (*as equal, patronisingly; as a 'student', from the assumption reader shares the same ideas and values; with (dis)respect; etc.*)
- Which values do you recognise in the text? (for example: *feministic; new age; religious; social-democratic; humanistic; conservative; capitalistic; individualistic; collaboratively; environmentally aware; nationalistic; etc.*)
- Which different 'discourses' and 'intertexts' do you recognise in the text? (*see above, and discourses reminiscent of law, text books, advertising, financial world etc.*)
- Are these values conflicting in anyway?

6 – evaluation

- Why is this text written?
- If you would write it for a different target group what and how would you adapt it?
- What other ways could you write about this topic (think about aim, audience, values and intertexts?
- Is it an acceptable text if you look at it from a liberal view of text structure (in terms of argument, structure, clarity and 'honesty')?
- How do you respond yourself to the text now? Compare with your own expectations you had written down at point 1.

I introduced this framework at the point of the lessons where we looked at the *Men's Health* text. The questions in the framework were not specifically geared to this particular text. So, even though one aspect of the second lesson related to Dutch articulation, the framework itself does not cover this aspect. The notion of Dutch articulation was not a general point to be discussed for each text we read, but seemed pertinent to this *Men's Health* text. There are six points in the framework, which relate to various stages in the interpretation process, as I had conceptualised this. These stages move gradually from content and description gradually to interpretating and problematising the text. The earlier points in the framework relate to looking at the text from an 'outside' perspective, whereas looking at the complexity of the text as cultuurtekst introduces discursive mapping which involves students looking at texts also from an 'inside' perspective.

In designing my framework I did not take account of the framework which O'Regan (2006) designed for his approach which he calls the TACO approach: Text as a Critical Object, as his study was not available then. My framework does indeed differ from O'Regan's in that his framework is designed to be interpretive, as well as analytical. My approach as I explained before was less explicitly analytical and partly formed the basis for discussion of text and content. Although O'Regan's TACO approach is more complex and more fully underpinned by philosophical perspectives, there are some similarities with my approach as a staged process of analysis and an aim to engage in 'discursive mapping' (Pennycook, 2006), so I will refer to his work in the discussion of my framework below.

The first point in the framework serves to invoke students' previous experience and expectations of the text in order to make them aware of the possible preconceptions they may have. This is not a pre-reading activity per se, because normally the students would already have read the text as homework in preparation for the class. However, the first reading of text as homework is primarily meant for students to read at a content level, in order to look up any vocabulary they do not understand. Point 1 in the framework then, is to ensure there were no misunderstandings which arose from unfamiliarity with the vocabulary or with certain (cultural) references to the text. Under the heading of what the text was about, I also included the recognising of main and subsidiary points in the text. This was because the aim of my lessons was partly to develop cognitive language skills.

The second point was designed to make students think more carefully about the immediate context of the text; the context of situation. This involved moving from the surface content of the text (which is discussed under point 1) to recognising what the text 'does'; what its aim or function is, and the way of bringing that about, such as the use of various argumentation schemas. Another aspect of this part of the framework refers to the target group: who is the text aimed at and how can you tell? Whereas the first point of the framework is intended to be purely at a description level, this second point in the framework moves the attention of learners on to the level of interpretation. This point in the framework constitutes the 'preferred reading', which O'Regan (2006: 113) describes as 'the *apparent* argument, perspective, or purview of the text as it appears to the reader and is therefore *preferred* in the sense that the text itself seems to indicate this preference.'

Point 3 of the framework, the notion of genre, bridges the notion of context of situation, i.e. social setting, and context of culture. I have given this a separate heading as it needs some special consideration, both in terms of reading as well as writing of text. In developing writing skills, it is crucial for the students to consider conventions of certain social contexts (Bakhtin, 1986; Fairclough, 1992). As far as reading a text is concerned, the issue of genre helps students to recognise the conventions associated with specific types of text and to consider why a text may deviate from these conventions and expectations.

The fourth point of this framework, text as text (i.e. text as a product), is designed to alert students to the textual aspect of text, which I see here as a more traditional, structuralist approach to text in language teaching. In this framework I am contrasting the notion of text with the notion of cultuurtekst. Under this heading students look at text in terms of cohesion and argumentation. The rationale for this was not only to develop cognitive language skills, but also to guide students towards the interpretation of text as cultuurtekst. I felt that, together with point 3 of genre, looking at the *effect* of the overall structure and cohesion of a text, would alert the reader to style as social language use, which would pave the way for seeing text as cultuurtekst. This point in the framework, as well as the previous two points, require critical work by the students which are on a par with the 'critical thinking' level defined by Pennycook (2001) as being an aspect of the liberal humanist paradigm. It is a level of critique which requires students to take up an 'outside' position towards the text they are reading.

The most important point for my purposes is point 5, that of cultuurtekst. In this section I want students to look at that aspect of cultuurtekst which recognises and maps the discourses and the voices in the text, and to see if the discourses are consistent with one another, or conflicting. The conflicting discourses are the most significant ones. For this aspect I borrowed from Wallace's framework (Wallace, 2003: 39) which focuses on how the topic and participants in the text are represented. I am encouraging students to recognise discourses by engaging their knowledge of previous texts, of intertexts, by asking: where have you come across this kind of 'talk' before? This discursive mapping, 'problematising practice' (Pennycook, 2001), applies to all texts, and not just to ones which show clear ideological positions, in terms of power domination. As O'Regan states (2006: 118) 'all texts are inserted into a matrix of social, political and economic meaning relations.'

The final point in the framework is an overall 'evaluation'. I use evaluation here, partly in line with Halliday (cf 1985) in attributing meaning to the text. However, it also has a more pedagogical rationale in the sense that it functions to summarise the points mentioned under 5, cultuurtekst, which can then be compared with the questions and answers which were given in the earlier parts of the framework. I followed Wallace's aforementioned Hallidayan framework with questions such as 'Why has this text been written?' which serves to make students aware that as well as text function, as part of immediate context discussed under point 2, there are ideological underpinnings to a text. Finally, I ask the students to look at the text from the liberal humanist perspective of text: Is it a clear, well argued piece of text?, before asking them to give their own response to the text. By comparing their answers under point 6 with earlier answers, I hope to alert students to the value or importance of analysing a text from different perspectives.

Important to mention is that my framework was not purely meant to help students interpret texts, but also intended to function as an 'awareness raiser' for students in producing text themselves.

The Text and my Analysis

The English translation of the text is in the appendix. I will offer a summary here.

The title of the text is: '*Huwbare mannen gevraagd*' ('Marriageable men wanted') with the subtitle: '*Pas op. Er wordt op je gejaagd.* ('Look out. They are after you'.) The text comes from a monthly publication called *Men's Health*. The publication is an international one, and the Dutch version carries the same English name. As far as I can tell, the texts are not translated from English, but written by Dutch authors for a Dutch audience. The particular issue (1999) which carried the text I was using for these classes, used the following editorial categories within the table of contents: 'Fitness and sport'; 'Relationships' (the category in which the article under discussion appeared); 'Psychology' (an article about stress); 'Nutrition'; 'Sex' ('How to keep going for longer'); 'Health'; 'Career'; 'Adventure'; and 'Fashion'. In addition there are a number of columns which all reflect the topics in the sections just mentioned. The categories and topics would suggest that the target group of *Men's Health* are ambitious, health and body conscious, fairly youngish men. The notion of 'success' is emphasised in many of the articles and columns.

Content and context

As described in the introductory paragraph of the text, the article is about single career women between 35 and 54 whose 'biological clock is ticking'. As the title states: 'Marriageable men wanted'. The women are represented on the one hand as aggressive young women who go out in the evenings to engage in '*mannen vernielen*' ('male-bashing'), and on the other hand as women who have a problem and need help, as they are incapable of maintaining a healthy relationship with a man, and are thus risking missing out on having a baby.

The 'preferred reading' of the text could be construed as advice or as a warning to men. In the last line of the introductory paragraph this is made explicit as the (male) reader is directly addressed in this warning:

Kijk uit, er wordt op je gejaagd.

Look out, they're after you. (literally: Look out, you're being hunted).

Equally, there is a whole paragraph with the heading: 'The career woman: instructions for use', in which advice is given. It starts with the following sentence:

Wat doe je wanneer je verstrikt raakt in een relatie met een vrouw die gehard is in de top van het bedrijfsleven?

What do you do when you get trapped in a relationship with a career woman who has been hardened in a top position in the business world?

There are some linguistic, as well as visual features of the text which suggest a half-serious as well as a half amusing undertone in discussing the particular 'social phenomenon' of the single career woman. Particularly the descriptions in the first few paragraphs, which describe some of the women in their 'male-bashing' exploits seem geared to getting some laughs:

Allen zijn ze op hun eigen manier even succesvol én .... even single. Nou ja, de meiden komen wel aan hun trekken hoor, dat is het niet. Dorien – 34, topbaan bij een bank – heeft al een paar jaar een relatie met een getrouwde vent. José – 36, manager bij een hotel in Utrecht – heeft een onmogelijke verhouding met een vage schilder met een alcoholprobleem.

All are in their own way equally successful and ...... equally single. Well, the girls don't go without, you know. Dorien – 34, top job at a bank – has had a relationship with a married bloke for a few years. José – 36, hotel manager in Utrecht – has an impossible relationship with some vague artist with an alcohol problem.

Similarly, the inset box with a quiz about 'how to recognise a desperada' clearly is not meant to be taken seriously, e.g.:

- *Ze heeft geen kinderen maar soms al wel de kinderopvang geregeld - 25 pt.*
- *Ze citeert moeiteloos enkele strofen uit 'Het dagboek van Bridget Jones, 59 kilo' -10 pt.*
- *Zeven van de tien zinnen die ze uitspreekt, begint met één van de drie volgende woorden: onafhankelijkheid, ruimte of respect - 20 pt.*

- She doesn't have any children, but has sometimes already arranged child care 25 points.
- She quotes with ease whole paragraphs from 'The diary of Bridget Jones, 59 kilos' – 10 points.
- Seven out of her 10 sentences start with one of the three following words: independence, space or respect – 20 points.)

On the other hand the thrust of the rest of the article seems fairly serious and informative. There certainly is a semblance of seriousness in its references to other sources. The dominant information source is that of the female psychologist, Labrijn, who has carried out 'exhaustive research' (*uitputtend onderzoek*) into this phenomenon. She has written a book on the subject and gives therapy to women with 'this problem'. Furthermore a documentary film by a Dutch female film maker set in New York is cited as proof that this problem is universal.

Representations and discourses

When deconstructing the text, the first paragraph sets the scene and gives the impression that 'the issue' of single career women is wide spread. They are characterised as a homogeneous group:

> *Ze verdienen geld als water en hebben alles wat hun hart begeert, behalve een man. Steeds meer hoogopgeleide carrière-vrouwen tussen de 35 en 54 raken in paniek omdat zich maar geen potentiële vader voor hun kind aandient. Ze zijn soms cynisch, vaak hard en altijd veeleisend…*

> They earn money like water and have everything to their heart's desire, except a man. More and more well-educated women between 35 and 54 are starting to panic because a potential father for their child has not yet turned up. They are sometimes cynical, often hard nosed, and always demanding…

The group characteristics are defined as:

> *Leuke, goed geklede, vlot gebekte meiden zijn het en ze hebben het helemaal voor elkaar.*

> Great, well-dressed girls they are, with the gift of the gab and they've really made it.

What it means to have 'really made it' is further defined in terms of possessions and appearances:

Designkleren, dakterras of balkon, vlot karretje onder de cellulitis-vrij getrainde billen, make-up van Clarins en Roc, koelkast met zalm en champagne en natuurlijk die job met uitdagende perspectieven.

Designer clothes, roof garden, nice trendy car under their cellulite-free trained buttocks, make-up from Clarins en Roc, fridge with salmon and champagne and of course that job with challenging prospects.

Moreover this group of women is represented as sexually aggressive:

Als de meiden uitgaan is zij [Suzanne] het die roept 'Kom vanavond gaan we mannen vernielen!', een kreet die een gevleugeld begrip is geworden in het groepje. Sarren, flirten, beetje zoenen, en net als hij denkt dat-ie jou heeft, toch weer afwijzen – aan veel meer komen ze niet toe.

When the girls go out, [Suzanne] is the one who shouts 'Come on, tonight we're going to destroy men!', which has become a battle cry in their little group. Provoking, flirting, bit of snogging and just when he thinks he has got it in the bag, drop him. Much more than that they don't get around to.

Initiating sexual advances seems to be the male prerogative.

Welke man heeft er geen avonden gespendeerd aan vrouwen waarin je een vermogen aan aandacht, humor en dineetjes investeert met nul komma nul aan (seksueel) rendement?

What man has not spent evenings with women, investing a fortune in attentiveness, humour and dinners with zero point zero (sexual) gain [profit]?.

The expected conventions of behaviour, it is clear, is for the man to take the woman out to dinner and bestow his attention and charm on her, with a clear expectation that this favour will be returned in sexual kind. The discourses on which the text draws are very similar to the ones which the *Men's Health* publication displays; discourses of success and status defined through possessions, job, a toned body and money. The latter is important; the quote above is located within a capitalist discourse, e.g. 'investing', 'fortune' and 'profit'.

These discourses of success take on a natural common sense assumption when applied to men. However, when applied to women, these discourses take on a negative connotation; it seems subversive and abnormal for women to have 'a top position in the business world'. Indeed the rest of the article makes clear that success is not a natural state of affairs, but it is a 'problem' for women. The first example of this is in the form of a woman in a documentary film, Laura Slutsky (!), who as a single career woman has 'developed strategies for being successful', which have led her to be 'confrontational and critical' in her relationships. Laura was told by her psychiatrist that 'her game was power'. She might win the battle with this, but she would lose the war.' Again, power and success are highlighted as problems. By describing Laura in relation to her psychiatrist, her desire to be powerful and successful is constructed in terms of an 'illness' or 'madness' (cf. Foucault, 1965). Moreover, the unnatural and aggressive aspect of this is emphasised by locating power in yet a different strand of meaning: that of fighting and war.

Another shift in tone then takes place. A discourse of psychological analysis is constructed as the female psychologist, Labrijn, is quoted, explaining that women's desire for success is occasioned through their *'jeugdervaringen'* (childhood experiences). Frequently, the father is absent, and because of this fatherly neglect women overcompensate by building 'a strong male ego' for themselves in terms of 'wanting to achieve a successful position in society'. But building up this strong outer protective layer

> *snijdt haar ook af van haar zachte kant. Haar creativiteit, haar vermogen evenwichtige relaties met mannen aan te gaan.*

> has cut her off from her soft side, her creativity, her ability to have stable relationships with men.

Labrijn continues:

> *Afhankelijk kunnen zijn is het taboe van de succesvolle vrouw.*

> Being able to be dependent is the taboo of the successful career woman.

Softness, creativity, being dependent are then constructed as 'natural' characteristics of women.

Another shift of personal self-development takes place as the psychologist describes therapy sessions in which women are trained in 'alternative behaviour'. Together with her clients she explores the behaviour that women themselves want to change. Moreover, Labrijn gives some practical tips to men who are in a relationship with a career woman. These reflect the discourse of self-development; on the one hand the shared responsibility is emphasised, and on the other, the importance of the man to protect himself and his own individuality:

> *Zoek en vecht samen uit wat wel en niet goed voelt in de relatie, ook als je voor jezelf geen pasklare antwoorden hebt. En blijf bij jezelf.*

> Work out together what does and doesn't feel good in the relationship, even if you have no ready made answers. And stick to your own convictions.

The final paragraph represents yet a different strand of discourse, which seems to be almost diametrically opposite to the discourses of the independent successful career woman. Instead, an intensely traditional image is presented; evidence of the successful results of the therapy sessions is given in the form of the marriage and birth announcements Labrijn receives from her ex-clients. Moreover, she herself points to how happy she is now since she has been in a 'really good relationship' for the past 5 years. Moreover, she also had her first child, she says 'beaming'. The last few sentences set the article within a wider context. Labrijn explains women of her age have been part of the generation which was conscious of feminism, and even though, she said, this was a phase that was necessary, it had led to a particular attitude towards men:

> *In die tweede feministische golf werden mannen individueel verant-woordelijk gemaakt voor allerlei maatschappelijke misstanden, voor de ongelijkheid. Dat heeft de attitude van je afzetten tegen mannen bevor-derd en onze generatie heeft daar last van. Ik denk dat er nu wel ruimte is voor een andere houding.*

> During the second feminist wave men were held individually responsible for all kinds of social injustice, for inequalities. That encouraged the attitude of contempt for men, and our generation suffers from that. I think now the time is right for a different attitude.

Feminism is represented here for its contempt against men. It would seem then, that the final discourse which emerges is that of anti-feminism. This final discourse, allows us, I would suggest, to read the whole article in the light of an anti-feminist perspective, or at least a perspective of fear of successful women, as success seems to be a male attribute.

The women in the text are represented in many different and conflicting ways. Through the range of representations and different discourses a picture is created where the discourses of power, success and sexual aggression are 'natural' for men, but unnatural for women, to the point that they are seen as 'ill' or at least as 'unhappy' when they display these male characteristics. What is natural for women is to be soft, creative and dependent, and to find happiness in a stable relationship and motherhood.

A discourse of self-development, both in terms of changing one's behaviour and gaining insight into oneself is also reflected in the text. Part of this discourse is the discourse of shared responsibility, ('work out together what does and doesn't work') and a discourse of individuality, at least when it applies to the male: 'stick with your own convictions'.

Dutch Articulation

Looking at the text as cultuurtekst as I did in the previous paragraph, means looking at culture and language at a 'generic' level. But I also felt that this text displays culture at a 'differential' level (cf. Risager, 2007), which I referred to in chapter 2 as 'Dutch articulation'. The topic of the text is clearly a global, or at least a western one; indeed students made intertextual connections, as chapter 5 will show, with American and English soaps and films. Yet my own interpretation of this text is that particularly the gender based discourse of women only finding fulfilment in motherhood was more likely to have occurred in the Netherlands. Whilst I realise I am treading on dangerous ground here, keen as I am to underline the pluriformity and multicultural aspects of society and avoid an essentialist interpretation, there are neverthe-less cultural and social specificities in society as a result of, at least in part, historical development. Certainly, in her history on Dutch women's writings between 1919 and 1970, Fenoulhet (2007: 1) highlights the 'extreme empha-sis on the nuclear family'.

Another Dutch discourse, as I saw it, was that of the semi-therapeutic one, which was quite prevalent in lifestyle publications in the Netherlands at the time (1999). On the other hand we could surmise that 'therapy talk', and the discourse of 'personal development' is part of many lifestyle magazines in the west. It has become so ingrained that we cannot even step outside it easily; it has become taken for granted to such an extent, that, even in a men's maga-zine, it does not seem out of place (at least not to me). However, I felt that a discourse which sometimes is referred to as 'touchy-feely', - the word already indicates a critical attitude - would be out of place in an English men's maga-zine. I also interpreted this particular discourse as an indication that strongly negative stereotyping of women and brazen sexism, as expressed in the first part of the article, was not acceptable, even in a glossy male magazine (which quite likely is also read by women), and needed to be toned down and wrapped up in a semi-serious therapeutic tone. Of course, the underlying sexism is still there, even, or maybe especially in the 'therapy-part' of the article. But the ther-apy discourse seems to make the sexism in the article more acceptable because of the tone of concern and caring it adopts, even using a literal female voice.

Using the Framework in the Classroom

In the first lesson students had not received the framework for analysis which I discussed above. I felt that it might make the class too formal and I wanted them to 'engage' with the text. For most of the other texts we had discussed in the course up to that point, I had given them questions specifically geared towards that particular text. In quite a few instances I found that following the questions one by one formed a hindrance to the flow of the discussion in class. In this particular lesson, then, the framework was intended to be more a guide for myself.

However, as I will show in chapter 5, in reality, it was very difficult to fol-low the framework. Whilst it had been designed to take student through the text progressively, the students themselves did not make that strict separation.

Frequently, in answering one of my questions, they would bring in issues that related to one of the other points in the framework. Initially, I did say on a couple of occasions; 'this will come later in the lesson', but as that frequently had the effect of stopping the flow of communication, I tried to steer students back to the point under discussion – and not always with success. Cooke and Wallace call this students 'not staying on task' (2004: 109). This happened even more frequently in the second lesson, as the students rather than pre-empting the next questions, used the text for their own purposes to 'talk *around* the text' (ibid), as I will show in the next chapter. As a result the framework was followed only in a very loose sense during both classes.

To prepare students for the second lesson, the cultuurtekst part of the framework, I gave students a copy of the framework and asked them to answer the questions related to point 5 as a homework task.

The Students

There are six students on this course, two male, four female. Five of the students have followed the whole programme in the department which included a language course in the first and second year and a year or a half year (varying between 3 to 8 months) spent in the Netherlands as part of the Year Abroad. The sixth student was a mature student, Chris, who was in his sixties and who followed an MA course at the department. All students have had experience of foreign language learning at an advanced level (i.e. at A-level or comparable) before they started this degree course. All students except one (Emma) started the degree course without any prior knowledge of Dutch. Students followed a variety of degree options which were either BA Dutch or a combination of Dutch with another modern foreign language.

All students are white, three are mature students (Chris, Emma and Eve), the other three either started their degree straight from school or after a gap year. All students were British, but students had a variety of background experiences. In addition there were two exchange students from the Netherlands, Marijke and Yasmin, who I had invited to take part in one of the classes which I use for data collection. I will describe the individual students below.

Emma

Emma was a mature student in her late twenties. She had lived and worked for a number of years in the Netherlands before she came to study at our department. She was the only student in the group who when she started her degree already had a high competence in Dutch. She was taking the BA Dutch programme.

Claire

Claire had studied in France for a couple of years doing a Baccalaureate, but had lived in Britain prior to that. She did not speak any Dutch when she started her study. She was taking the BA Dutch and French programme.

Andy

Andy had taken A-levels at a British school. He did not speak any Dutch before starting his study. Like Claire, he was taking the BA Dutch and French programme.

Sarah

Sarah had taken A-levels at a British school. She also started Dutch completely from scratch. She was studying BA Dutch and German.

Eve

Eve was in her mid-twenties which classified her as a mature student. She had lived for a brief period in Amsterdam working in a bar. She had a smattering of Dutch when she started her BA Dutch programme.

Chris

Chris was a mature student in his sixties. He had worked his whole life. He was taking an MA course at the Dutch department. He had learned Dutch many years ago and wanted to catch up on his language skills. His Dutch competence was particularly grammar-based and his writing style tended to be very formal.

Marijke

Marijke was an exchange student from the Netherlands. She was studying literature at the University of Groningen. She also undertook some work practice while she was at the department. In this capacity she did vocabulary work with students in a literature class.

Yasmin

Yasmin was an exchange student from the Netherlands. She was studying at the University of Amsterdam and was of Turkish descent.

In chapter 5, I use classroom data mainly, but not exclusively, relating to Claire, Emma, Sarah and Marijke, because their responses tended to provide the richest segments of data. In chapter 6 in providing a general overview of my findings, I also discuss some interview data relating to Claire and Sarah. I decided to focus on these two students because of their contrasting approaches to the cultuurtekst pedagogy. One of the students, Claire, could be said to be a 'model student', as she engaged well with this pedagogy. Claire has also, together with Emma and Marijke, contributed more than the other students to the classroom discussions. I selected Sarah for this study, because the data relating to her are significant: she resisted my pedagogy throughout the course and she was very open and frank about this.

Conclusion

This chapter described the context in which my study took place and I set out the conceptual framework which I developed to look at texts as part of what I call the cultuurtekst approach. I draw attention to the tensions, 'ruptures' and frustrations which were part of this study in terms of a number of areas, which included 1) the conflicting pulls of language teaching discourses in the context of my work; 2) the organic nature of the study, with paradoxical and 'messy' data and a constant interplay between data, theory and reflection; 3) and in the classroom itself, when students did not always 'play ball' or even resisted my pedagogy.

In the next chapter I look at the classroom data of this study in which these tensions emerge clearly.

Notes

[1] The semantico-grammatical category is one of the four principles under-pinning the functional-notional syllabus. The category holds that particular meanings are embedded in grammar.

[2] Student feedback was generally positive about the improvement of their language competence. The most pleasing comment (for me) on one student questionnaire was that the course had been 'very thought provoking'. On the other hand it needs to be said that my impression was that only the more academically motivated students engaged enthusiastically with the texts, whereas others treated the texts and activities as just another language exercise.

CHAPTER 5

Tensions in the Classroom

Introduction

In this chapter I look at what happened in the classroom data during the two lessons in which we discussed the *Men's Health* text, using the framework for analysis which I described in chapter 4. During the first lesson we discussed the text as 'text' and looked at it from the perspective of the immediate context, or the context of situation, which, as I described in chapter 4, I had conceived of as a pared down version of Hymes' model of communicative competence.

During the second lesson we looked at the text as a cultuurtekst, i.e. we looked at it at the level of the context of culture. For the second lesson I had invited two exchange students from the Netherlands to enhance the intercultural aspect of looking at text as cultuurtekst. I have explained in chapter 4 how these two lessons fitted in with the syllabus as a whole.

I had conceptualised both lessons to be distinct from one another, with lesson 1 focusing on the situational context, pedagogically speaking supporting the second, cultural and intercultural, layer of reading. Both levels of reading would require students to approach the text from a critical perspective, but I had envisaged students taking a critical approach to the text from an outside, seemingly objective stance in lesson 1 and a critical approach of critiquing the ideological stance in lesson 2.

To be able to answer the overall question of this study 'How do students engage with the cultuurtekst-pedagogy?' I focus in this chapter on what different ways of reading my focus in these two lessons yielded.

More particularly, I look at whether the cultuurtekst layer of reading would enable students to 'be intercultural', whether they recognise the range of (conflicting) discourses in the text, and whether reading the text at a textual level in the first lesson would pedagogically speaking support the reading of text as cultuurtekst in the second lesson. Finally I look at whether the notion of Dutch articulation is a fruitful one to pursue as part of a cultuurtekst approach reading.

A number of tensions emerged from these data, tensions which were located both in the fact that students' conceptualisation of the text and of the pedagogical activity itself were not always straightforward. It is particularly how students engaged with the text through 'dialoguing' and 'languaging' which led me to understand the importance of students' own experience in interpreting the text, and particularly how these experiences can be utilised and given a greater role in the classroom.

Lesson 1: Text as 'Text'

The Progress of Lesson 1

This first lesson took place with all six students in the group, 2 male, 4 female. The students had read the text as homework and I had asked them to underline and look up the words and expressions they did not know. At the start of the lesson we quickly went through any queries students still had at a semantic level. I had not given students a copy of my framework for analysis, so the discussion was to a large extent teacher-led.

Whilst lesson 1 was geared towards looking particularly at the level of 'text' as a product and in relation to the immediate context of the aim, audience, function and structure of the text, students did start to deconstruct the text and issues of representation and voice also surfaced. I followed the structure of my framework for analysis loosely. The first 20 minutes or so of the lesson were taken up by me explaining the task, i.e. that we would look at the text twice over the course of two different lessons, that in each session we would look at it in slightly different ways, and that Dutch students would be joining us for the second session. I also explained briefly what these two different ways of looking at text were and that in the second session we would focus on text as 'cultuurtekst', i.e. looking at discourses and possible intertextual references. Students had heard of the terms 'discourse' and 'intertext', as they had been mentioned in other classes, but it seems fair to say that the understanding of these concepts was still somewhat vague. I only explained these in a cursory manner. This was partly because in previous years when I piloted my course, students had shown resistance to explicit analysis in class. They felt the language class was for learning language skills, not for doing text analysis. Equally in previous lessons in the course with the cohort of students on whom I am basing this study, students had responded very negatively when I mentioned the word 'discourse'. One student, Chris, said: 'It's always 'discourse this and discourse that. It's just jargon', referring to another (literature) course. Other students were nodding in agreement. I felt at that time that we could talk about the issues by referring to terms such as 'ideas', 'values', and 'network of ideas', as these terms seemed less 'loaded' to students. After all, my aim was not necessarily for students to carry out a full discourse analysis of texts, but rather to raise awareness of underlying assumptions in texts. I did not purposely avoid the term 'discourse', but I felt we could talk about all the issues which a critical look at texts would throw up in language with which students felt comfortable. As it turned out some students occasionally used the term 'discourse' themselves, and whilst students sometimes searched for terms and phrases, they were able to express complex ideas fluently and at times in an academic voice.

The level of participation of individual students in this lesson was more or less on a par with that of other lessons during the year. Noteworthy is that the male students did not contribute very much to the lessons, though this was partly reflected in all lessons, as the female students tended to be very articulate and eager to engage in classroom discussions. Both male students signalled signs of resistance towards this particular text. Chris particularly disliked the text and said several times it was a very 'bad' (*slechte*) text. He commented once that the writer was probably drunk when he wrote it. Andy participated more than Chris, but tended mainly to contribute only when being addressed directly. Andy commented that he had not much to say about the text, because it did not relate to him. Both Andy and Chris rejected the triviality of the text. Andy commented later in his interview that he felt the topic would have been better discussed using a 'better' text. With this I assumed he meant an academic text, or one from a 'quality' newspaper. The female students in the class on the other hand clearly were invoking personal experiences and intertextual references, even in this first lesson. In my discussion of the data of this first lesson I am guided by the topics of the framework: content, function and text structure. A more specific selection of data was guided in the different ways of reading the text. I will now turn to the discussion of the first point in the framework; that of 'content'.

Discussing Text Content

Aligning with or Going Beyond the Text

In line with my framework, the first point I wanted students to engage with was the surface content of the text. My aim with this question was to elicit an awareness of the surface content, or 'preferred reading' of the text, what the text seemed to be about, at a first reading. Even though in my framework I had formulated other questions relating to content, particularly whether students recognised the theme of the topic and in what situations they might have heard or read about it, it turned out to be difficult to follow this format as the discussion tended to stray from the point at times.

My own interpretation of the surface content of the article was guided by the introductory paragraph in the text, as well as by recognising a particular rhetorical structure, often referred to in the Dutch mother tongue writing pedagogy as the 'problem-solution' structure (cf. Steehouder, 2006 (1979)). (We had discussed these rhetorical structures in texts a few weeks earlier.) Applying this structure to text, the 'problem' would then relate to a 'certain type' of women (single successful career women between 35 and 54) whose 'problem' is that they are not capable of loving and lasting relationships and were thus lacking a partner to have a baby with.

The question of what the text is about is of course very open and ambiguous. In effect I am asking students to give a concise summary in one sentence. And as we had not at this stage looked at the text in terms of its textual structure, the students responded from first impressions. Moreover, as I explained in chapter 3, readers bring their own experiences to bear upon interpreting text, so a wide range of interpretations is to be expected. This highlights the issue that summarising out of context – a standard pedagogical task in much of language teaching – is not a disinterested activity. We can only summarise a text if we know what the reason for the summary is and from which perspective we need to summarise.

The students gave indeed a range of different answers:

Eve

Eve: ...dat dat soort vrouwen nu bestaan en een beetje gevaarlijk zijn voor mannen [...] vrouwen die op jacht willen en jonge mannen willen pakken. [...] ja niet gevaarlijk, maar hoe zeg je dat nou? opletten

G: Ja een waarschuwing voor mannen.

Eve: ...that these kind of women now exist and are a bit dangerous for men [...] women who want to hunt and catch/ grab young men [...] well, not dangerous, but how do you say that: 'take care'?

G: Yes, a warning to men.

Andy

Andy: Het gaat over dat sommige vrouwen nu een mannelijke identiteit hebben.

G: Wat is het mannelijke daaraan? Wat is het mannelijke aan hun identiteit?

Andy: Dat ze hard zijn geworden..

Andy: It's about the fact that some women now have a male identity.

G: What is male about it? What is male about their identity?

Andy: That they have become hard...

Sarah

Sarah: eh... ik vond het een beetje grappig. Het gaat over hoe mannen ook gebruikt kunnen worden.

G: Als hoofdpunt of als bijpunt?

Sarah: .... er zitten een heleboel tips in over hoe je deze situatie kunt ver-mijden.

Sarah: I found it a bit amusing. It's about how men also can be used

G: As main point or as subsidiary point?

Sarah: ... there are lots of tips in the article about how to avoid this situation.

Claire

Claire: Kijk voor mij is dit de ideale vrouw die de ideale man wilt.

Claire: For me it's about the ideal woman who wants the ideal man.

Emma

Emma: Ik denk dat het echt gaat om vrouwen die echt denken dat ze niet zonder een man kan; dat ze echt een man nodig hebben.

Emma: I think it really is about women who really think they can't live without a man, that they really need a man.

The question of what the text was about was made even more difficult because of the range of conflicting discourses and the various textual elements in the text (e.g. the visual page lay-out of the text which included different headings, photographs and various text boxes). The students' interpretation of the text content showed that rather than trying to weigh up the different text elements together and to decide what the main thrust or point would be, they focused on only one aspect of the text. In doing so, students' answers depended on what they had selected as a significant aspect of the article.

Even though my question was intended to be one of surface content, students did go beyond that already, and tried to analyse the content in relation to an aim or an underlying meaning; they gave an 'evaluation' of the text, as Halliday (cf. 1985) calls it. Wallace (2003: 43), referring to Wells (1991), points out that it is inherent in readers, even very young ones, to discuss the implications of the text.

All students presented their answer with a confident voice and took the question to be a standard pedagogical one needing a definite answer. They did not query the ambiguity of the question, nor the ambiguity of the article.

Text Alignment: Discourse of Hard and Aggressive Women

The aim of this first stage of reading the text had indeed been to 'stay close to' the surface content of the text, and not to query any of the underlying ideological assumptions or the truth claims made in the text. However, even if students stayed close to the text, there were still significant differences in their responses.

Eve applied a common reading strategy to determine what the text was about. She looked at the first paragraph, where frequently the main point is introduced. In this introductory paragraph the text explicitly addresses the presumed male audience and says: 'take care: you're being hunted'. In her interpretation Eve is aligning herself with the text's presentation of what the main issue is; namely to say that 'these' women exist and men should be warned against them. She is interpreting what the text is about from a text functional perspective; the text aims to achieve something, and that aim is to warn men against these women. In seeing the content of the text as related to its function, she is in line with Hymes' paradigm where text function or aim is one of the features guiding communication.

However, in describing the women in the text as 'scary', Eve also evaluated the text. She presumably referred to the paragraph in which the women were described as enjoying 'male-bashing' when going out with friends in the evening. In focusing on this particular representation, rather than on any of the other various representations of women in the text, Eve saw the main point of the text as embodied in that particular discourse. Eve is confident in her interpretation of the text; she does not add qualifiers or modal particles.

Andy, similarly to Eve, feels the text is about a certain 'type' of women, but he pinpoints a different representation as the main point. By saying that they have a male identity, Andy may be referring to the part of the article which is written in a therapeutic discourse, where the male characteristics that women have taken on are explained as a response to their perceived lack of paternal contact. Andy does not elaborate on this, nor does he say the article *represents* the women as having a male identity. Instead he states that the text is about the *fact* that some women have a male identity. And as such he is staying with the thrust of the article. He says this in a seemingly objective voice by presenting his view as factual statement and by not adding a qualifier such as: 'according to me'. The meta-communication that Andy uses is in line with traditional educational discourse where the teacher asks a questions and the student responds. A qualifier in such cases is not necessarily a convention that needs to be followed.

Sarah's answer is interesting, because on the one hand she seems to align herself with the text position, yet on the other hand she is looking outside the text to interpret the main issue of the article. Sarah, like Eve and Andy, also uses a confident voice and uses no qualifiers such as 'I think', so she seems to be confident about her interpretation. However, she is also explicit about her own response to the article: she thought it was a bit amusing. Sarah is also evaluating the text; she is assigning meaning to it. Like Eve, she also sees the article in

Sarah

terms of its discourse of women who are 'dangerous' for men, but Sarah transforms that discourse into one of 'exploitation'; the text is about the fact that men can also be 'used'. So, Sarah sees the main focus of the article not so much in terms of 'the fact' that 'these kind of women' exist, but instead, she focuses on the *effect* these women have on men. Whereas Eve and Andy saw the article in the light of women, Sarah is seeing the text in relation to men.

However, Sarah also evokes her knowledge of society to attribute meaning to the text. By using the modifier 'ook' (*also*) Sarah transposes the issue of women being used (by men) to men being put in the same role. Being used is not just happening to women, Sarah seems to be saying. Moreover, Sarah, like Eve also assigns a functional meaning to the text. By stating that 'there are lots of tips in the article about how to avoid this situation' (of being used by women), Sarah sees the aim of the text also as informative for men, which could have a real impact on the readers' lives (avoiding a particular situation).

Even though the three students above, Eve, Sarah and Andy all hinted at the particular discourse of 'aggressive women', their answers still showed considerable differences, showing the complexity and ambiguity of the question of what the text is about. Eve stayed closest to the text by focusing specifically on the introductory paragraph, whereas Andy and Sarah were already 'evaluating' the text. In mentioning the amusing aspect of the article, Sarah pointed to the 'preferred reading' of the text. All three students had interpreted the task as a traditional language classroom task, and followed the academic discourse for that. They gave their answers in a seemingly objective voice. They also stayed on task in seeing text in relation to the immediate context.

Going Beyond the Text: Different Discourses

Two other students, Emma and Claire, did not just stay close to the text position of the discourse of 'hard' women, as Eve, Andy and Sarah had done. They both allowed a greater role for cultural context in their interpretations. But each of them drew on a different discourse in the article. Claire took on a position of critique from the start. By saying that the text was about the ideal woman wanting the ideal man in the set of data above, Claire is not only evaluating the text, in relation to its immediate context, she is relating it already to a context of culture. It is not clear how she has come to this interpretation, or indeed what she means by 'ideal', although in making this statement, Claire is, like Sarah, clearly referring to the text-producing environment and indeed discursive formations. She comes back to this interpretation later on in the lesson when she seems to refer to the pressure women are under to conform to certain lifestyle characteristics (e.g. have a great body, wear great clothes, have a great car etc.). In making this connection, she is also evoking her life experience and knowledge of media discourses by seeing the text in the light of these previously encountered discourses. She comes back to this text fragment several times in the lesson.

In contrast to the other students, Claire makes clear that she is not just stating what the content of the article is, but what *she thinks* the text is about; *Kijk voor mij is dit...* [Look for me this is about...]

Emma has yet another response to the question of what the text is about. Like Claire, she is not aligning herself with the position of the hard and aggressive women, and she brings her own evaluation and interpretation to bear on the text. She, like Claire, is explicit in stating she is giving her own interpretation (*ik denk dat het echt gaat om...*, I think that it is really about...). Her interpretation centres on one of the aspects of the article which focuses on women who are unsuccessful in their relationships, as represented through the therapeutic discourse of women who go into therapy to help them to have 'stable and mature' relationships. That she feels strongly about her interpretation is shown by the fact that she used and repeated the word '*echt*' (really) several times. She did not explain her interpretation nor why she specifically focused on only this particular discourse. Both Claire and Emma were already engaged in 'discourse mapping', even if they did not do this explicitly.

In summary, in the individual answers as to what the text is about, students focused on the various content aspects of the text, which represented a range of discourses; aggressive women (who are 'bad' for men), women who have a male identity, pressures on women to be perfect, and women who feel they are incomplete without a man.

In doing so, they discuss the text at a range of levels: functional, cultural (identity and representations) and intertextual (implicit references to other media representations). So even if the question of content was intended to focus students' awareness on the superficial text level, students interpreted the task as an invitation to go beyond the text, to evaluate the text and critique the ideas and truth claims implicit in it. Even in the answers which stayed closest to the text, and indeed the intended task, students inscribed their own meaning onto the text and evaluated it in relation to what could lie behind this text.

However, the contrast in these representations, the aggressive woman versus the image of fulfilled motherhood, was not seized upon by any of the students at this stage, and in fact never became a point of focus in either of the two lessons, despite my efforts to draw students' attention to it. Each student saw the text only in the light of *one* discourse, i.e. single-voiced discourse, whether about 'aggressive women' or about 'women as mothers'.

Discussing Text Function

Different Positions of Critique

From the initial statements about the content of the texts, students gradually started to collaborate to make sense of the text around the questions which focused more specifically on the pragmatic aspect of the text (audience/aim) as well as structure and argument. My intention had been to focus specifically on this immediate context of text production, but students continued to relate the text further to its wider cultural context.

In my own answer to the question of what the text was aiming to achieve, I indicated that there were two sections in the article where the reader was addressed directly; in the first paragraph this consisted of a warning (as Eve had indeed noticed earlier), and further on in the article, as Sarah had noted above, the reader was presented with advice on 'what to do when trapped in a relationship with a career woman'. However, apart from these paragraphs which indicated a warning and advice, at the surface level the article as a whole seemed to present itself as an informative text, albeit in a humorous tone, setting out the phenomenon of 'single career women' and its 'associated problems'.

Claire focused on the latter notion in saying that the function of the text was (in part) a commentary. However, as the data below show, Claire's position shifted immediately from taking part in the classroom exercise of looking at what the text was aiming to achieve, to critiquing the text itself for its positioning. She used both levels of criticality I referred to in chapter 4; on the one hand she criticised the text for not achieving its aim, and on the other hand she critiqued the text (albeit implicitly) for its ideological view:

Claire: Ik denk dat er zijn een paar serieuze commentaren want je denkt, ja... er zijn vrouwen die hebben problemen, maar ja sorry hoor, dit is niet normaal. er zijn veel vrouwen die ik ken, maar ik ken geen stereotiep... Dit is een heel streng stereotiep.

G: Welk stereotiep?

Claire: De eerste, op het begin.... 'leuke goed gebekte meiden, zalm in de koelkast'... ja....

Emma: Ik weet niet wat hij hiermee wil zeggen. Hij noemt een aantal vrouwen op die een bepaalde leeftijd zijn en een bepaalde levensstijl, maar wat wil hij daarmee zeggen? Is dat een probleem van alle vrouwen? Of van de vrouwen die hij toevallig is tegengekomen?

G: Ja, maar Claire zegt hij heeft het over een bepaald verschijnsel en jullie zeggen ook... je herkent dit verschijnsel, zo van de succ...

Claire and Emma: de succesvolle carrièrevrouw

Emma: Maar gaat dit altijd hand in hand met dit [gedrag]?

Claire: Ja, precies, precies.

Translation

Claire: I think there are a few serious comments because you think, yes...there are women who have problems, but sorry, this is ridiculous.

I know many women, but I don't know a stereotype[ical one]… this is a very strong stereotype.

G: Which stereotype?

Claire: The first… at the beginning… 'good looking girls with the gift of the gab, salmon in the fridge'… yes…

Emma: I don't know what he intends to say with that. He talks about a few women of a certain age and leading a certain lifestyle, but what does he want to say with that? Is that a problem of all women? Or just the women he has happened to have met?

G: Yes, but Claire said… you recognise the phenomenon, that of the succ…

Claire and Emma: of the successful career woman

Emma: Yes, but is that always accompanied by this [behaviour]?

Claire: Yes, exactly, exactly.

Rather than staying with the task of identifying the aim of the text, which Claire brushes off with the comment that it could be seen to be a commentary about problems that women have, she immediately turns to the implication of the text by relating it to her own experiences and evaluating it in accordance with those.

Claire makes use of her personal experiences at two levels. In stating that the text aims to be a serious commentary she legitimises the topic, it seems, and confirms that 'women who have problems' do exist. So she does not dismiss the text as ludicrous or not worthy of discussion outright (although which 'problems' Claire is referring to is again not clear: women who are 'hunting', women not having successful relationships, women harassing men, women feeling the biological clock?).

But Claire also makes use of her lifeworld knowledge as she starts to deconstruct the text. She looks not just at the text, but she uses – implicitly - the context of her own experiences as a reality check against which to gauge her own response to the text; there isn't anyone she knows who is like this. Claire is moving on from 'text' to critique its representation.

By asking students to look at the text at a textual level in relation to immediate context, I had assumed students would take on an 'outside' position (i.e. looking at the text for its textual intricacies and specificity at a seemingly objective level). This outside perspective is surrounded by its own conventions of 'educational talk', where in class students usually employ an 'analytical voice'. However, as Claire is taking on a position of critique and using her experience of the world to look at text at a cultural level, she, in contrast with the convention of this approach, switches to using a 'personal' voice: 'well, I'm sorry, but this [stereotype] is ridiculous'.

Emma then contributes to Claire's analysis and critique by trying to link the excerpt quoted by Claire with the motivation or intention of the author. Emma is also critical of the text in different ways. On the one hand she criticises the author's lack of clear purpose and his lack of intellectual rigour in using stereotypes. But, at the same time she also takes a more critical cultural perspective on board; she starts to consider that the excerpt is a generalisation which suggests all women display the same lifestyle characteristics. Both Claire and Emma are starting to relate the text to social and cultural perspectives and knowledge, Claire critiquing the text for not according with reality, Emma for its generalisation.

Text Alignment in Order to Understand the Male Perspective

Sarah on the other hand, provided a very different take on the idea of what the text aimed to achieve. Since the students had brought the discussion on to a cultural level, I wanted to build on this by focussing their attention on what these particular stereotypes might signify. The stereotypes to which Claire above had referred, were a set of lifestyle characteristics that successful career women displayed, such as having a house with a balcony, luxury food, snazzy car and so on. But when I ask, in response to Claire's statement in the set of data above, why the author might have chosen those particular clichés, Sarah interpreted my question not as an invitation to refer to the social world or other views she may have had. Instead she brought the discussion back to the textual level referring to the aim of the text, which was indeed the aim of this pedagogical activity in the first place. In doing so, Sarah introduced the notion of the intended reader:

Sarah: Ik denk dat hij zo begint om ze zo aan te trekken, ze zijn daarin geïnteresseerd... als je aan een leuke goed geklede mooie vrouw denkt, dan als je als man dat artikel leest dan denk je van 'he mmmm' interessant en dan wat is het, hoe gaat het verder, dus het is eigenlijk... het trekt precies de mannen aan... dus het werkt alsof het zo'n vrouw is, 't zegt: hier is een groepje mooie vrouwen en we gaan hun houding bespreken en dat... dus het brengt de man die de tekst leest, in, zeg maar, om eh om het verder te gaan lezen en aan het eind is het zo andersom dat eigenlijk eh dan willen ze niet meer... dan zijn ze niet meer in deze vrouwen geïnteresseerd want ze zijn eigenlijk een beetje kinderachtig.

[...]

Sarah: Ja maar volgens het artikel... dus aan het eind dan is dan wordt de mannen vrijgelaten, zeg maar, van de vrouwen in de tekst.

G: Hoe wordt hij daardoor vrijgelaten...?

Sarah: Omdat gewoon hoe het aan het eind is dan zou hij niet meer geïnteresseerd zijn in de vrouw want het lijkt alsof ze een beetje stom is en nergens naartoe gaat.

G: Waar zie je dit precies? aan het eind hè, ja 't eind is interessant hè, Claire noemde het eind ook al...

Sarah: Ja ik denk niet dat het oppervlakkig is want 't gaat over de relatie met hun vader. Als je kijkt daarnaar dan zie je dat het is een sociologische en psychologische analyse over wat er in hun hoofden zitten. Dus eigenlijk denk je: ze zijn een beetje gek, het is eigenlijk... ze weten niet wat ze willen. Ze willen gewoon alles wat ze denken te kunnen krijgen. Dus eh 't gaat eigenlijk over de manier waarop mannen oppervlakkig in deze vrouwen geïnteresseerd zijn, maar de doel van de tekst is eigenlijk te zeggen: nou deze vrouwen zijn niet goed voor je want ze kunnen niet goed met je praten, want ze kunnen alleen maar over hun praten en...

G: Ja ze zijn niet goed voor je en ze zijn alleen maar met zichzelf bezig.

Sarah: Ja.

Translation

Sarah: I think that he starts like that to attract them. [To draw the male readers into the article] They are interested in that... if you think about a nice well-dressed beautiful woman, then when you read the article as a man then you think: mmmm interesting and then:...what is it? How does it continue? So really. It attracts exactly the men... so it works as if it is one of those women, it says: here is a group of beautiful women and we are going to talk about their attitude and that... so it brings the man who is reading the text in, as it were, to eh to read further and at the end it is the other way round that actually eh then they don't want them anymore... then they are not interested in these women anymore, because really they are a bit childish.

[...]

Sarah: Yes, but according to the article... so at the end the men are released as it were from the women in the text

G: How is he released by that?

Sarah: Because, well just how at the end he is not interested anymore in the woman because it seems as if she is stupid and going nowhere.

G: Where do you see that exactly? The end is interesting isn't it, Claire also mentioned the end...

Sarah: Yes, I don't think that it is superficial because it is about the relationship with their father. If you look at that then you see that it is a sociological and psychological analysis about what is in their heads. So actually you think… they are a bit mad, it is really… they don't know what they want. They really want everything that they think they can get. So eh it is really about the way these men are superficially interested in these women, but the aim of the text is really to say: these women are no good for you because they can't really talk with you, because they can only talk about themselves and…

G: Yes, they are not good for you as they are only concerned with themselves.

Sarah: Yes.

Sarah is constructing a different context in which to interpret the aim of the text by referring to the intended reader. In explaining why these stereotypes were mentioned in the text, Sarah focuses on the rhetorical structure of the text. She sees a parallel between the way that the text is structured as if it were a metaphor for the women themselves; the quote which Claire called stereotypical, (the description of women in terms of lifestyle characteristics) Sarah regards as a rhetorical effect: the male reader would be attracted to these women because they are good looking, and so would be inclined to read further. But, further on in the article, Sarah says, the male reader would realise these women are 'stupid' (*stom*). With her interpretation Sarah brings the discussion back again to the textual level; both in term of how the text is constructed which leads her to conclude that the aim of the text is to say to the reader: 'these women are not good for you'. The text function is then, as Eve had suggested in the first set of data, a warning to men.

Assigning a function to a text takes account of a social context; the immediate context in which the text functions as a communicative act. Sarah did indeed consider a social context: that of the male reader who needs to be warned against 'these' women. By describing this text function from the perspective of how a male reader might approach this text, it might seem that Sarah is trying to read the text interculturally: she is trying to understand the 'other'; the 'other' being the male author as well as the male reader for whom the text is intended. It would seem that Sarah is trying to relate the text to the context of reception, but as she is not referring to previous knowledge, or experiences of the context of the intended readers of the text, she is taking her cue from the text itself. So by explaining how a male reader might read the text, she is actually 'imagining' this context.

Like Emma and Claire, Sarah focuses just on one of the discourses in the article; but unlike Claire and Emma, she does not see the article to be about women who are out to hunt or hurt men, but women who are 'stupid' and 'a little bit mad'. She seems to refer to the part of the text which describes women in therapy in order to deal with their inability to have long-term relationships. She does not see the text as representing women as such, but as a description of how women 'are'.

Sarah, like Emma and to a lesser extent Claire, also feels sure about her interpretation is the 'correct' one. In one of her interviews she later states that she really doesn't see how you can interpret the article in any other way.

Discussing Text Structure

Conflicting Discourses

My intention with focusing on textual structure was to encourage students to recognise the different ways in which the women in the text were portrayed. This would then prepare the way for seeing the text as cultuurtekst and the multiple and contrasting discourses embedded in it. In the course of the discussions so far, students had located their comments regarding the text always within one particular representation of the women, one particular discourse. Students were not necessarily aware that they saw the text in terms of a *representation*. In this lesson, I did not use the meta-language of the cultural studies oriented analysis, which makes up the cultuurtekst part of the framework we would discuss in the next lesson. Students seemed to regard their interpretation as 'obvious'. As I had said before, students felt confident about their interpretation, and at no point did they seize on the conflicting answers that each student seemed to give in terms of what they thought the main point or aim of the text was. Students then read the text as, what Kramsch (1993: 27) calls after Bakhtin, a 'single-voiced discourse'.

Only Claire had voiced her concern with the conflicting discourses. When I asked earlier in the lesson whether there was an argument in the article, she said:

> Claire: *Maar ik denk dat het begint met een idee en dat het eindigt niet met hetzelfde idee, of in het midden is er een… there's wires crossed.*
>
> Claire: But I think that it starts with an idea and it does not end with the same idea, or in the middle there is eh… wires crossed.

In the data below, I am trying to focus students' attention to the contrast of the discourses in the beginning and end of the article; what Claire described as 'having its wires crossed'. The set of data below starts with me asking how women are represented at the end of the article (i.e. in terms of fulfilled motherhood) in comparison to the beginning, where women were first described in terms of 'ladette' behaviour out to 'destroy men', and in the paragraph following that, where they are represented in terms of their consumerist lifestyle. Claire and Emma disagree in their interpretation:

G: ... *je zei eerder het is een vreemd eind van de tekst heel anders... de vrouw wordt aan het eind totaal anders beschreven dan aan het begin. Hoe wordt ze anders beschreven?*

Emma: een beetje zielig.

G: *Wordt ze als zielig beschreven? Vanuit wie gezien? Vind jij dat ze zielig is of vindt de schrijver dat?*

Sarah: wWt betekent zielig?

G: *Pitiful, iemand waar je medelijden mee zou hebben.*

Claire: Maar de vrouw op het eind zegt... eeh ja, 'mijn relatie gaat nu al vijf jaar hartstikke goed: dat is echt heerlijk'. Maar het is... wennen... 'zeker voor vrouwen van mijn generatie'. Dus voor haar, zij is een andere vrouw, ze heeft geleerd en nu ...alles gaat goed, nu heeft zij een man en een kind en zij heeft... ja...

[Claire and Emma talk at the same time, but I think Emma says]:

Emma: Dus hij heeft toch eigenlijk wel bereikt wat het doel was waar al die vrouwen naar streven.

G: *ja maar dat is de psychologe dus...*

Emma: ja, maar dat is dus het man-en kindverhaal.

Translation

G: ... You said before that the text has a strange end... very different... at the end the woman is described very differently from the beginning. How is she portrayed differently?

Emma: a bit '*zielig*' [pitiful].

G: is she described as pitiful? From whose perspective? Do you think she is pitiful or does the author think that?

Sarah: What does 'zielig' mean?

G: pitiful, someone whom you would pity.

Claire: but the woman says at the end: ... eeh [she quotes] 'yes, my relationship has been going really well now for 5 years and that is really wonderful', but it is... getting used to... 'for women of my generation'. So for her, she is another woman, she has learned and now... everything is going well, she has a man and a baby and she has... yes...

[Claire and Emma talk at the same time, but I think Emma says]:

Emma: so he has achieved what the aim was of all those women.

G: Yes, but she is a psychologist so...

Emma: Yes, but that is the husband and child narrative.

Emma does not take my question as an invitation to describe what that particular representation was, but she momentarily steps outside the classroom discourse of text analysis, and uses a personal voice by making a value statement: the women (as described at the end of the text) are to be pitied. Claire disagrees with that particular value judgement; after all, she says, the woman in the text describes herself as happy. She has learnt [from her therapy] and now everything goes well. Claire further quotes from the text itself, saying that women of her (i.e. the female psychologist's) generation have 'had to learn', but now 'everything is going well'. Claire is trying to find evidence in the article to describe this particular discourse, but Emma responds to Claire by switching the focus from the text and the portrayal of women in that last section, to the author: 'he has achieved what the aim was for all those women', and she concludes by saying: 'that is the 'husband and child narrative'', which she explained earlier as the way that women are seen as reaching fulfilment only through motherhood. So Emma seems to suggest that since the article finished with this particular representation, this shows that the representation of women as fulfilled by their relationship and 'happy motherhood' is the 'solution' or most important discourse of the article: he [the author] achieved what all those women want. Emma looks at the text from a critical ideological perspective; she critiques the intensely traditional view of women finding happiness only in marriage and motherhood, but in this critique she is not considering any of the other discourses and representations. The discourse or representation of women as taking on the 'male' characteristics of achievement and success, she did not mention.

Claire is much more prepared to see the text in its complexities of conflicting discourses, and is still struggling to make sense of the text. Emma is not. She is sure of her interpretation.

Conclusion Lesson 1

The focus of this first lesson was to look at text on a textual level and in relation to the immediate context. What emerged was that, even at this level of looking at text, many different interpretations are possible. The range of answers students gave to the first question about the content of the text showed how complex and ambiguous such a question is. Indeed, I take a view that text interpretation is a process in which readers use their experiences and lifeworld knowledge to *give meaning* to the text, not to *extract* pre-existing meaning (see chapter 3). However, that does not mean we should allow for a limitless number of interpretations in pedagogical activities. I believe, along with Wallace (2003: 16) that we can talk about a range of 'preferred readings' of text. The answers to the question about content showed that students do not look at text in a disinterested way. Even if students try and stay close to the text in their answers, they still inscribe meaning, they 'evaluate' the text, and see it in relation to its context in relation to its effect on the world; e.g. the text is about women who have a male identity, the pressure to be 'perfect', or about how women 'use' men, or, in total contrast, that women only gain happiness through having a stable relationship and a child: what one student called the 'husband and child narrative'.

This may show that seeing text as stable, which is in effect the assumption underlying questions such as what the text is about, is an artificial and ambiguous task.

Another significant aspect to emerge from the data of this first lesson, is that in ascribing meaning to the text, students tend to focus on only one of the discourses within the text, rather than seeing the text in its entirety and with a complexity of multiple discourses. Critical thinking merged with critique of ideology in some instances.

Lesson 2: Cultuurtekst

Of the group of 6 regular students Sarah and Andy were not present in this lesson, but two exchange students from the Netherlands, Yasmin and Marijke joined this class. I had invited them to create a dialogic space in the classroom as well as an intercultural element in which students could discuss various interpretations and relate to other texts which drew on similar or significantly different discourses. Because I wanted to introduce the idea of 'Dutch articulation', i.e. what I perceived to be the intensely traditional discourse on women, I also thought the presence of the Dutch students might add an extra layer of interculturality. To ensure the Dutch students were prepared for this class I had given them a few articles we had discussed during this block on gender, and the framework for analysis that guided our discussions. I had also briefly discussed with the Dutch students the issue of 'cultuurtekst' and I had given them a photocopied handout of a few pages from a book by Maaike Meijer, in which she discusses the notion of cultuurtekst. This meant that the Dutch students were more explicitly prepared for this class on a theoretical level than the regular students of the class, as these had not received the text by Maaike Meijer. As I explained in chapter 4, I had not been explicit throughout the course about its underpinning theories, as I had assumed, partly based on previous experiences in other classes, that students would not appreciate theoretical discussion or information as part of a language class.

To prepare the regular English students for this particular class I had asked them to complete a homework task. This task was to write down their answers to the cultuurtekst section under point 5 of the analysis for framework we used (see appendix). These questions were designed to get students to recognise which discourses underpinned the text, and asked how the topic and subjects in the text were talked about; how the reader seems to be addressed; which discourses or intertexts they recognised, and whether these were in any way conflicting with one another. All of these questions asked for specific references to linguistic points of vocabulary or grammar to explain their answer. Sarah was the only student who had not carried out this piece of homework. Emma had given her own interpretation to the task and rather than treating it as an academic and analytical exercise she wrote a spoof on the original text as if it was an article in a glossy women's magazine.

The Progress of Lesson 2

The aim of the second lesson was to discuss the text as 'cultuurtekst': text as a cultural construct through discursive mapping. I had wanted to draw students' attention to the prominence of particular discourses in the text, and how these took on an aura of 'truth'. The issues of representation had surfaced in the first lesson, but I wanted students to recognise the cultural locatedness of the text, i.e. the different discourses and values, and to see whether the range of different discourses added an extra layer of meaning to the text.

The lesson moved from eliciting some initial responses from the Dutch students to discussing issues of representation: how maleness and femaleness was constructed and what particular values, intertexts and discourses were recognisable. Finally we moved to the question whether this issue is talked about differently in England and Holland; in other words was there a Dutch articulation? By the exercise of discursive mapping, as well as looking at 'Dutch articulation', I asked students in effect to look at both a 'generic' and a 'differential' level of language and culture (see chapter 3).

After the short discussion around the initial responses of the Dutch students, I had asked students to do an exercise in pairs to look specifically at how men and women were represented in the text and to make a list of words and expressions which showed that. The aim of the exercise was to encourage students to see these different discursive formations through looking at the language used. By doing the exercise I hoped to make the (conflicting) discourses visible. After this exercise we looked at the text in sections by which I hoped that the students would recognise the different voices with which women were represented. So far in the first lesson only Claire had picked up the issue of the different representations. In the second lesson which I discuss below, students were 'dialoguing' more with one another and responding to one another's comments than in the previous lesson.

On the whole the Dutch students took a fairly equal part and the English students were not particularly more interested in what the Dutch students had to say in comparison to themselves. The Dutch students were perhaps a little reticent and less likely to respond as this was a new group and also a new way of looking at texts. The English students felt very comfortable in their comments about how things were 'done' in the Netherlands; as they had lived there during the year abroad, they felt their observations were valid.

My role during this lesson was less fore-grounded than in the first lesson. Whereas I asked questions to initiate discussions, responded to students' answers, and asked students to elaborate on certain points, on the whole I took a background role. Students were dialoguing and engaged in the discussions, frequently without any prompting from me.

I did not use the questions on the framework explicitly, as it had become clear during the first lesson, that working our way through the framework rigidly stopped the flow of the discussion. Nevertheless, there was a progress in the lesson as I had the framework questions in my mind, and through the discussions the notion of discourses and values in the text were gradually made more explicit by the students. However, this process did not take place neatly in a linear way and also led to misunderstandings amongst students as they sometimes were more interested in discussing the issues which were thrown up as a result of having highlighted the discourses, rather than seeing the text as the micro cosmos in which these discourses were reflected and recreated. It turned out that the presence of the Dutch students helped to make the discussion more focussed. I will start with the latter point below, and then move on to discuss how students engaged with the text and its underpinning values in an increasingly intercultural and ethnographic manner.

Role of the Dutch Students: Towards an Understanding of the Socio-cultural Context

My expectations of the role of the Dutch students had been that the English students would be more to the point in their answers, because they had experience of discussing texts in previous classes, albeit not using an explicit framework. As it turned out, it worked the other way round. The inclusion of the Dutch students in the lesson immediately raised the level of discussion, as their responses prompted more dialogic responses from the other students.

In giving their first responses to the text, both Dutch students straight away took an evaluative stance to the text and considered, without being prompted, what might lie behind the stereotypical representation of women in the text:

G: Wat is jullie eerste reactie op de tekst... puur persoonlijk en waar ging de tekst over naar jouw gevoel?

Yasmin: Heel herkenbaar, ja. Als je naar programma's kijkt als 'Sex in the city' en 'Ally McBeal' dan gaat het echt daarover. En dit artikel, ja dat was niet iets nieuws... ik herkende alles.

G: Je herkende, wat precies?

Yasmin: Nou zeg maar die hoger opgeleide vrouwen die een man wil om haar leven, zeg maar, compleet te maken en dat lees je ook in tijdschriften als Cosmopolitan en normale kranten ook en dergelijke, voorgekauwd spul was dit... ja dat heb ik heel vaak gelezen.

Translation

G: What is your first reaction to the text... purely personal reaction and what was the text about, you feel?

Yasmin: Very recognisable, yes, when you look at programmes like 'Sex in the city' and 'Ally McBeal' then it is really about that. And this article, yes it was nothing new... I recognised everything.

G: You recognised what exactly?

Yasmin: Well, those well-educated women who want a man to make their life, well, complete. You read that also in magazines like 'Cosmopolitan' and also normal newspapers, hackneyed stuff this was, yes I have read this often.

The dialogue continues:

Marijke: Dat was mijn reactie ook wel. Om nou te zeggen... ja, ik herken het natuurlijk ook wel, ik heb ook artikelen gelezen dat je ook over al die series op tv over vrouwen...

Claire: Ja, dat stereotiepe ook.

Marijke: Ja en als ik dan denk van... ja, ik herken het omdat ik er vaker over heb gelezen, ik herken het niet als verschijnsel in de maatschappij... ik heb dit soort vrouwen nog nooit gezien. Ja, eigenlijk vind ik het een beetje belachelijk dat mannen vernielen, ik vind dat heeeel kinderachtig. Zijn er echt vrouwen... is er een hele beweging van vrouwen die dat soort dingen serieus doen?

Yasmin: Ja, je leest er wel verhalen over, maar gebeurt het ook op grote schaal? Ik ken persoonlijk niemand die zo is.

Translation

Marijke: That was my reaction as well. Well... yes, I recognise it of course, I have also read articles like that and all those series on tv about women...

Claire: Yes, the stereotypes...

Marijke: Yes and when I think... yes, I recognise it because I have read about it more often, but I don't recognise it as a phenomenon in society... I have never seen these women. Yes, actually I think it is a bit ridiculous... that 'destroying men' thing, I find it veeeery childish. Are there really women... is there really a whole movement of women who are really doing that kind of thing?

Yasmin: Yes, you read about it, but does it really happen on a large scale? I personally don't know anyone who is like that.

Yasmin first responds by saying she recognised the issue of highly educated women who want a man to make their life complete. But she immediately made explicit that she recognised the *ideas* by having read about them in glossy magazines as well as in 'normal' newspapers. So Yasmin located the article in an intertextual relationship with global media discourses. The Dutch students were not just criticising the article for using stereotypes (although they did that too), but they were at the same time relating the article to the wider issue that these stereotypes indeed existed and were not only recognisable, but were hackneyed (Yasmin). This was a collaboration: Yasmin initially felt that the article portrayed something very recognisable, but Marijke takes her point further; she recognises the stereotypes because she has read about them so often, but she considers that these stereotypes do not relate to reality. Marijke, then, separated the 'cultuurtekst' (the underlying ideas in the text) from actual reality.

During the next exchange Emma considered what could be behind the creation of such stereotypes in the media, and how these ideas could become dominant, considering they do not relate to reality. And again in the ensuing dialogue, a collaboration takes place between Emma and one of the Dutch students, Marijke, who helped to make a more explicit link with the cultural context of the article:

Emma: *Misschien dat soort benoemingen dan, van mannen – of vrouwen vernielers, misschien is dat ooit een keer gezegd als grapje, en is dat gewoon opgenomen in de maatschappij en is dat opgenomen door mannen, of ja, door wie, en misschien van daar is het een verschijnsel in de geschreven... eh pers geworden, want ja, ik denk, ja, er zijn vaak genoeg vrouwen inderdaad die toch gewoon gelukkig zijn om alleen te zijn en die inderdaad op een beetje fun uit zijn, die wel eens een man versieren. 't Is niet zozeer dat ze een man willen vernielen, maar net als mannen, die willen verder niks... (onverstaanbaar)... ja, en daar houdt het dan mee op.*

Marijke: *Ja, 't kan ook best wel dat je... want het is natuurlijk een heel interessant onderwerp, iets zoals dit, dus als je er ook maar een klein beetje aan ruikt of iets opvangt wat een beetje in die trant zit van vrouwen die een man gaan vernielen, dat klinkt heel interessant en dan kun je daar ook een prachtig artikel over schrijven wat al die mannen ook als een gek gaan zitten te lezen... ik bedoel, 't blijft gewoon een ontzettend interessant onderwerp, man versus vrouwen.*

Emma: Ja precies, kijk wat een man doet, als een man uitgaat en een vrouw versiert, nou dat is gewoon normaal, niemand kijkt daar van op, maar als een vrouw dat doet, dat wordt nog steeds gewoon beoordeeld.

Marijke: Misschien is dat dan wel de waarde of het beeld dat je eruit kunt halen, hè, dat 't van vrouwen niet... dat 't niet bij ons beeld van vrouwen past om uit te gaan en mannen te versieren.

Translation

Emma: Maybe that those kind of labels: 'destroying men/male bashing' or women, maybe that has been said once as a joke and that label has just been taken over in society and taken over by men or yes, and maybe from there it became a phenomenon in the press, because yes, I think there are often enough women who are indeed just happy to be on their own and who indeed are out to have some fun, who would like to get it off with a man, not that they want to destroy a man, but who just like men... and who do not want anything more than that (inaudible) and... well that's all there is to it.

Marijke: Yes, it is also possible that you... because it is of course a really interesting topic, something like this, so if you sniff at it only a little or if you catch something in the sense of women who are going to destroy a man, that sounds very interesting and then you can write a wonderful article about it which all those men are going to read like mad... I mean, it remains such an interesting topic: men versus women.

Emma: Yes, exactly, look what a man does... when a man goes out and gets it off with a woman, that is just normal, it is expected. But when a woman is doing that it is still being criticised.

Marijke: Maybe that is the value or the image you can recognise, that it doesn't fit in the image we have of women to go out and pick up a man.

Emma's initial suggestion that the description of women as 'mannenverniel-ers' ('destroyers of men'/'male-bashers') had come into use purely by accident, through a joke that then became part of an accepted notion in society, does not consider in any way its social or cultural origins, ideologies or power relations. Emma's suggestion does not really refer to any previous knowledge or experience either, it seems. It is an attempt at explaining an existing and recognisable discourse as not located within a particular socio-cultural context, but as a chance happening. Marijke then takes Emma's suggestion on board, but instead of accepting Emma's version, she locates the emergence of 'labels' within the commercial text-producing environment; the magazine needs to attract readers, and gender relations, after all, constitute a very interesting topic, Marijke says.

Emma builds further on this and this time she does make a link with the socio-cultural context. She relates the representation of women as being sexually aggressive to cultural conventions: what is 'normal' behaviour for a man is not deemed acceptable in a woman. It is Marijke who makes this even more explicit and brings this back to what the text then might signify as a whole; that 'chasing men' is not part of the acceptable image of women in our society. Marijke is already referring to discourse here: the implicit conventions and assumptions of how women should behave.

So Emma, even though she thought she was agreeing with Marijke, approaches the text initially from a perspective outside society. Marijke tries to formulate it from a socio-cultural perspective and tries to engage with the values underpinning the text straight away, which Emma then responds to. The students then are starting to engage with the notion of how gender is constructed in the article; they have started to 'map' the discourses through their dialogic interaction. In the set of data I discuss below, Claire takes the mapping of discourses further still.

Reading from Inside or Outside Perspectives

The fairly heated exchange below shows the very different approaches between Emma and Claire in terms of conceptualising text and context. Claire was discussing the particular fragment in the text[1] (which Emma and Claire had also disagreed over in lesson 1), which she said was being stereotypical. Claire had just mentioned that she thought these stereotypes consisted of women being represented as having masculine traits:

G: En jij vindt dat mannelijk. Wat is er mannelijk aan?

Claire: Ik vind dat mannelijk want de vraag die ik citeer over seksueel rendement... voor mij is dat heel mannelijk, want ik vind dat dat is hetzelfde als de vrouwen in het eerste voorbeeld en dus voor mij is dat eh hij doet een eh 't franse woord 'rapprochement' eh ja...

[er wordt gelachen]

Claire: Wat is dat in het Nederlands of Engels? 't Brengt dat eh...

Marijke: Toenadering.

Claire: Ja...

G: Hij brengt die twee dingen bij elkaar.

Claire: Ja.

G: Maar hoe...wat is er nou precies... hoe komt het dat dat op elkaar lijkt... het feit dat vrouwen eerst worden beschreven met wat ze dragen... designer clothes, cellulitisvrij... getrainde billen...

[er wordt gelachen]

G: Je zou kunnen zeggen dat daar een soort...

Claire: Op zich is dat mannelijk want...

Emma: Neeeee! Waarom?

Claire: Ja, dat hele...

Emma: Als je succesvol bent, bent je dan mannelijk als vrouw?

Claire: Nee, maar...

Emma: Maar dat zeg je dan.

Claire: Nee, ik vind dat als je dat vind belangrijk, ja ik vind dat een beetje mannelijk.

Emma: Dus jij wil gewoon onderdanig blijven aan een man en met geld...

G: Emma, Claire zegt volgens mij niet dat dat mannelijk is, maar dat de schrijver het presenteert als mannelijk, dat de maatschappij dat zo vindt.

[door elkaar praten en lachen]

Claire: Maar wanneer je een lijst maakt met alle dingen... ik...

Emma: Hij beschouwt het als mannelijk.

Claire: Ja, als je geen namen hebt, als je zegt dat hij eh Maarten en zijn drie vriendin eh, vrienden, dan voor mij is dat misschien niet zo, ja, misschien niet die billen

[er wordt gelachen]

G: Nou, die billen zijn wel belangrijk natuurlijk. Waarom zijn die...

Claire: Seksueel.

G: Omdat hij toch de vrouw daardoor als seksueel aantrekkelijk neerzet.

Emma: Dus als ze dan dit allemaal hadden maar toch die cellulitis dan was er toch niet zo...

[onverstaanbaar door het door elkaar praten]

Claire: Luister... dakterras of balkon, ja vlot karretje, ja niet die cellulitis, hoe zeg je dat voor mannen, is dat eh... hoe zeg je...

sommige studenten: Sixpack.

Marijke en Yasmin: Wasbord.

Claire: Wasbord, ja make-up niet, maar koelkast met zalm en champagne en die job met uitdagende perspectieven, ja voor mij dat kan mannelijk ook...

Eve: Typisch zo'n bachelor...

[...]

G: Dus het is... de vrouw wordt beschreven in die succesvolle... economisch succesvolle termen en het prestatiegerichte... eh hij zegt ook op een gegeven moment eh... hij definieert het mannelijk zijn als eh prestaties verrichten... op blz... ik weet niet zo gauw.

Marijke: Ja, op blz. 49 aan het einde... 'zo bouwen ze een door het leveren van bepaalde prestaties'.

G: Ja, inderdaad, [ik herhaal het]... is een mannelijke identiteit, ja dus met andere woorden, prestaties leveren is een mannelijke eh karaktertrek.

Emma: Ja, dan ben ik het met je eens dat het inderdaad zo gepresenteerd is, maar...

Claire: Ja, ja.

Emma: Maar...

G: Ja, je bent het niet eens met wat ie zegt.

Emma: Nee.

Translation

G: And you find that male? What is male about it?

Claire: I think that it is male because the question which I'm citing about sexual gain for me that is very male. I think that that is the same as the women in the first example and this for me he is doing... eh the French word is 'rapprochement' eh yes...

[*Laughter*]

Claire: What is that in Dutch or English? It brings that...

Marijke: Approach.

Claire: Yes.

G: He brings those things together.

Claire: Yes.

G: But how... what exactly... how come that that looks like one another... the fact that women are first described by what they wear... designer clothes, cellulite free trained buttocks

[*Laughter*]

G: You could say that there is a kind of

Claire: In a way that is male...

Emma: Noooo... why?

Claire: Well, the whole...

Emma: When you are successful as a woman, you are being male?

Claire: No, but...

Emma: But that's what you then are saying.

Claire: No, I think that if you find that [kind of thing] important yes, I think that is a bit male.

Emma: So you want to remain submissive to a man and with money...

G: Emma, I don't think that Claire is saying that it is male, but that the author presents it as male, that society thinks it is male.

[*Students talking and laughing*]

Claire: But when you make a list of all those things... I...

Emma: He thinks of it as male.

Claire: Yes, if there wouldn't be any names given... eh Maarten and his three friends, then for me [it could be about men]... well, perhaps not those buttocks

[*Laughter*]

G: Well, those buttocks are important of course... why would they be...

Claire: Sexual.

G: Because he is portraying the women still as being sexually attractive.

[...]

Claire: Listen... roof terrace or balcony... yes, trendy little car, well, not the cellulite, how do you say that for men...?

Marijke and Yasmin: Six-pack.

Claire: Six-pack, yes, not the make-up, but the fridge with salmon and champagne and the job with prospects... yes, for me that can be male.

Eve: A typical bachelor...

[...]

G: So, the women are described in those successful economically successful terms and focused on achievement... eh... he also says somewhere... eh... he defines being male as eh... achieving... on page... I don't know...

Marijke: Yes on page 49 at the end: 'that's how they build a… by achieving things'.

G: Yes, indeed. Achieving… is part of the male identity, yes, so in other words I repeat what was said is a male characteristic.

Emma: Yes, then I agree with you that indeed that is how it is presented, but…

Claire: Yes, yes.

Emma: But…

G: Yes, you don't agree with him.

Emma: No.

Claire and Emma had discussed the same text fragment (the one about designer clothes etc.) in the first lesson, and they had both agreed that it represented a negative view of women, but they had each interpreted it differently. Emma had seen this fragment as representing women as superficial, being only interested in clothes and make-up, whereas Claire had seen it in terms of the representation of an 'ideal' that women would need to live up to. Those interpretations were forgotten now, and both Emma and Claire seem to agree that in this fragment women are described as being successful, having achieved a certain status due to these materialist possessions.

Claire notes that this particular representation of describing women in terms of success is gendered: success is represented as a male characteristic. But Emma does not seem to recognise that Claire is making a statement about a representation in the text and she assumes that it is Claire's own opinion that success constitutes a male characteristic. Emma steps outside the meta-communicative style of the classroom discussion and seems to forget we are engaging in the pedagogic activity of analysing a text. She feels so strongly about this that she almost launches a personal attack on Claire: '*Dus jij wilt gewoon onderdanig blijven aan een man en met geld…?*' (So you want to stay submissive to a man and with money…?).

When I am trying to build on Claire's point that the way that the women are presented is almost in male terms, and when I try and articulate that in terms of economic success and a focus on achievement (which the author later in the article explicitly defines as being a male characteristic), only Marijke latches on by pointing out where in the text this is said. Only then does Emma agree that, yes, this is an issue of representation, but states yet again that she doesn't agree with the view that success could be seen as a male characteristic.

Emma then seems to firmly remain outside the article, not trying to understand the text as discursive formations, but responding to the statement almost as an item for debate. Claire, on the other hand is trying to understand the text fragment in the context of the article itself and link it to its socio-cultural environment. By doing so, Claire is moving away from looking at the text as a product, and is starting to see the text as cultuurtekst, i.e. the discourses which underpin the text. Claire made use of her socio-cultural knowledge to come to this analysis and took on a position of critique. But, paradoxically, Emma's strong criticism of the text using her personal experiences or views, formed a hindrance to a position of critique as she saw the text in relation to a discussion about content, not a discussion about discourses. Claire saw this fragment in terms of culturally located ways of presenting male and femaleness, Emma saw this as a statement of truth, and she drew the discussion on to personal terms. This might suggest that a *strong* emphasis on personal experience, which is not being reflected upon, can be detrimental to being critical and even be stereotype confirming.

However, as a result of the interplay between theory, data and my own reflection, I realised in the later stages of this study that Emma's response to the text cannot be solely explained by her taking a position outside the text. It was precisely her emotional response to Claire's pinpointing of the particular discursive forces in society which represent success and independence as the prerogative of men, which alerted me to the fact that Emma was engaging with the text, and more so with Claire's responses to the text, in a critical way, critiquing the ideologically motivated content, and how a truth-certainty is maintained about gender. Her emotional response was directed at these particular discursive understandings, even if she mistakenly believed that Claire personally held that particular view. Through asking Claire directly whether she would like to remain dependent on a man and his money, Emma brought both the personal *and* political domain into the classroom. Since I felt uncomfortable with the emotional and passionate tone of the discussion, I intervened, without giving this personal political element a chance to develop. However, the next set of data shows a moment in the class where that did happen. It shows that students' engagement with their personal experiences can indeed be a step towards a critical engagement with the discursive forces of the text-producing environment.

Lifeworld Knowledge: Being an Intercultural Reader

The fragment below shows that instead of being a hindrance to engaging with text meaning, referring to one's own experience of the world could indeed aid the process of being critical in problematising the text, and being intercultural. The personal and cultural can combine to aid students to become intercultural readers. When the exchange below took place in the lesson, I felt at the time that the discussion had moved away from the text and that students used the text merely as a vehicle for a discussion about the topic. My aim throughout the lesson had been to get students to focus on the text and to point to the language in the fragment to prove their points, so I was initially disappointed that discussions like the one below developed, even though I recognised the value of having debates like this. Looking at the exchange now, I think it shows that students did have a meaningful and intercultural dialogue by collaborating in their interpretative discussion and making use of their personal experience. In doing so they were critical from an inside as well as outside perspective. Students were both intercultural in the sense of understanding the complexity of culture (cf. Blommaert, 1998; Holliday et.al, 2004) and they were 'being intercultural' (Phipps and Gonzalez, 2004) in trying to understand the 'other', in this case 'the male', in relation to their own experiences. Students tried to understand the text and its underpinning discourses; they also critiqued, as a group, these discourses, which in turn led them to look at their own situation in a different light again.

Claire: Maar we zeggen één ding en we denken een ander ding. Ik denk dat ik heb hetzelfde probleem, ik zeg altijd ik kan doen wat ik wil, ik kan carrière hebben of niet, wat ik wil, maar ook in mijn gezin [mijn eigen familie, GQ], ze zegt altijd, wanneer is het huwelijk, wanneer komt de kinderen en dat is een heel, ja, ik vind het heel moeilijk en ik denk dat dat is een normaal probleem van vrouwen in deze tijd, ja de... hoe zeg je dat?

G: Ja de rol, de veranderende rol.

Claire: Ja, de rol, je kan alles zijn of niks zijn, maar het is moeilijk om een balans te vinden.

Marijke: Ja, blijkbaar vinden mannen dat ook heel moeilijk dat ze niet goed weten wat ze nou van een vrouw moeten verwachten en dat daarom zo'n artikel ook gepubliceerd wordt omdat dat daarop ingaat van wat voor wat willen vrouwen nou eigenlijk en hoe zitten ze in elkaar...

G: En wat willen ze zelf?

Emma: En wat willen mannen?

G: Ja, precies dat bedoel ik.

Emma: Willen ze een hoer hebben of een moeder?

G: Een hoer en een madonna.

Claire: Ja, een hoer in de slaapkamer en een moeder in...

Marijke: [lacht] Ja, in de huiskamer of zo...

[door elkaar praten. Iemand zegt]:

In de keuken

G: Ja, inderdaad. Zit er ook iets in van jaloezie? Dat de vrouw...

Claire: Alles kan hebben.

G: ...een bedreiging vormt? de man is nu zijn positie kwijt als degene die presteert, mannelijke identiteit is het leveren van bepaalde prestaties.

Claire: Dat is het feministenidee dat ik heb de laatste tijd ook met mijn Franse professor zo gepraat. Zij zegt dat sinds het begin van de tijd, mannen hebben een probleem, want vrouwen kunnen de kinderen hebben en mannen niet en dus mannen hebben vrouwen eh 'repressed'?

Marijke: Onderdrukt.

Claire: Onderdrukt... enne nu vrouwen kunnen een carrière hebben en een huis en een baan en ze kunnen alleen wonen als we wilt, ja we kunnen alles doen en dat is een grote probleem voor mannen en ze weten niet wat ze willen en ze moeten denken...

Marijke: Maar dan zou je kunnen zeggen dat dit artikel... juist die nadruk op de carrièrevrouw die, zeg maar, helemaal de plank misslaat, een bescherming is van hé, het is altijd van ons geweest om een carrière te hebben en om te presteren en nu doen die vrouwen het ook, maar kijk eens naar ze, ze kunnen er niks van, 't gaat helemaal mis met ze, dus om dat ook een beetje te beschermen van 'ja, maar het is toch ook een beetje van ons', want, ja, al kunnen ze het wel... toch niet zo goed als wij.

G: ja, dus wat spreekt daar dan..., als we dat dan bijvoorbeeld vergelijken met Liesbeth Wietzes artikel van de man als dinosaurus, de mannen hebben hun positie verloren, ze zijn meelijwekkende wezens geworden, eh het was een heel extreme visie van haar, ze bracht het heel extreem, omdat het polemisch bedoeld was, maar herken je daar misschien iets in, zeg je, ja er is een bepaald maatschappelijk verschijnsel niet zozeer het maatschappelijk verschijnsel zoals hij het beschrijft over die agressieve jonge vrouwen, maar is er een maatschappelijk verschijnsel dat mannen, of vrouwen ook, in de war zijn, niet meer precies zoeken zoeken naar...een andere vorm...

Emma: Ja, ik weet het niet, het is heel moeilijk, maar ik ben niet in de war, als vrouw zijnde heb ik geen probleem dat ik ook een carrière wil en desnoods kinderen en getrouwd zijn.

Marijke: Maar denk je dat dat gaat lukken ook als je dat allemaal wil?

Emma: Dat weet ik niet en als het niet lukt, ok, daar heb ik ook geen probleem mee.

Claire: Maar ik denk ook dat de vrouw niet kan accepteren dat het ok is om geen man te hebben. Er is een...

Emma: Vrouwen kunnen dat niet accepteren?

Claire: Nee, de maatschappelijke mensen, ja, vrouwen, ik denk dat het misschien is het... het is dom, want ik weet dat zonder man kan ik gewoon functioneren op een normale wijze.

Marijke: Ja...

Claire: Ja, er is misschien een <u>soort</u> idee en...

Marijke: Maar er is toch ook een soort restant van dat hele traditionele dat je toch ook een, dat je toch het idee hebt dat je een man nodig hebt en als je dan ook kijkt naar 'Ally McBeal' en al die series, je zit er toch ook op te wachten dat ze eigenlijk een vriendje krijgt?

Emma: Maar is het ook niet zo tegenwoordig dat er voor mannen een beetje een nieuw concept is dat zij gewoon een vrouw nodig hebben voor eh eh 'companionship'?

Iemand zegt Gezelschap.

Emma: Gezelschap, want mensen als wezens, ik denk zijn niet bedoeld om alleen te zijn, man of vrouw, 't maakt niet uit. Misschien is het dan voor mannen, misschien moeten ze een hoofd er...

Claire: Get their head around it.

Emma: Ja, het idee dat die mogen ook kwetsbaar zijn, die mogen ook zeggen, ja eigenlijk wil ik best wel een vrouw.

G: Ja en denk je dat dat hier ook enigszins naar voren komt?

Emma: Nee.

[er wordt gelachen]

Translation

Claire: But we say one thing and we think another thing. I think I have the same problem, I always say I can do what I want, I can have a career if I want and what I want. But also in my family, they always say, when is the wedding, when will you have children, and that is, yes, I think that is very difficult, and I think that that is a problem of women these days, yes, the... how do you say that?

G: Yes, the role, the changing role

Claire: Yes, the role, you can be anything or nothing, but it is difficult to find a balance.

Marijke: Yes, apparently men also find it difficult that they don't know what to expect from a woman, and that is why an article like this is published because it discusses what kind... what women actually want and what makes them tick.

G: And what they want themselves?

Emma: And what do men want?

G: Yes, exactly that is what I mean.

Emma: Do they want a whore or a mother?

G: A whore and a madonna.

Claire: Yes, a whore for in the bedroom and a mother in

Marijke: [laughs] Yes, in the living room

[*Talking and laughing. Someone says*]:

In the kitchen

G: Yes, indeed. Do you think there's an element of jealousy? That the woman

Claire: Can have everything.

G: ...forms a threat? The man has lost his position as the one who achieves success; male identity is [seen as] achieving success.

Claire: That is the feminist idea. I also talked about that with my French lecturer. She says that since the beginning of time men have a problem because women can have children and men can't. That's why they have 'repressed?

Marijke: Oppressed.

Claire: Oppressed... and eh... women now can have a career and a house and a job and they can live on their own if they want. Yes, we can do anything we want and that is a big problem for men and they don't know what they want and they have to think...

Marijke: But you could say that of this article... especially the emphasis on the career woman who has got it all wrong [in her private life] is a protection of... eh... this has always been our [domain] to have a career, to achieve, and now women do it as well, but look at them, they go to pieces, so to protect that a bit as well, yes, this is also ours... because even though they can do it, they can't do it as well as we can.

G: Yes, so what can we if we compare that for instance with Liesbeth Wietze's article 'the man as dinosaur', men have lost their position in society, they have become sad creatures... it was an extreme view... she presented it in a very extreme way because it was intended to be polemical, but do you perhaps recognise something that there is a phenomenon in society, or no not a phenomenon the way he describes it about aggressive women, but a phenomenon that men, and women as well, are confused, don't know exactly... are looking for new ways...

Emma: Well, I don't know, it is very difficult, but I am not confused, as a woman, I have no problem with the fact that I want a career and possibly children, and be married

Marijke: But do you think that you will manage it, if you want all of that?

Emma: I don't know, and if I won't manage it, then that would be fine too.

Claire: But I also think that the woman can't accept the fact that it is ok not to have a man.

Emma: Women can't accept that?

Claire: No, society... people, yes, women, I think that... maybe it is... it is silly, because I know that I can function normally without a man...

Marijke: Yes...

Clair: Yes, maybe there is a <u>kind</u> of idea and

Marijke: But there is still a remnant of that very traditional... that you still have the idea that you need a man and also when you look at 'Ally McBeal' and those TV series... you are waiting for them to finally get a boyfriend?

Emma: But, is it also not the case that there is a new concept for men that they need a woman for eh eh [she says in English] 'companionship'?

Iemand zegt: Gezelschap.

Emma: Companionship, because people as beings, I don't think they are meant to be on their own, man or woman, it doesn't matter. Maybe it is then for men, they need to get their head...

Claire: Get their head around it.

Emma: Yes, the idea that they can be vulnerable as well, that they can also say: Actually, I would quite like to have a woman [female partner, GQ].

G: Yes, and do you think that this comes across in any way in the text?

Emma: No.

[*Laughter*]

The classroom exchange above occurred at the point in the lesson straight after I had guided students through the different representations of women in the article. I had wanted them to consider how these different and conflicting representations, i.e. women as 'aggressive hunters of men', as 'excessive lifestyle consumers', and as 'mothers,' created a different layer to the text. Claire answered by relating these different representations to her own life and suggesting that women may think or say they have the freedom to be what and who they like to be, but that in reality they are under pressure to conform. So she implied that whilst women might think they have all they want, they are nevertheless strongly influenced by expectations of society, that is to say the discourses which are enacted by their friends and family. It is difficult to gain a balance between those discourses, she seemed to say. Claire was thus reflexive in her answer.

Marijke then made an explicit link with the article suggesting that men clearly find it difficult to balance these various changing expectations women themselves and society have. Emma then turns the discussion towards men: they don't know what they want: a whore or a mother. She elegantly (and perhaps unwittingly) brings two discourses in the article together; that of the sexual representation of women in one of the early representations in the article and the end of the article, which could indeed be termed the madonna-discourse: the traditional mother.

The discussion amongst the students then becomes political: (suppression of women throughout history), and psychological (envy of women's reproduction abilities) before it turns personal again about whether students themselves think they can combine the different roles of being a career woman with that of being a mother. Finally, Emma talks about relationships between men and women.

At this stage in the lesson, students were not any longer trying to make sense of the text. They had made the text their own and were collaboratively creating meaning, in trying to relate the text to their own reality and their own experiences. As I said, my initial feeling during this exchange in the lesson itself was that they were almost 'hijacking' the text. Cooke and Wallace refer to this as 'talking around a text' when a text carries 'too much meaning in a personal experiential way' for the students to maintain the required distance to stay 'on task'. Students wish to 'make meaning in different ways' than the questions asked by the teacher (2004: 109). But looking at the data, students are doing more than merely talking around the text. They are discussing the issues which arose from the text as a critique of society and highlighting the power differentials that women still face. The style of meta communication had indeed changed from analytical talk of standing outside the text to a dialogue and collaborative style of talking, referring to personal experiences, as well as discourses in society. In fact, students are even quite explicitly referring to the issue of discourses. Claire calls it *een soort idee* (a kind of idea), which Marijke specifies as *een soort restant van dat hele traditionele...* (a remnant of the very traditional...). In this discussion, then, students are using the insights gained through the text analysis, taking these further in a discussion using both the ideas that were gained through the classroom activity of the text analysis, relating these to their own experiences, before applying these ideas which had been gained through a more personalised discussion, back to the text. This way they were seeing the text as cultuurtekst, in terms of its conflicting and multiple discourses: the expectations of being successful and independent versus the expectations to be married and have children, which Claire highlighted as being part of everyday reality for women. They also saw the conflicting discourses of 'the whore and the madonna', as Emma phrased the expectations of men towards women, which indeed highlighted the way the article had represented women.

By using the dialogic space students collaborated to engage in both discursive mapping, and in discussing how they themselves were affected by these expectations and discourses in society. Students were engaging through 'languaging' (cf. Phipps and Gonzalez, 2004), or 'dialoguing', as I call it, using the article as a starting point, but then conversely relating their discussion again to the article. They referred to a range of personal experiences to engage with the text, from giving examples of their own experience, to relating the discussion to other academic discussions (e.g. Claire referring to a literature class in French), and students talking about their expectations for their own future.

The personal here helped to engage students and make them see the cultural and social significance of the article. Marijke particularly brings the discussion back to the article. She also queries Emma in her confident statement that she will have no problems integrating being a woman with having a career. She makes it personal and at the same time queries underlying assumptions, both in the text, but also in the attitude of the students themselves.

By standing both inside and outside the text and through dialoguing, students were able to use the personal to be intercultural. They were intercultural at a generic level: recognising the cultural values embedded in the text and the complexity of society of which this text is a product. However, the lesson also addressed being intercultural at a more specific level and local level. I conceived of this as Dutch discourses, and I turn to this next.

Dutch Articulations

Even though the topic discussed was transcultural, and certainly not specifically Dutch, as mentioned, I felt this particular texts showed what I called Dutch articulations in the text. Students had indeed recognised the global, or at least western, relevance of the text and made intertextual references to American and English soaps and films. I asked students whether they felt that this issue would have been written about in a similar way in an English magazine aimed at men. As I describe in more detail in chapter 4, my own interpretation had been that the extreme traditional positioning of women as needing to find fulfilment through motherhood, would not have been acceptable in an English publication, not even in a men's one. This discourse was made more acceptable by another discourse which also carried a Dutch flavour: that of therapy and self development, which, I thought, would equally have been out of place in an English magazine aimed at men.

In the fragment below I am trying to bring this discussion into the foreground. The exchange student, Marijke, responded as I had expected, saying that this kind of discourse certainly does not surprise her, but the regular students of the class did not seem to want to pursue this line of analysis. As in the previous set of data, they 'talked around the text' and focused on the difference in conventions in how people talk about relationships: what can you say and what not? The students are relating it to previous knowledge and experience gained when living in the Netherlands. Marijke took on the role of 'learner' about English culture. The discussion which I had hoped to kick-start on whether there was Dutch articulation to some of the discourses employed, became a content-oriented one, based on personal experience, or at least what they had inferred and observed about differences in relationships in England and the Netherlands:

> Claire: *Ja, maar ik moet zeggen ik heb in MH in Engeland gekijkt wanneer ik was in Waterstone's en MH in Engeland is niks te doen, of er is een klein artikel over seks maar al andere artikelen zijn over sport en health hoe je kan een betere sixpack hebben.*
>
> G: *Ja, wasbord dus.*
>
> Marijke: *[lacht]*
>
> Claire: *Ja, en een betere... 'deze schoenen voor voetbal'.*
>
> G: *Niets over relaties.*
>
> Claire: *Nee, niets over relaties.*
>
> *[...]*
>
> Marijke: *Maar denk... dan wat je ook zei dat over MH dat het alleen maar over sport gaat, dat praten over relaties, dat dat niet helemaal kan, dat dat te open is?*
>
> Claire: *In Engeland het kan niet ja, ik denk dat in Engeland je kan het niet publiceren in een Engelse mannelijke publicatie.*
>
> G: *En dan met name het vrij serieuze over relaties en het therapeutische gedeelte...?*
>
> Claire: *Nee, nee want ik denk dat in Engeland we praten niet over deze soort dingen, want ik denk mannen, maar ook vrouwen praten niet in dezelfde manier over seks.*
>
> Emma: *Nee.*

Claire: *In Nederland is het heel... je hebt 6 mannen en 6 vrouwen die woont bij elkaar en misschien ik weet het niet, praat je over seks en dat soort dingen.*

Marijke: *[lacht]*

Claire: *Maar je praat over relaties.*

Marijke: *Ja, dat gaat.*

Claire: *Maar ik denk in Engeland ik praat niet met mijn vrienden over mijn relatie behalve dan in een meer generale manier.*

Translation

Claire: Yes, but I have to say, when I was in Waterstone's I had a look, and in MH in England there is nothing, or just a small article about sex, and all other articles are about sport and health... how you can have a better 'sixpack'...

G: Yes, 'wasbord'.

Marijke: [laughs]

Claire: Yes, and a better these shoes for football.

G: Nothing about relationships.

Claire: No, nothing about relationships.

[...]

Marijke: But do you think, that what you said, that MH is only about sport, that talking about relationships that it is not possible/acceptable, that it is too open?

Claire: In England you can't do it, yes, I think that in England you can't publish it in an English publication for men.

G: And then particularly the fairly serious tone about relationships, that therapeutic part?

Claire: No, because I think in England we don't talk about these kind of things, because I think men, but also women, don't talk in the same way about sex.

Emma: No.

Claire: In the Netherlands it is very... you have 6 men and 6 women who live together and maybe, I don't know, you talk about sex and that kind of thing...

Marijke: [laughs]

Claire: But you talk about relationships.

Marijke: Yes, that is…

Claire: But I think in England I don't talk with my friends about my relationship except in a more general way.

Claire had taken an intercultural stance by looking at an English version of *Men's Health* for comparison. Her analysis, that it did not contain anything about relationships, was taken further by Marijke. She was interested to what degree you could infer whether there is more of a taboo on talking about relationships in England than in the Netherlands. The exchange is perhaps a little essentialist in its focus and conducted at a very general level, but I had encouraged that by my initial questioning about 'Dutchness'. Whilst the dialogue was not leading to discourses in Dutch society regarding women, that I had scaffolded the discussion towards, the dialogue was nevertheless intercultural. An interesting side effect was that the intercultural dialogue was taking place in both directions: the statements about English society made by Claire, led Marijke to ask further questions. Interesting is that the English students were more confident in their observations about cultural difference. Marijke did not focus on cultural differences, and in her interview she said she had no idea what 'Dutch values' were, as she, as a native speaker, had never thought about it in those terms.

The students may have taken on an intercultural stance in the sense that they were thinking about the issue of the wider cultural context in the Netherlands and Britain, but they were not extending this to continuing the position of critique of discourses. Nevertheless, the students were reflecting; Claire used both the evidence of what she had inferred from the article, and something which Marijke had said earlier on in the discussion and then related it to her own experience. On the other hand, the discussion did not rise above the level of stereotypes, and students were not aware of the fact that they were colluding in stereotypes.

I then aim to bring the discussion back from the 'talk around the text' to the pedagogical task at hand, i.e. looking at the underpinning values in the text and whether these could be said to constitute a Dutch articulation. I want to find out from Marijke whether she feels the underpinning values in the text are in any way 'recognisable' to her:

G: [question directed at Marijke] Wat vind jij, heb je het gevoel dat… komt dit op jou vrij herkenbaar over, dat je deze waarden in een tijdschrift hebt of vind je dat ook vreemd, als je tenminste in ogenschouw neemt dat dit tijdschrift op mannen is gericht?

Marijke: Ik vind het niet vreemd dat ze iets zoals dit publiceren. Ik heb niet het idee dat dit heel erg buiten de toon valt van wat er verder in Nederland te lezen is, nee.

Claire: Dit is een normaal artikel in MH in Nederland.

Marijke: Ja, niet dat ik MH lees, maar... [lacht]

[...]

Eve: Er is veel meer vrijheid in Nederland om te schrijven wat jij bedoelen wat jou mening is, veel Nederlanders geven hun mening zoveel makkelijker aan dan Engelse mensen. Het is meer sociaal acceptabeler om te zeggen wat je voelen over hoe het dan is, want dat is jouw mening.

Claire: Je hoeft niet te vragen over hun mening want ze zegt het...

[door elkaar praten]

Emma: Maar dat [Nederlandse, GQ] mannen makkelijker over gevoelens praten of makkelijker dan Engelse mannen over gevoelens praten, dat kan ik je wel vertellen. 't Is echt tanden trekken soms.

[...]

[door elkaar praten]

Claire: ...over seks ik denk dat seks is niet zo problematisch en een soort idee. In Nederland er is meer sex education op school, je bent jonger, 't is meer...

Emma: Het is gewoon in Nederland.

Claire: 't Is normaal, het is topical.

Eve: De Engelsen vinden het zo moeilijk om over seks te praten.

G: Actueel.

Claire: Ja, actueel en in Engeland het is taboe.

Emma: Het is alledaags bijna in Nederland, niet dat iedereen de hele dag over seks praat, maar...

[door elkaar praten]

G: ...maar hier in deze tijdschriften kom je dat toch ook tegen in Engeland, in Cosmopolitan heb je toch ook een heleboel seks.

Emma: Ja, maar dat is...

Claire: Dat is niet...

Eve and Emma: Dat is voor vrouwen...

Claire: Ook het is over goede seks...

Emma: Ja, maar dat is ook echt niet...

[...]

Claire: Ze zegt dat seks is niet altijd perfect en het gaat niet altijd goed en dat in relaties zijn er momenten dat je hebt problemen, maar in Engeland is het altijd, ja je moet, hoe zeg je 'orgasm' in het Nederlands?

Emma: Orgasme.

Eve: Het is elke keer, ja je moet een multiple orgasm...

Claire: Ja, precies.

[lachen en door elkaar praten]

Emma: [onverstaanbaar]... seksueel

Claire: Ja, ze moeten over seks praten in een soort closed of, ja, het is een soort perfect idee, ja en je praat over dit perfecte idee, maar het is alleen maar...

Eve: Alleen maar de 'beautiful people'.

Claire: Ja, en je bent niet in hetzelfde soort...

Marijke: Het is niet persoonlijk?

Claire: Ja precies, het is een soort ideaal.

Translation

G: [question directed at Marijke] What do you think? Do you have the feeling that... does this come across as fairly recognisable... that you find these values in a magazine, or do you find that strange as well, considering this magazine is aimed at men?

Marijke: I don't find it unusual that they publish something like this. I don't think this is very different from other things you can read in the Netherlands. No.

Claire: This is a normal article in *Men's Health* in the Netherlands.

Marijke: Yes, well not that I read *Men's Health*, but...

[...]

Eve: There is more freedom in the Netherlands to write what you think, what your opinion is, so many Dutch people give their opinion so much easier than English people, it is more socially acceptable to say what you feel, to say how it is because that is your opinion.

Claire: You don't have to ask their opinion, because they say it.

[Students all talk at once]

Emma: But [Dutch, GQ] men talk more easily about their own feelings than English men talk about their feelings, that much I can tell you. Sometimes you really have to pull it out of them.

[*Students all talk at once*]

Claire: ...about sex I think that sex is not so problematic and a <u>kind of</u> idea in the Netherlands, there is more sex education at school. You are younger, it is more...

Emma: It is normal in the Netherlands.

Eve: The English find it so difficult to talk about sex.

Claire: ...and in England it is taboo.

Emma: It is almost everyday in the Netherlands, not that everyone talks about sex all day, but...

G: But in the magazines here in England, in Cosmopolitan there is also a lot of sex.

Emma: Yes, but that is not...

Claire: that is not...

Eve and Emma: That is for women...

Claire: And it is about good sex...

Emma: Yes, but that is not really...

[...]

Claire: She says that sex is not always perfect and it doesn't always go well, and that there are moments in relationhips that you have problems, but in England, it is always, yes, you have got to... how do you say 'orgasm' in Dutch?

Emma: 'Orgasme'.

Eve: It is everytime, yes, you must [have] a multiple orgasm...

Claire: Yes, exactly.

[*Laughter and everyone talks at same time*]

Emma: Yes, it is very extreme... [not audible]

Eve: [not audible] Sexual.

Claire: Yes, they have to talk about sex in a kind of closed, or yes, it is <u>a kind of</u> idea about perfection, yes, and you talk about this 'perfect-idea', but it is only...

Eve: Only beautiful people.

Claire: And you are not in the same [league?]

Marijke: It is not personal?

Claire: Yes exactly, it is a kind of ideal.

Marijke indeed feels the values reflected in the article are similar to those in other publications in the Netherlands, which might suggest there may be a Dutch articulation to some aspects of the text. My question was aimed at discourses in the media, and Marijke's answer does indeed focus on this. However, the students did not follow up on the representations in the media, but instead continued the theme of attitudes of 'openness' in attitudes and communication, which the discussion around the text had thrown up for them. In comparing these attitudes between the Netherlands and England, students followed essentialist notions of national cultures. Eve's general observation that Dutch people have a direct style of communication is applied by Emma to different communicative behaviours between English and Dutch men when it comes to talking about feelings. She seems to make use of her own personal experiences by emphasising: 'that much I can tell you'.

From that point the discussion starts to focus on sex, but Claire relates this to her cultural knowledge of the Netherlands. She suggests that because there is sex education at schools, it is easier for people to talk about sex. However, rather than just making an observation, using her cognitive schemata, she touches on a more complex point; she says that talking about sex is 'a kind of idea' (*een soort idee*). Claire seems to suggest that because sex is talked about from a younger age at school, it becomes part of culture, almost like a discourse. The other students do not pursue the more complex point Claire is making, but they confirm the fact that talking about sex is just more common in the Netherlands.

When Eve focuses on the comparative element ('the English find it so difficult to talk about sex') both Emma and Claire confirm this, but I feel that the students are colluding in a stereotype. I want them to query this further and I counter their comments by stating that there is a lot of talk about sex in English magazines as well. This leads students to consider the way Dutch magazines write about sex compared to English publications, such as Cosmopolitan. It is Claire again who considers these differences and she suggests that Dutch magazines will write about sex in the context of relationships and that they would also focus on the fact that sex is not always perfect. English magazines (i.e. Cosmopolitan), on the other hand, write in a 'closed way' about sex, as if sex should be perfect all the time; it is not about personal experiences, but an 'ideal' to live up to (Eve: 'multiple orgasms'). Again Claire comes close to suggesting that there are different discourses surrounding sex, i.e. conventions in talking about sex and the assumptions and expectations which surround it. Also interestingly, Claire focused again on the pressure that glossy magazines exert to conform to the image of an 'idealised' lifestyle, which Claire mentioned a few times in relation to the article in *Men's Health*.

Whilst I had wanted to focus on Dutch articulation and discourses in the *Men's Health* text, students changed that focus to a comparative one, looking at the differences in the Netherlands and England in communicative styles in the way people talk about feelings and about sex. Whilst partly I felt students were colluding in stereotypes, they also, Claire in particular, attempted to relate both their personal experience and their cognitive and lifeworld knowledge to reflect on these differences.

I felt slightly uncomfortable about discussing issues comparatively, as this so easily leads to an unproblematic confirming of national stereotypes. Of course, I had encouraged the comparative stance in trying to make students consider the idea of a Dutch articulation, but articulation focuses on discourses, rather than on the 'facts' of people's behaviour, which is how the discussion was developing. On the other hand, students were reflecting on their own experiences when they had been in the Netherlands during their residency abroad. Whilst I think students were in danger of over-essentialising their experiences, Claire points towards a way in which topics like these could be debated in a more constructive and intercultural way, with students reflecting critically on their own experiences. She hints at the fact that there are discourses, which she referred to as 'kinds of ideas', surrounding sex, which may differ from country to country (or indeed from social group to social group), because of historically developed attitudes, or indeed, as Claire suggests, because of the educational curriculum, which is a powerful conductor of values and discourses. Focusing on discourses rather than the 'facts' of people's behaviour, allows for a more comprehensive and problematised view of the notion of a possible national articulation.

In comparing the two different sets of data, i.e. the one where students were engaged critically in mapping discourses and were discussing these on a transcultural basis, the data set above relating to Dutch articulation in contrast reverted the topic onto a national level. These different data show the tension between these perspectives, transcultural and national, which I think are part and parcel of language teaching which takes into account the complexities of language and culture. Both sets of data showed students engaged in 'dialoguing' about issues which related to culture, language and clearly to students' own lives. The data also show the importance of collaboration in the meaning making process. The fact that one set of data showed students taking a more complex stance to the topic in hand, and a more essentialist approach in the second one, also shows that the context of discussion is important. This context was partly created by me by asking students to focus on Dutch articulation. But students themselves also created the context together. If one student introduced a different perspective, i.e. Eve in the last set of data introducing the notion of differences in communication styles between the English and Dutch, then others were prepared to follow that line of conversation. In doing so, students showed responsibility and engagement towards one another in their discussions, as well as an intellectual curiosity towards new and other perspectives.

Conclusion

What emerges from the classroom data is that the personal experience and reflections of students, the collaborating and dialoguing together in class is as important as the analytical activity of looking at the text from the various perspectives encompassed in my framework. In the first lesson students took a greater distance towards the text, took on an outside position, and seemingly approached the task of discussion as a traditional pedagogic activity, where a 'correct' answer is expected. Generally speaking it was not until the second lesson, when we looked at the cultuurtekst perspective, when students started to take a more dialogic approach to the text, relating the text to their personal experiences, which in turn influenced their interpretation of the text.

Over the two lessons, the discussion in class became more 'dialogic' as the lessons progressed, both in relation to the text - students engaged with the text at various levels, but also in terms of class discussion - students initially answered my questions directly to me, but soon started to respond to one another and collaborated (or clashed with one another on a couple of occasions) in interpreting the text. On the whole, it could be said that students' understanding of the text gradually moved from the level of text as product, to text as cultuurtekst, recognising underlying values. However, this was not a neat and linear progress. There were significant learning moments, but students' understanding of the discourses in the text remained frequently at an implicit level. At times, it also felt that students had negated their earlier understanding of the text. Students used a variety of approaches to interpret the text and these approaches also differed from student to student.

There were occasions where the students were intercultural in their attempts to understand the text from the inside, i.e. engaging with the cultural meaning of the text in relation to their own lived experiences. They also tried to understand and critique the values contained in the text. In that sense students were ethnographic and engaging. However, students did not reflect on their own interpretation of the text, so as such they did not make their own reality 'strange'. This was not surprising, as I had not invited students to be reflexive. I only conceptualised the notion of text ethnography and its reflexive aspect as a result of this data analysis. Students did, however, take a position of critique as they reflected on the ideological underpinnings of the text and its representation of normalising the discourse of women being soft, gentle, caring and dependent.

Interestingly, the deeper insights by students occurred when they moved away from the exercise of text analysis and made the discussion their own.

The 'talking around the text' became the most dialogic, insightful and even academic discussions of the two lessons, where students recognised the power structures that regulate women's personal life choices in terms of career and motherhood.

Whilst in the first lesson, students conceived of the discussions at the 'text level' as a more traditional learning task, responding to questions and tasks, in the second lessons students created their own dialogic space in which they collaborated to talk around the text, which at times also took on elements of discursive mapping. Students moved from particular interpretations and readings to other ones, even if these seemed to be conflicting. In doing so they created their own changing, what I call, 'context of discussion', a shared experience of learners engaging in the task of making sense of a text, mapping discourses and relating it to their own experiences. Students' readiness to engage in different interpretations or articulations showed their responsibility to one another in the classroom discussions. The dialogic space in the classroom gives rise to a fluidity of the 'context of discussion', opening up opportunities for sharing experiences, for expressing thought in a continuing shifting exchange of ideas, emotions and experiences.

The notion of Dutch articulation did not lead to any insights or, even considered discussions. The Dutch student, Marijke, did acknowledge that the discourses in the text were recognisable in terms of what was published in the Netherlands, but this point was not taken up further by anyone. I think in retrospect, the notion of articulation would need to be developed further as it is at a very subtle level that this takes place. The evidence from the classroom discussion suggests that the idea of a national articulation leads to uncritical comparisons and feeds into confirming stereotypes. However, one student did introduce an interesting notion, by implying that ways of talking about a topic, such as sex, can be nationally articulated to a degree, depending on to what degree it is included and how it is talked about in education.

Nevertheless, I believe the tendency to confirm stereotypes shows how careful we need to be in focusing on national patterns. Even if there may be a Dutch articulation in texts, or indeed discourses, this is only a particular tendency at a particular time and in a particular environment. Such an articulation is only one of various other articulations and of other discourses. Since students had difficulty making sense of the multiple discourses, or voices in the text, and had a tendency to interpret the text only in the light of one of these, focusing on a 'national' articulation carries with it the risks of confirming or creating new stereotypes which should probably not be tackled until students have a fuller and more balanced understanding of the complexities of national identity.

Notes

[1] 'Designer clothes, roof garden, nice trendy car under their cellulite-free trained buttocks, make-up of Clarins and Roc, a fridge full of salmon and champagne and of course that job with challenging prospects...'

CHAPTER 6

Conclusion: Embracing Tensions

Introduction

This book explored an approach to language and culture teaching as part of a general language class, which I called the cultuurtekst approach - a way of reading texts as culture. The underpinning rationale for my cultuurtekst approach is that language and culture are complex, and that teaching language as if both language and culture are stable notions creates a distorted representation of the cultural and social reality of people's lives.

The study on which this book is based consisted of a deeply reflexive process, which originated in my disquiet with contemporary language teaching practices at the time I started my study. This reflexivity consisted of a constant interplay between ideas and practice. On the one hand, I reflected on theories of language, culture and of pedagogy in order to develop the approach. Conversely, in looking at how students responded to my approach I reconsidered the theoretical premises on which language teaching practice is based, including my own practice. I developed notions such as 'being a text ethnographer' and 'Dutch articulation', and utilized the notion 'discourse mapping', as an important rationale of the cultuurtekst approach as a way of being a critical intercultural language user. The reflexive process of looking at my own practice was a profoundly uncomfortable one. In listening word for word to my tape recorded lessons, and looking at transcripts of these over and over again, I was confronted with everyday failings, such as not picking up on points students made, cutting off students, misinterpreting comments, leading discussions too much or not leading them sufficiently and many other of these awkward deficiencies, which most of us are probably liable to as teachers. More significantly, however, because of what at times seemed to be only embryonic understandings and, perhaps more worryingly, because of the resistance shown by one student, Sarah, in particular, I started to doubt whether my approach was a worthwhile addition to teaching methodology. Was my contribution to the development of a new paradigm in fact worth exploring further?

However, in this micro observation of my own teaching I became aware of two things. First of all, after the discomfort of potential failings, either in actual teaching or the methodology, was dispensed with, I realized that neither learning nor teaching are linear and straightforward processes. During the lessons it was exactly the hesitations, the ruptures, the discomfort in students which indicated valuable learning moments, much more so than the occasions where confident answers were given. Equally, it was when students responded in personal ways, rather than in distant, seemingly objective intellectual ways, that real engagement took place. Moreover, it was the resistance of Sarah in particular, which pointed not to the failing of this approach, but to the fact that I had, in her words, not gone 'far enough' with it. An important conclusion then is that whilst students had taken a step towards discourse mapping, interculturality and understanding the complexities of culture and being a text ethnographer, what was lacking was precisely the consideration and reflection on students' own subjectivities. And by extension, it was through my reflections on my own subjectivities, my own teaching and the discomfort I had felt, that I was able to progress in my own lessons to open up more space for personal engagement.

Before I come back to this later in this chapter, I summarise and conclude the findings of this study here, relating these to the theoretical concepts I developed, before discussing how this contributes towards thinking about a new paradigm of language teaching which fits in with the current demands of preparing students for their future complex mobile lives, linguistically, culturally and personally. In discussing the findings I will also refer to significant data from student interviews, which indicate these learning moments and processes.

The Student Interviews

For the purposes of this book I have looked in detail at the classroom data I collected during my study, and which I analysed in chapter 5. I am not affording the same amount of time and space to the interview data in this chapter as I did to the classroom data in the previous one, because the interview data were intended particularly to triangulate the classroom data. In this final chapter, where relevant, I refer to some of the interviews to illuminate some of my research findings in greater detail. In doing so, I focus on only two students, Claire and Sarah, particularly because of their contrasting views.

Out of all the students, Claire had engaged most with the conflicting discourses in the *Men's Health* text and with the cultuurtekst pedagogy. In the interviews, however, Claire showed that she was still struggling with the concept of cultuurtekst to some extent. Yet her conceptualisation of cultuurtekst in relation to her own lived experience added substantially to my own interpretation and theorisation of cultuurtekst for language pedagogy, as I will show below.

Similarly, Sarah's responses added significantly to my understanding of how students can engage with the idea of cultuurtekst, and how their assumptions of what communication is have a bearing on how they conceive their language learning. Moreover, it also helped me to locate the further conceptualisation of cultuurtekst pedagogy in a philosophical context. Even though Sarah had not been present during the second lesson, which was part of the analysis of the previous chapter, I have still opted to refer to data of Sarah's interviews here, because her resistance to my approach offered valuable insights into her learning experiences in relation to my pedagogy, and indeed has consequences for my reflection on how to take this pedagogy forward.

To understand the depth of Sarah's resistance, I need to point out that a few weeks into the course Sarah had approached me to ask whether she could be excused from attending the classes and just take the course on a self-study basis. She did not like the course because of its focus on 'style' in relation to the audience and purpose of the text. As the data show, Sarah had not even started to engage with the notion of discourses. It has to be remembered here that, as I mentioned in chapter 4, I had at the start of the course used the term 'style' in order to refer to 'routinised ways of talking' about certain topics, as that seemed a more acceptable notion to students because of its more obvious link with the idea of improving one's language skills in the class, rather than the term 'discourses'. But the idea of people adapting their language use in different situations had had a profound effect on Sarah. She suddenly felt that she could not communicate effectively anymore with people because she was worrying and wondering about what to say and how to say it, whereas before that would have come automatically. The idea that people use different kinds of languages in different situations, that people 'switch codes' was very unsettling in a psychological way. In fact, she mentioned at the time, 'it had rocked her to the core'; it made her feel that on the one hand she could not trust people anymore to say exactly what they meant, and that on the other hand, it made her very self conscious about her own use of language in English, both in writing and speech.

We managed to resolve the conflict between us by agreeing that Sarah would attend classes and do her homework, but that she did not have to participate in class discussions if she did not want to. After a few lessons, Sarah started to participate fully in class, but it always remained clear that she continued to be resistant to this approach.

The Research Findings

Introduction

The overall question I attempt to answer in my study is 'How do students engage with the cultuurtekst pedagogy?' The sub questions in relation to the two lessons in which the *Men's Health* text was discussed were: 'What different levels of reading do the two perspectives of text and cultuurtekst yield?', and whether students make the journey from 'text' to 'cultuurtekst'. In answering both these questions I was particularly interested in whether students would recognize the complexity of the discourses at the cultuurtekst level of reading, whether these different levels of reading would also relate to different levels of criticality, including that of engaging with the text as a text ethnographer, and finally, whether students recognized any Dutch articulation in the text.

Below I discuss the ambiguities between text and cultuurtekst which emerged both from the classroom data and the interviews, and how this linked to criticality as well as, in the case of Sarah, views of communication.

From Text to Cultuurtekst: Different Ways of Being Critical

As I showed in chapter 5, over the course of the two lessons students gradually moved from seeing the text as 'text' to seeing text as 'cultuurtekst'. However, this progress was not neat and linear, and there were considerable differences between students. Understanding of the text at a cultuurtekst level seemed to be incidental - occasional nuggets of insights, which students would not necessarily build on later. It became clear that it is not easy to separate the different ways of reading as students move in and out of different positions towards the text. It also became clear that we cannot separate reading a text for its content, structure and immediate context as a stable entity separate from cultuurtekst, because students invested the text with cultural and social meaning, even when reading the text at the textual level, as was the case in the first lesson. However, despite attributing meaning to the text, at the textual level of reading, students did so in the light of only one of the discourses reflected in the text. During these discussions, some students stayed close to the text and aligned themselves with the text or the author, but others went beyond the text, and were indeed aware the text was showing representations, rather than facts. Moreover, in the first lesson, students talked in a very confident manner about their analyses, as they seemed to interpret the task to be one of a traditional language classroom: that of assuming a 'correct answer' was required.

Discussing the text at cultuurtekst level in the second lesson, on the other hand, did seem to give students more insights; students became less confident in their voice as they interpreted the task as needing more careful consideration.

It is the hesitancy with which students try out ideas as part of dialogic group discussions, which I considered to be important learning moments. Questions which assume a correct answer do not allow any space for dialogue, engaging with other ideas, or for reflection. In the lesson focusing on the text as cultuurtekst, there was more 'discussion around the text', and students used these discussions to re-interpret the text in the light of what had been said. Again there were considerable differences between students. There were occasions where students showed an intercultural stance in their attempts to understand the text from the inside, i.e. engaging with the cultural meaning of the text in relation to the context of text production as well as engaging with their own lived experiences. Interestingly, the deeper insights by students occurred when they moved away from the exercise of text analysis and made the discussion their own. The 'talking around the text' became the most dialogic, insightful and, even academic, discussions of the two lessons, where students critiqued the power structures embedded in the text, i.e. those that regulate women's personal life choices in terms of career and motherhood. Moreover by relating their experiences again to the texts, students were also becoming aware that the text was making 'claims to truth'.

Claire

Whilst tentative conclusions after the second lesson pointed to a deeper engagement with the discourses in the text, the interviews with the students showed that some of the learning of the cultuurtekst lesson had not necessarily been transferred. Claire, for instance, had shown most understanding of and engagement with the discourses in the text during the lessons, including the conflicting ones, and had recognized these to be culturally significant. During one of her interviews, however, she took a different view; that these conflicting discourses showed a lack of clarity and poor argumentation. She showed her unease with the notion of cultuurtekst as she describes the process she followed in reading the text.

First she reads the text as a language learner making sure she has understood all of the vocabulary, then she reads it for content, critiquing both the stereotypical representations in the text as well as empathising with the women in the text who are dumped by their lover for a younger woman, before addressing the text at cultuurtekst level:

> Claire: When I did the, well, what I tried to do was read it for the vocabulary so that I understood it fully because it was annoying to leave (...) and then read it again on the train without writing anything and without having read your [framework], and then it was that I started to see the kind of... I find it very patronizing, em, there are lots of sentences that I don't like, the whole cliché, cliché thing, you know, oh her true lover left her for

a younger woman. Well, you know, that's quite a horrible thing to have to deal with, you know, you don't have to be patronizing about it.

But then, when I read it with, what I did was when I needed to write out the text that you wanted for the cultuurtekst question, I wrote down all the questions that were asked and then I read it each time so I went through it thinking, how are women portrayed here or how are the people in this story portrayed, and then kind of underlining a word and using some of the things that I saw, and the more I read it, the more I realised that it's not a very, well, that the argument isn't very good because it sort of skips from one thing to the other, and it never actually says anything, it kind of moves around and around this point but it never makes any statement about, you know, or conclusion.

Claire's representation of her process of reading is significant for various reasons. Her reading at the content level is not just a 'preferred reading', looking at the position from which the text asks to be read (see chapter 3), but her response to the text in this phase of reading was one of both critical and personal engagement. One the one hand she critiques the stereotypical, patronising and mocking approach of the text. But at the same time she responds from a personal perspective: she talks with a voice of empathy with the women who are being dumped by their lover for a younger woman. In my own framework of reading I had not taken account of this personal engagement which was also a significant point to emerge from my classroom data. But whilst she is critical of the text in terms of its ideological stereotypical representations of women, her critique here occurs at the content and textual level of reading. She sees the final cultuurtekst level of reading as an *academic* exercise, answering the questions about representations. Rather than this resulting in a firming up of the critique of discourses, it led her to a more traditional perspective of reading: being critical of its poor argumentation.

It seems then that her view of cultuurtekst carries within it a traditional view of text as containing stable meaning and text as a product. This dual view of text could be the result of giving students a framework which carries within it these two views. Critiquing representations is for Claire achieved through an engagement with the content from the perspective of people being represented in the text. She tries to inhabit the place of the 'characters', as it were, and to see the world momentarily through their eyes.

However, later on in the interview, she comes back to the distinction between text and cultuurtekst more specifically and this time she relates the notion of personal experience and interest with the idea of cultuurtekst.

Claire: [...] because we talked about it as a cultuurtekst not just necessarily as an article, because as an article you can take it apart.

G: Right

Claire: You know, but as a cultuurtekst it's very interesting, because it, you know, it talks about a cultural phenomenon, which you know, and I found the way it used, you know, because if you think, you know, I don't read many things by men, so I think that's quite interesting and, you know, yeah. No, I found it a very, I thought yesterday was really good fun, I really enjoyed it, because it was, you know, especially as you're talking about something which is actually quite interesting for someone my age, you know, talking about politics or economics is something that is not so relevant to me now, em, but social values, sex, things like that, is quite a sort of, that is something I would realistically discuss with a friend, you know, you're not kind of making a you know, fake situation.

G: Well, it's very much part of life and society.

Claire: Exactly

Claire sees text, or 'article' as she refers to it here, as a product you can analyse, 'you can take it apart'. She juxtaposes this with reading or discussing the text as cultuurtekst, which she interprets now as 'talking about a cultural phenomenon' you can relate to and engage with as you would in your everyday life: 'it's something I would realistically discuss with a friend'.

Whilst in the first fragment she indicates that the academic cultuurtekst exercise of looking at the way women were represented, made her realise the text was not a 'good text' in the traditional sense, Claire's conception of reading as cultuurtekst is quite different. Here she relates cultuurtekst not as an academic exercise looking at representations, but as reading as a 'communicative experience', relating the text to one's own (or other people's) experiences. For Claire this happened particularly when discussing the text in class. It was this communicative experience as dialogue which personalized the cultuurtekst phase of reading. Whilst Claire does not mention it in this fragment above, this experience becomes intercultural if the text is produced in an environment, and is about a social group, the reader is not familiar with. By relating the text to everyday lived experience and reflecting on that, Claire is reading, at least to some extent, as a text ethnographer. With Claire engaging with the text as a reader for her own interests, a topic she can relate to and would realistically discuss with friends, her description of the process of cultuurtekst seems to parallel the dialogic spaces which opened up in class when students engaged with the text by 'talking around it'. Reading 'as an experience', and classroom discussion as a real life activity, not a 'fake situation', as Claire called it, might then provide students with an opportunity to see things from different perspectives.

In summary, in her retrospective engagement with the text in the two sets of data above, Claire employed various positions of criticality. She had critiqued the text from a liberal humanist conception of critical thinking. From this perspective the text did not stand up to scrutiny as a 'good text'. She also employed ideology critique. From this perspective the text consisted of stereotypical representations. And furthermore, Claire employed also a personal level of critique; she critiqued the text, as it were for its misrepresentations and mocking approach, as if the women in the text were characters of flesh and blood with whom she could empathise. Through inhabiting the represented characters, she saw the world temporarily from their perspective. An approach in reading which is not unlike the idea of sympathetic imagination with is afforded in literature.

Sarah on the other hand, read the text in a very different way, one which is more distant and from a liberal humanist perspective. However, as we will see below, personal engagement also played a role for her, but in quite a different way from the way that Claire engaged with the text.

Sarah

Sarah rejected the notion of cultuurtekst quite strongly and she had not engaged with the idea of discourses. It must be remembered, however, she had not taken part in the second class where we discussed the text at a cultuurtekst level. In one of her interviews, when I ask Sarah what the notion 'cultuurtekst' means for her she says she feels it is to do with lifestyle. She distances herself from this particular genre, or 'cultuurteksts' as she perceives them, because they are 'manipulated' and written for specific audiences.

> Sarah: So I don't, so for me it's em it's quite clear when I read an article in a newspaper or a or a em whatever piece in a lifestyle magazine, that it's that it's just em that it's quite, well, manipulated for a particular audience to try and appeal to a certain type of em frame of mind.
>
> G: Mm.
>
> Sarah: And I don't, I don't like the idea of em of em being so manipulated, so I'd rather not read them.

Sarah thoroughly dislikes the idea of being manipulated through language. As she had said to me at the start of the course, she had previously always thought that people were 'honest' in their communicative behaviours and stayed true to themselves by speaking the same way regardless of who one spoke to or what one wanted to achieve.

With relating cultuurtekst particularly to the genre of lifestyle texts, Sarah may think of cultuurtekst as linked to 'low' culture; the popular mass media, which may contradict Sarah's own sense of culture and identity. Later in the interview when asked what kinds of texts she does read, she says that she prefers to read books, 'founts of knowledge', and would much rather learn about topics in class that are personally interesting to her, such as, for instance, Erasmus, rather than 'these cultuurteksts'.

What is interesting is that Sarah considers lifestyle publication as the same genre as newspapers. Her dislike of texts being manipulated is less geared to critiquing ideology, it would seem, then to an 'ideal' view of communication, as she makes clear below.

But the process of having discussed texts in class according to the questions in my framework for analysis, had led her to reflect deeply on the nature of communication. Her resistance to the course was not only caused by the fact that the texts seemed to be manipulated, or by her sense of identity as a reader who wants to read texts of a certain academic, or perhaps literary, standing, she also worried about how as readers you can interpret texts 'correctly'. For her the issues of 'trust' and 'honesty' emerge. As a reader you not only need to be able to trust a writer not to manipulate you, conversely when you write you need to trust your readers to interpret your text the way you intended:

Sarah: So you can, so you can, not only does the writer make choices and so structure a text that it says what he wants to say, but also a reader by interpreting it in different ways understands it differently, so that's why the whole idea of, that's why I think you get lost, anything you read or you listen to or anything, any kind of communication, there's such a lot of room for error, just because em if you are going to interpret it one way or another and you mean it one way or another.

G: Yeah yeah.

Sarah: There's so much potential to em confusion.

G: Yeah.

Sarah: Despite it being what you might call a better communication, it doesn't mean, I don't know a good communication has got to do with listeners as well as speakers or readers as well as writers.

G: Yes, yeah.

Sarah: And you can't, and so to, so you have to rely on your audience and so that's why if you're going to, if you think you can manipulate them, well if they can't rely on you, em I suppose (...) so I think the whole trust thing is that you read a, it would be nice to be able to read a text and em for them not to be playing with you and it depends on genre so if you, I don't know, if you're like criticizing things and don't mind reading crap then you can quite happily read different things that I wouldn't be able to read because I, I don't know, I don't like that so...

G: Right, okay.

Sarah: Does that make any sense?

Sarah is clearly trying to make sense of very complex ideas about communication which the course has made her think about. Firstly, she is very much aware of the complexity of the process of a communicative event and the important role the reader has in interpreting a text. Secondly, she contrasts what she knows is happening in communicative events with what she feels *ought* to happen.

To start with the first point, Sarah realizes that in communicating, not only does the writer need to make linguistic choices, the reader also has to be able to decode those. Whereas in earlier comments, Sarah seemed to hold on to a view of text as stable and universal, here she is introducing the importance of the reader's interpretation. However, Sarah sees the reader's role as a potential problem, since there is such a large potential for error and misunderstanding. Sarah assumes that the writer has a particular meaning which the reader must interpret 'correctly'. This fits with Sarah's interpretation of the *Men's Health* text in class, where she tried to align herself with the author (as I described in chapter 5). Sarah's view of communication accords with that of the structuralist model - a view of communication which many students hold subconsciously, that in sending a message in a communicative event the message has to arrive exactly as the sender had intended it.

Sarah sees the relationship between audience and writer or speaker as one of trust. As the reader you need to be able to trust the writer that he is not going to manipulate you. Sarah seems to hold to a view of 'ideal communication' which is similar to one of the maxims of Grice's cooperative principles: that of being truthful. Sarah's view of reading is one of text as 'text' and not as 'cultuurtekst'. Her criticality is rooted in the liberal humanist view of 'critical thinking', rather than seeing text in relation to contexts.

Whereas we saw that for Claire discourse critique was achieved through relating the text at a personal level and looking through the perspective of the women who were represented, seeing them as real characters as it were, for Sarah it worked the other way. She resisted the course, precisely because of affect. She felt uncomfortably because discussing texts brought to the fore the different personalities and backgrounds of students in the class:

> Sarah: But I realise that, well, it's a course with a clear aim and a clear method to follow up, but at first I found it difficult because I don't like, I don't like it.
>
> G: Right, well tell me a bit more about...
>
> Sarah: So if you read the specific, anything, any kind of specific text we looked at, em, say, I don't know, it maybe depends on generation or em background or anything, like, so different people will read the same text in a different way. It could be a way of finding out about the person I suppose by their interpretation of it, I suppose you can't really get away from that can you?
>
> G: Yeah, no.

Sarah: So em unless it's a subject that really doesn't affect you personally, then you can't really leave your own background or ideas behind. And so although you, although you're just discussing one text, if you read it with different people like we did, you'll see that it meant different things to different people, say em that text about [London] or something, em, we did quite near the end [...]

G: Oh right, yes.

Sarah: Yes, so that said something different to, I suppose we looked at it all in different ways, Andy, Emma, and I suppose our class was quite good because, for this course, because you couldn't get probably six more different people, all next to each other in the same class.

G: Did you find that useful? Did you feel that em there was a dialogue going on between you as a class, and was that beneficial?

Sarah: Well, I did think that em it's quite interesting, because if you just forget the texts but look at the class, I think that em for whatever reasons, in the end people identified with each other differently than at the beginning.

G: Was that with one another or with the texts?

Sarah: Yeah, with one another, and I actually think it might have to do with probably to do with the course because it was so much based on discussion and interpretation [...]

Sarah's experience in class of discussing texts with the other students showed her that the texts meant different things to different people. We saw earlier that Sarah has a strong notion of correct interpretation. But what Sarah finds significant here is not whether people's different interpretations are valid, but that people's interpretations say something about who they are. The way you interpret the text says something about your identity. Sarah turns it around: not only does your experience, your lifeworld knowledge inform your interpretations, it also reveals who you are.

As Sarah makes this point in the context of citing an example of what she did not like about the course, we can surmise that Sarah feels uncomfortable about the idea of revealing something about herself. Reading a text the way we did in class, has a challenging aspect because it forces students to engage and show something of their personality and experience with other people. Sarah may be worried about giving too much of herself away by interpreting a text.

An interesting notion emerges from this. Whereas the previous set of data pointed towards the fact Sarah holds a stable view of communication, in the data above, by making a link between interpreting a text and what it reveals about someone's personality, Sarah comes closer to a social view of language and communication. She acknowledges that there are multiple interpretations of a text, depending one's experiences and even personality. Even if Sarah deploys the notion of personality and identity as unchanging, by seeing a strong correlation between interpretation and who you are, in this set of data she is holding an almost dialogic view of text.

Even though the lessons stopped short of making a more explicit link between students' interpretations and their experiences and lifeworld knowledge, including discourses they have been familiarized with, Sarah already made this link. Although for Sarah this link was less in terms of social knowledge, but rather related to a stable individual identity.

In the next set of data Sarah makes the link between personal experiences and communication more explicit. Whereas in earlier data she may have felt uncomfortable about unintentionally revealing things about herself, below she states quite explicitly the connection between individual personalities and communication:

> *Sarah: But we're talking about communication, communication is (...) so you could say it's endless, so yes, it's endless because em em there's superficial communication and there's all different types going on at the same time and so if you're talking about communication, to really talk about communication, you do have to ask all those big questions so and we haven't done that, so that's why well...*
>
> *G: Ah okay, so you feel that's what you would've liked to address more.*
>
> *Sarah: I suppose, okay I suppose, it didn't occur to me before but now we're talking, I suppose, there are other aspects of communication, em, that we haven't talked about at all, so...*
>
> *[...]*
>
> *G: And what sort of questions are they? What sort of questions would you have liked to have addressed?*
>
> *Sarah: Well. I suppose em if you're talking about communication, then yes, ways, genres are quite safe em types of text where you look at em a text and say where's it from and what is it called and all the, that's kind of safe, and when you go down into and then you can, then the problem is that that's when it gets personal and so if that hasn't occurred to other people then fine, so then if you really wanted to know about what somebody is writing and why, and then you'd have to go sort of it would also become em em, it would have to do with individual personality and em yeah, I don't know.*

Sarah feels the course should have gone deeper and further in addressing the 'big questions'. The course had stayed at a safe level, talking about 'superficial communication' and genres and ways of writing. These big questions, Sarah suggests, relate to the individual; they are about finding out what somebody is writing and why. Whereas I had designed the course to address those questions about what is communicated, how and why at a social, political and cultural level, Sarah felt these questions should be explored at a psychological level: what influences an individual to communicate in a particular way and to what degree this is related to personality. Rooted in a view of language as stable and communication as expressing individual thought, Sarah's view contrasts with my aim to look at language at a social level. Nevertheless, my intention as I set out in the first chapter had been to rearticulate aspects of the liberal humanist paradigm, particularly the idea of expressing thought. Even though in Sarah's experience these views clashed, it is precisely in the dialogic space in the class-room, where students were expressing thought both as a collaborative social activity and conceptually in relating language to its cultural discursive contexts. Whilst Sarah was worried about revealing too much of herself, it would pre-cisely by trusting the communicative other which would make dialogic rela-tions possible.

So for Sarah, the personal was an extra analytical layer to lead to insights into why we as individuals communicate the way we do. For Claire the personal helped her to be critical of the text partly as a responsibility to the women rep-resented in the text: she spoke with a voice of empathy. For Claire the personal also had an ethical perspective: during class she had also shown a concern with the injustice of the stereotyping and gender inequality.

Sarah also showed an ethical stance, but for her that was located in the use of language: not obfuscating arguments and making sure that readers could interpret correctly what you as a writer wanted to convey.

Being a Text Ethnographer and Intercultural Communication

The process of critical engagement with the ideas in a text, as I have found through analysis of my data, is partly occasioned by students reflecting on their own experiences. I have called this process 'being a text ethnographer'.

Being a text ethnographer, I contended in chapter 3, is looking at text both from an inside and an outside perspective. However, I do not conceive the inside perspective as trying to understand the text from the perspective of the author or even of the intended audience. Helping students to engage with oth-erness in a text is more likely to come about in engaging with ideas within the text. Ideas, moreover, which do not have to be understood and agreed with, but can also be critiqued from their discursive and ideological perspectives – their claims to truth. However, the research findings showed that the richest moments of engaging with texts and the ideas embedded within were those moments where students abandoned the text temporarily and related the ideas to their own life, their experiences and their knowledge about society. It is this aspect of 'engaging with' which comes close to being a critical intercultural language user. The most intercultural moments were then largely instigated by the students themselves.

However, despite this engagement, students stopped short of reflecting on their own interpretation of the text and their own culturally located position as a reader. So as such they did not make their own reality 'strange'. This was not surprising, as I had not invited students to engage with that level of reflexivity during the classes. In fact, I had only conceptualised text ethnography as a result of this data analysis. This notion of reflexivity as part of reading a text as a text ethnographer is an area for further theoretical development.

Dutch Articulation: The National Dilemma

Mapping discourses is not only a critical activity. It is also a way of conceiving of the relationship between language and culture at a generic level, rather than the one language, one culture relationship which has influenced much of national focused language teaching. Cultuurtekst forms this bridge between language and culture; it is the space where different meanings can be created and rec-reated. It reflects as well as constructs culture, the latter through discourses. These discourses reflect transnational concerns and ideas, and so do not limit looking at cultural environment as a national process. Yet, due to historical processes and structures in society, which are formed along national lines, these discourses, I contended in chapter 2, may take on a national articulation. As I explained, I do not mean that a national articulation relates to essential-ist practices, behaviours or ways of conceptualizing our world around us, but rather that certain accentuations may be more prominent, or more accepta-ble in public discourse in certain social and cultural environments, including national ones. These articulations are not stable in themselves, but can also be rearticulated in different contexts and over time. This Dutch articulation is not a feature of all texts, but it seemed prominent in the text I used for this study, in its very traditional gendered perspective on women and the implication that their natural roles are to be mothers and wives.

As chapter 5 showed, students did not recognize the Dutch articulation that I had identified in the article, as they felt this text could have been written in the same way in an English publication. They saw the text not in a national, but in a global perspective. Students recognized instead the global intertextual references of British and American soaps and films. Marijke, one of the Dutch exchange students, was the only student who had been prepared to consider the notion of a Dutch articulation, although she phrased this very carefully. The text, she said, was not incongruous with other things published in the Neth-erlands in certain social environments. However, none of the other students pursued this notion of a Dutch articulation.

In class the notion of Dutch articulation did not lead to any significant insights, except confirming stereotypes. The notion 'backfired' as it were. In the interviews students were more prepared to consider the notion, although Claire and Sarah saw this in different ways. Claire tried to understand texts from the context in which they are produced, whereas Sarah saw Dutch articulation as related to the content of the text: a text about Dutch culture.

> Claire: And that is always going to be problematic and I suppose in a way I'm much more aware of Dutch texts and the cultuurtekst behind them because I actually have to research and I have to read it with my eyes very very open and see all the different things and I think to myself, well, I don't understand that, is that because that's a cultural thing, is that a cultural difference or is it just because I don't get the grammar or whatever, whereas in French and English I don't tend to think about that.

Claire is aware of her position as a culturally located reader. Being an intercultural reader, i.e. not being the intended audience, actually helps in understanding the cultural articulations of a text, Claire suggests, as it forces her 'to read with her eyes very very open'. As a bilingual speaker of English and French she does not have to think in the same way when reading a text in those languages as when she is reading a Dutch text. Being a foreign language reader then makes you stop and think and be more reflective about the text. It helps you to stand 'outside' the text and consider the particular cultural meanings.

> Claire: But I do think that it's a, it's an interesting way of looking at a piece, especially if for instance, I mean it's always interesting to look at other cultures, but to look at your own culture, to look at an English text written by an English person for an English audience, and to look at the analysis, you know, look at the way it's written, em, I do, I tend to do that a lot more than I look at the actual culture and the discourses behind it and the, it's affected by other things, em, I don't tend to look at the culture because it just seems natural to me.
>
> G: Yes.
>
> Claire: And I suppose one of the things that I've learnt in the last year is that, to look at it from someone else's point of view, in a way, and so when I write I try and think about other people, but also when I read I try and think about well gosh, how are people going to interpret that or how are they going to understand it.

Claire explains that when reading English texts she does not look at 'the culture' or discourses because they seem natural to her, whereas, she seems to suggest, she does do that with Dutch texts: 'it is interesting to look at other cultures'. She then explains that what she learnt from the course is writing from a reader's perspective. By linking these statements, Claire seems to be saying that her awareness of discourses and culture is helpful in addressing people from different cultural groups. So Claire sees her responsibility towards her own readers then also in intercultural terms in the sense that when she writes, or even when she reads, she almost tries to 'step into the shoes of the other', by imagining how they will interpret the text. Claire is seeing being intercultural in an ethnographic way: a sympathetic imagination of the possible reader.

Sarah on the other hand interpreted Dutch articulation as the content of text about a culture, which was only significant and valuable when treated in a comparative way:

> *Sarah: Well, I think em because we sort of mentioned that before, haven't we, and that what I said em em was that you can only talk about em a sort of certain way of doing things in one place or another if you compare two, so where you've got a text say for example the nostalgia text or the text [about London], for example, that's where you've got a Dutch person in an English context, so when you're comparing two, then it might be more obvious, where as if you are just looking at the text, so if it's like a Dutch text about, just in a Dutch, in Dutch society, say like the what was it, the text, the Men's Health or other lifestyle magazine or whatever, it's not comparing Holland particularly with any other country.*

> *G: No.*

> *Sarah: So I don't really, I think it depends on the content of the thing, not in terms of what it's saying but em whether it's Holland as opposed to something else, if there's, if it's like comparing or there's two contexts, but it did say, didn't it in the [London text] it was saying that this is different in Holland or something.*

Sarah interpreted my question about recognizing a particular Dutch articulation in the text as asking whether we can learn anything about Dutch culture, i.e. 'Dutch ways' of doing things. She feels that any specific Dutch aspect will come through only if the text is *about* a Dutch person in an English context or vice versa. So Sarah assumes that any understanding or insight into Dutch society from a text relates to the *content* of the text, rather than the way the content is written, reflecting underpinning cultural values, ideologies and discourses.

It is in retrospect not that surprising that students did not engage with the idea of a Dutch articulation in the way I had intended, i.e. as a discursive articulation in a particular historical national context. The concept of 'discourses' is complex enough for students to consider in its own right, and Sarah had not engaged with this notion. The idea of a 'flavour' or articulation of a discourse is indeed very subtle, and for students to recognize this would require them to be enculturalised in a range of discourses in various areas of social and cultural life current in both, and possibly other, countries.

Intertwining a cultuurtekst approach focusing on discursive mapping in global perspectives, with an approach that highlights cultural particularities in the form of looking at Dutch articulations, is one of the tensions that underpin this study. This study showed that dealing with this 'national dilemma', as Risager phrases it, is not easy in the classroom.

Finally, in terms of comparing the two students whose interview data I discussed in this chapter, it may be tempting to conclude that Claire was more successful as a student engaging with this pedagogy than Sarah, as Claire's engagement was more in line with my intention. However, Sarah's discomfort had led her to go through the greatest transformation as a learner. In turn it led me to realise that discomfort is perhaps a necessary process in education. Being intercultural, and trying to engage with other ideas, will mean stepping outside the familiar. It is about exploring the possibilities of who we can be, and how we can relate to one another. It is not only about being intercultural, it is also about being human.

Conclusion: Tensions, Ambiguities and Incompatibilities

The study on which this book is based has been born out of and marked by tensions and ambiguities. These tensions were present from the very start of the study and were part of the context in which it took place – a traditional university which was characterized by a strong adherence to the liberal humanist paradigm in language education, but operating in a wider context which emphasises instrumental aims.

Tensions were also located in the actual pedagogy itself. Looking at texts as products, employing an approach to criticality which is rooted in the liberal humanist paradigm, i.e. that of taking critical distance, conflicts with the cultuurtekst level of looking at texts. The latter employs a poststructuralist critique, looking at multiple discourses in texts, which I referred to, following Pennycook (2001), as 'discursive mapping'. This means looking at texts as a meaning making process, whereby the cultural contexts of both the text producing environment, but also that of the reader, have a bearing on the interpretation. The tensions between these two perspectives led to some confusion where students critiqued the text on the one hand for its ideological positioning and on the other for its poor argumentation and structure.

I already referred earlier to the conflict embedded in my pedagogy of the centrality of discourses in the cultuurtekst approach and the concept of 'Dutch articulation'. This particular tension led to students referring in discussions to wider global contexts and intertexts and their personal experience on the one hand, yet reverted to national stereotyping on the other.

These tensions, conflicts, resistances and seeming incompatibilities not only formed the backdrop of the study, but also inform my conclusion and point to the way forward. I am arguing that the different perspectives on text, educational philosophies and criticality are not necessarily incompatible as such. After all, ambiguities are part and parcel of students' everyday realities. They live with diversity, with supercomplexity, with cultural, linguistic and philosophical tensions. One of the important conclusions of this study then is that language teaching needs to embrace these tensions if it is to develop pedagogies which acknowledge cultural complexities on the one hand and the existence of cultural patterns on the other.

In chapter 1, whilst rejecting the tenets underpinning the liberal humanist paradigm, i.e. the assumptions of objectivity and truth, and its denial of humans as being, at least in part, shaped by cultural forces, I argued for a re-articulation of some of its concerns. These were located, I contended, in 1) the idea of criticality and intellectual engagement in language classes, 2) the notions of morality, which I interpret here as a concern for others, and 3) the importance of Self.

I have discussed the different perspectives on criticality in detail throughout this book as one of the tensions which I am embracing. The concern for others is an element which I did not purposefully include in my pedagogy, but it emerged naturally as students engaged with the text and its fictional characters in discussions. This concern for others also emerged in students' writing as they showed an awareness of the other they were addressing. In a similar vein, the emphasis on Self and individual agency emerged, as students themselves engaged with the text and with one another explicitly referring to their own personal experiences.

In this way, the three elements which I highlighted contributed to and fed into one another. This criticality embedded in the cultuurtekst approach was then partly achieved through the intellectual engagement with the text and through a consideration of the analytical questions I had asked in class and the framework I used. However, it was equally the personal engagement as a group, the more intimate dialoguing with one another and relating the discussions to themselves that led to this criticality. The dialogic space in the classroom which students created themselves, opened up an imaginative, personal and intimate human perspective through which collaboration and exploration of ideas took place. In doing so, students showed empathy and placed themselves into the shoes of others and into their future imagined selves. It was through sympathetic imagination that critical interculturality started to take place.

Pedagogical Implications

Because of the time which has lapsed between the data collection and the completion of this study, my pedagogy has since had time to evolve as I reflected on the implications of my findings. After the initial data collection, but before the analysis of the data, I responded particularity to the resistance shown by Sarah. I also felt that the overt critical analytical stance of my pedagogy could irritate students as their main aim for this course is to improve their language skills, i.e. they do not feel they need to learn how to analyse a text. As a result my initial response was to tone down my cultuurtekst approach, so that discussing texts in class is not seen as explicit 'text analysis', but instead as 'talking about the text', which is part and parcel of conversations building up linguistic skills. My cultuurtekst pedagogy initially became even more implicit than the one I described in this book.

However, since I have analysed the data and completed the study, I have come to the conclusion that rather than making my approach less explicit, I should make it more so. In order to deal with the tensions thrown up by using conflicting perspectives in class, I should embrace rather than avoid them. Indeed, when looking at texts and carrying out tasks, I now explain explicitly from which view of text and criticality we are operating; whether we are looking at text structures, whether arguments are convincing and whether we focus on writing solidly argued texts ourselves, or whether, in contrast, we are engaging in discursive mapping. I do not tiptoe around the notion of discourses any more, but address these explicitly in class, if relevant. My pedagogy is still one of explicit heteroglossia; we read texts from a large variety of genres - each text including multiple voices and discourses - which we analyse whilst discussing the issues thrown up by these. This way, students adapt their writing more consciously to a variety of readers, drawing on discourses more consciously and explicitly.

The personal in language learning also needs to be embraced more explicitly. I now ask students on occasion to relate their own experiences to the texts we read and the tasks we do in class. I also ask students to reflect on their own interpretations of texts and how these relate, not only to their particular set of experiences, but especially to their understanding of these experiences in relation to discursive forces. Moreover, I ask students to be reflexive about their own writing in relation to their own and the other (culture's) context: why they have written a particular text in a particular way. Bringing the Self into students' language tasks like this, resonates with the point that Sarah referred to in her interview: that the course should look at what makes individuals communicate the way they do. So far, I have only included this reflexivity as part of class discussions, but in future I will embed this more thoroughly in the syllabus by asking students to write down these reflections in diaries.

Being explicit to students about the conceptual framework I use is not an insignificant point. It goes against the expectations students have about what a language class should be. Moreover the concepts which are touched upon are possibly also in conflict with students' views of what language, culture and communication are, and how they interrelate. Provided students feel they are at the same time gaining practical language skills, being open to students about the concepts and conflicting perspectives can avoid resistance such as shown by Sarah. In the end it was not so much the fact that my course addressed notions with which she disagreed, it was the fact that I did not address these issues more explicitly and in further depth. If you touch on issues of communication, 'real communication', she asserted, you can't leave issues hanging mid-air.

Even though my cultuurtekst pedagogy took a global perspective from the start, the notion of a Dutch articulation brought the national back into focus. This particular notion, I showed, proved not to be that useful, and to be fully exploited also needs to be used explicitly for it to make sense to students without it leading to stereotyping. However, I have since only referred to the notion on very rare occasions. Indeed it has become almost an incidental part of my pedagogy. Students themselves tend to take cosmopolitan perspectives in class, as one of my examples of such a task below shows.

By linking students' experiences with practical language tasks we can create opportunities in class for communicative encounters where students can engage their own beliefs and belongings to imagine themselves to have real impact on the world – creatively and responsibly with an interest in and concern for their communicative partners.

Example

My study consisted of only two lessons out of a whole year long course where I focus on reading and awareness raising. All the same, I have observed that that awareness of how language and culture interrelate also benefits students' language skills, as they will learn to think about and consequently adapt their own language use as part of showing responsibility in communicative events.

Claire had said in one of her interviews that when reading in the foreign language, she was 'reading with her eyes very very open, – with an alertness to cultural connotations. I am arguing that in using the cultuurtekst approach, students apply this awareness to the way they communicate in general – with an alertness to cultural connotations and to how relations are constructed discursively. I discuss here two examples of tasks which I am using now in my pedagogy where students write or speak 'with their eyes very open'.

Whilst I reject instrumentalism in its focus on skills at the expense of personal development, ethics and engaging with criticality, that does not mean that language classes cannot include work related tasks. My examples below use work related contexts and I illustrate how my approach differs from functionalist skills-based teaching. In instrumentalist-oriented language classes and text books, the task of giving an oral presentation, for instance, tends to be accompanied by advice on structuring, how to introduce and finish a presentation, and by providing some useful phrases. In a cultuurtekst-oriented approach preparing students for an oral presentation could indeed include some of these aspects (after all, students need to know the conventions before they can choose whether they want to deviate from these or not), but emphasises particularly the relational aspects of positioning themselves towards the audience. This means a reflection on how they are creating and conducting relationships. It is through evoking the personal that students can start looking at communicative situations critically.

In my advanced language class I start preparing students for an oral presentation by asking them to reflect on their own previous experiences, either in a personal social sphere or a work environment where they have had to present information. This led to considerations of how their previous holiday jobs, for instance, such as working in the visitor centre of London Zoo or being a tour guide for Dutch tourists in Notre Dame in Paris, had been instances where they had to consider and make decisions on their positioning of others, as well as their positioning of themselves towards their imagined 'clients'. In this process students recollected situations in which they had to make on the spot decisions on how to present information in ways that could be understood, and showed concern for their communicative partners.

The next stage of this particular task is to look at other presentations found on the internet and students try and imagine themselves in the role of the intended audience. How do they feel they are being positioned as an audience? Do they feel they are treated with respect? How does the context inform the presenter's style? Has he/she taken note of their possible viewpoints and previous knowledge? Are there particular assumptions which are underlying some of these presentations? When students prepare their own presentations in a work context of their own choosing, they try and get under the skin of the imagined role they have set for themselves and also that of their imagined audience, so they can decide what to present and how to do so. Elsewhere I describe how students engage creatively with this task from a position of justice, equality and respect for one another – how they utilize their cosmopolitan empathy. They do not address an imagined monologic other, but a complex one which necessitates them using multiple voices (Quist, 2013). Their presentations feel authentic and do not employ the bland ready-made style which tends to be found in course books using vocationally-oriented language tasks.

Another example in my current course is the task of writing emails or letters in a work-oriented situation. Students start with reflecting on uncomfortable writing situations they have experienced where they were unsure how to address their addressee or what tone to adopt. The writing task I give them has a clearly described context of relations, e.g. they have to imagine themselves to be the Head of a school who writes to parents to explain particular changes in the structure of the school. Students consider what tone to use, how to position themselves as the Head, and how to position the parents. Students then read out their finished work in class and receive feedback from the other students, who imagine themselves in the position of the receivers of the text. Students often comment on whether the text is too authoritarian to their liking or conversely too hesitant in its tone, and differences in opinion about this are discussed. Frequently this leads to hilarity as students, unsolicited by me, start to relate these different styles and indeed discursive constructions, in this case to do with education, to the individuals who wrote the texts. They often joke about whether this tone fits with the perceived personality of the text writer.

In engaging in tasks such as these which combine the personal and the critical in very practical language tasks, students create dialogic spaces where they can discuss in intensely personal and intimate ways why they have chosen the communicative styles they have been using. This comes close to what Sarah had said she had wanted to gain from the classes.

My pedagogy is still evolving, but by reflecting on discourses, multiple voicedness, and on interpersonal and intercultural relations, we do not only offer chances for students to being intercultural, but also to being human - to use their sense of responsibility towards, and engagement with, others. This can be applied to all manner of genres and tasks using all manner of language varieties and purposes, from academic to journalistic to creative writing – all of which invite students to reflect on conscious linguistic choices and encourage experiencing the communication process. These reflections also bring to the fore the fluid process that communication is; it brings a realisation of the changeability of communicative situations, the 'ruptures', the fragility of our own positions, and of text as culture. It also engages students' cosmopolitan attitudes using their sympathetic imaginations (Quist, 2013).

Towards a Theory of the Personal and the Critical: Embracing Incompatibilities

The practical examples of the language tasks above, which combine an ethical, individual as well as a critical perspective with vocational concerns is not meant to be a simple marrying of liberalist and instrumentalist approaches. The accentuation of cosmopolitan and ethical concerns which may have found its origin in the liberal humanistic paradigm transcends that particular philosophical perspective, and can just as easily be taken on board by the poststructuralist critical perspective of discursive mapping.

The seeming incompatibility and tensions which underpin this study in the perceived philosophical conflicts in many of the concepts I have been advocating, is perhaps not as much of a problem as is sometimes assumed. In this I am reminded of the term Romantic Conceptualism, an art scholarly term, described in 2006 by the Dutch critic Jan Verwoert to refer to conceptual art. The two terms are not as incompatible as they seem. Conceptual art, whether installation, video or performance, is often associated with a cold intellectual approach to art and rigorous attention to simplicity of form. However, many conceptual art pieces do in fact frequently draw attention to the actual processes of producing meaning, relying on memories and expression of emotion. The conceptual is thus being romanticized. In a similar way an intellectual engagement with text, language and writing can draw on the actual processes of meaning making and include personal reflections, creativity, a concern for others, and relating one's own every day communicative experiences to the wider cultural forces.

We are at the turning point of another shift in language teaching. One which affords a greater role for personal stories and self exploration. The call for romanticism as a new paradigm has been mooted by Ros i Solé and Fenoulhet (2013) who propose a 'Romantic turn' in language learning, emphasising an engagement with learners' subjectivities, emotions and an acknowledgement of the discomfort of interculturality.

In the seeming incompatibility of the personal and the critical, I am reminded of the traditional Sufi image which Elif Shafak (2011) conjures up of the upside down tree, extending its roots in the air. Its life force, its cultural environment, is provided by the arc of the vast blue sky full of the promise of possibilities. In a similar way our students feed from this vastness to create their own stories as they go about their journey: critical, accepting, adopting, adapting, making choices and creating their own stories of belongings.

Bibliography

Anderson, B. (1983, 2005) *Imagined Communities: Reflections on the Origin and the Spread of Nationalism* (2nd ed.). London: Verso.

Andersen, R. (1988) *The Power and the Word: Language, Power and Change.* London: Paladin Grafton Books.

Apple, M.W. (1990) *Ideology and Curriculum* (2nd ed.). New York and London: Routledge.

Arnold, M. (1869, 2006) *Culture and Anarchy: an Essay in Political and Social Criticism*, Bibliolife.

Atkinson, P. et al. (2001, 2007) Editorial Introduction In: *Handbook of Ethnography.* London: Routledge.

Austin, J.L. (1962) *How to do Things with Words*, Oxford: Oxford University Press.

Bailey, S.N. (1994) 'Literature in the modern languages curriculum of British universities'. *Language Learning Journal.* 9, pp. 41-45.

Bakhtin, M. (1981) *The Dialogic Imagination (Four Essays)* ed. M. Holquist, Austin: University of Texas Press.

Bakhtin (1986, 1996) *The Problem of Speech Genres.* In: Speech Genres & Other Late Essays. Austin: University of Texas Press.

Barnett, R. (1997) *Higher Education: A Critical Business.* Buckinghamshire: Open University Press.

Bartlett, F.C. (1932) *Remembering: A Study in Experimental and Social Psychology.* Cambridge: Cambridge University Press.

Barro, A. et al. (1998) 'Cultural practice in everyday life: the language learner as ethnographer'. In: M. Byram and M. Fleming (eds) *Language Learning in Intercultural Perspective: approaches through drama and ethnography.* Cambridge: Cambridge University Press.

Baumann, G. (1996) *Contesting Culture: discourses of identity in multi-ethnic London*, Cambridge: Cambridge University Press.

Beheydt, L. Review article of 'Hoe maakt u het? De Nederlandse taal in haar culturele context'. *Neerlandia Extra Muros*, XXXVI, 2 mei 1998.

Beheydt, L. (2003) 'Vreemde ogen dwingen'. *Kroniek cultuur en maatschappij der Nederlanden*; jaargang 41, 2. Also available online at: http://snvt.taalunieversum.org/Taalunieversum/nem/artikel.php?ID=35 [Last accessed October, 2013].

Besamusca, E. (2006) 'Landeskunde: wat is dat?' Paper at *Neerlandistiek in Contrast, Zestiende Colloquium Neerlandicum*. Univerisity of Gent, 20-26 August, 2006.

Besamusca, E. and Verheul, J. (2010) *Discovering the Dutch*. Amsterdam: Amsterdam University Press.

Billig, M. (1995) *Banal Nationalism*. London: Sage Publications.

Blommaert, J. (1998) *Different approaches to intercultural communication: A critical survey*. Centrum voor Islam in Europa. Available online at: http://www.flwi.ugent.be/cie/CIE/blommaert1.htm [Last accessed October, 2013].

Blommaert, J. and Jie, D. (2010) *Ethnographic Fieldwork: A Beginner's Guide*. Bristol: Multilingual Matters.

Brumfit, C. et al. (2005) Language study in higher education and the development of criticality. *International Journal of Applied Linguistics*. 15 (2), pp. 45-168.

Byram, M. (1989) *Cultural Studies in Foreign Language Education*. Clevedon: Multilingual Matters.

Byram, M. (1991) 'Teaching culture and language: towards an integrated model'. In: D. Buttjes and M. Byram (eds), *Mediating languages and cultures*, Clevedon and Philadelphia, Multilingual Matters.

Byram, M. (1992) 'Language and culture learning for European citizenship'. In *Language and Education* 6 (2-4) pp. 165-176.

Byram, M. (1997) 'Cultural Awareness as vocabulary learning'. *Language Learning Journal*. 16, pp. 51-57.

Byram, M. (1997) *Teaching and Assessing Intercultural Communicative Competence*. Clevedon: Multilingual Matters.

Byram, M. et al. (1994) *Teaching-and-Learning Language-and-Culture*, Clevedon, Philadelphia and Adelaide: Multilingual Matters.

Byram, M., and Zarate G. (1994) *Definitions, Objectives and Assessment of Socio-cultural Objectives*. Strasbourg: Council of Europe.

Byram, M. and Fleming, M. (eds) (1998) *Language Learning in Intercultural Perspective: approaches through drama and ethnography*. Cambridge: Cambridge University Press.

Byram, M. et al. (2001) *Developing Intercultural Competence in Practice*. Clevedon: Multilingual Matters.

Canale, M and Swain, M. (1980) 'Theoretical bases of communicative approaches to second language teaching and testing'. *Applied Linguistics*, (1), 1.

Canning, J. (2009) 'A skill or discipline? An examination of employability and the study of modern foreign languages.' In: *Journal of Employability and the Humanities*. 3, 1-12.

Carr, W. (1995) 'Education and Democracy: confronting the post-modern challenge'. *Journal of Philosophy of Education*, 29 (1), pp. 75-91.

Clark, R. (1992) 'Principles and practice of CLA in the classroom'. In: Fairclough, N. (ed), *Critical Language Awareness*, London and New York: Longman, 1992, pp. 134-137.

Cohen, L. and Manion, L. (1985) *Research Methods in Education* (2nd ed.). Hampshire USA: Croom Helm.

Cohen, L., Manion, L., and Morrison, K. (2007) *Research Methods in Education*. London and New York: Routledge.

Coleman, J.A. (1996) *Studying Languages: A survey of British and European students*. Centre for Information on Language Teaching and Research.

Cook, G. (1989) *Discourse* Oxford: Oxford University Press.

Cooke, M. and Wallace, C. with Shrubshall, P. (2004) 'Inside Out/Outside In: a study of reading in ESOL classrooms'. In: Celia Roberts et al (eds) *Research Report: English for Speakers of Other Languages – case studies of provision, learners' needs and resourses*. National Research and Development Centre for adult literacy and numeracy.

Cope, B. And Kalantzis (1993) 'Introduction'. In B. Cope and M. Kalantzis (eds) *The Powers of Literacy: A Genre Approach to Teaching Writing*, London and Washington, D.C.: The Falmer Press.

Cope, B. and Kalantzis, M. (1993) 'Histories of Pedagogy, Cultures of Schooling' In: *The Powers of Literacy: A Genre Approach to Teaching Writing* (eds), B. Cope and M. Kalantzis, London and Washington D.C.: The Falmer Press. pp. 41-45.

Council of Europe (2001) *Common European framework of reference for languages: learning, teaching and assessment*. Cambridge: Cambridge University Press.

Cummins, J. (1979) 'Cognitive Academic Language Proficiency, linguistic interdependence, the Optimal Age Question and some other matters'. *Working Papers on Bilingualism* 19, pp. 121-129.

De Leeuw, E. et al. *Contact! Nederlands voor andertaligen*. Amsterdam: Intertaal.

Dearing, D. (chairman) (1997) 'Higher Education in the learning society'. *The National Committee of Inquiry into Higher Education*.

Deleuze, G. and Guattari, F. (1988) *A Thousand Plateaus*. London: Athlone.

Denzin, N. and Lincoln, Y. (eds) (1994) *Handbook of Qualitative Research*. Thousand Oaks, CA: Sage.

Devos, R. et al. (2009a) *Vanzelfsprekend*. Leuven, Den Haag: Acco.

Devos, R. et al. (2009b) *Nederlands voor anderstaligen: van theorie naar praktijk*. Leuven, Den Haag: Acco.

Eagleton, T. (1984) *The function of criticism*. London: Verso.

Eagleton, T. (2000) *The Idea of Culture* Malden, Oxford, Victoria: Blackwell Publishing.

Emig, J. (1983) 'The Relation of Thought and Language Implicit in Some Early American Rhetoric and Composition Texts'. In J. Emig (ed) *The Web of Meaning: essays on writing, teaching, learning and thinking*. Upper Montclair, N.J.: Boynton/Cook Publishers Inc.

Fairclough, N. (1989) *Language and Power*. London: Longman.

Fairclough, N. (1992) *Critical Language Awareness*. London and New York: Longman.

Fairclough, N. and Wodak, R. (1996) Critical Discourse Analysis. In T. van Dijk (Ed.) *Discourse analysis*. London: Sage.

Fenoulhet, J. (2007) Making the Personal Political: Dutch Women Writers 1919 – 1970 London: Legenda, Modern Humanities Research Association and Maney Publishing.

Fenoulhet, J. and Ros i Solé, C. (2010) *Mobility and Localisation in Language Learning*. Oxford: Peter Lang.

Foucault, M. (1965) *Madness and Civilization: a history of insanity in the age of reason*. New York: Random House.

Freire, P. (1970) *Pedagogy of the oppressed*. New York: Continuum (M.B. Ramos, trans).

Gee, J.P. (2009, 1990) *Social Linguistics and Literacies: Ideology in Discourses* (3rd ed.). Abingdon: Routledge.

Geertz, C. (1973) *The Interpretation of Cultures* New York: Basic Books.

Glaser, B. and Strauss, A. (1967) *The Discovery of Grounded Theory: Strategies for Qualitative Research*. Chicago: Aldine Publishing.

Giroux, H.A. (1992) *Border Crossings: Cultural Workers and the Politics of Education*. New York: Routledge.

Gramsci, A. (1971) *Selections from Prison Notebooks*. Edited and translated by Hoare, Q. and Nowell Smith, G. London: Lawrence and Wishart.

Grice, H.P. (1975) 'Logic and Conversation' In: P. Cole and J.L. Morgan (eds) *Syntax and Semantics*, Vol. 3: Speech Acts, New York: Academic Press.

Guilherme, M. (2002) *Critical Citizens for an Intercultural World*. Clevedon: Multilingual Matters.

Gumperz, J.J. et al. (1979) *Crosstalk: a study of crosscultural communication*. Southall: NCILT.

Gumperz, J.J. (1982) *Discourse Strategies*. Cambridge: Cambridge University Press.

Habermas, J. (1984) *The Theory of Communicative Action: Reason and the Rationalisation of Society* (Vol. 1). London: Heinemann.

Hall, E.T. (1956) *The Silent Language*. New York: Doubleday.

Hall, S., (1983) 'The problem of ideology – Marxism without guarantees' In: B. Matthews (ed), *Marx 100 years on*. London: Lawrence & Wishart.

Hall, S. (1985) 'The rediscovery of 'ideology': return of the repressed in media studies'. In: V. Beechey and J. Donald (eds), *Subjectivity and Social Relations*, Milton Keynes and Philadelpia: Open University Press. p. 46.

Hall, S. (1996) 'Who Needs Identity?' In S. Hall and P. Du Gay (eds) Questions of Cultural Identity. London: Sage, pp. 1-17.

Hall, S. (1997) 'Cultural Revolutions', a dialogue between Martin Jacques and Stuart Hall. In: New Statesman, 5 December 1997, pp. 24-26.

Hall, S. (2001) 'Foucault: Power, Knowledge and Discourse'. In Wetherell, M., Taylor, S. and Yates, S.J. (eds) Discourse Theory and Practice. London: Sage.

Halliday, M.A.K. (1978) Language as a social semiotic, London: Edward Arnold.

Halliday, M.A.K. (1985, 1989) In: Halliday and Ruqaiya Hasan (eds) Language, context, and text: aspects of language in a social-semiotic perspective (2nd ed.). Oxford: Oxford University Press.

Halliday, M.A.K. (1994) An Introduction to Functional Grammar (2nd ed.). London: Edward Arnold.

Hammersley, M. and Atkinson, P. (1983, 1995) Ethnography: principles in practice (2nd ed.). London and New York: Routledge.

Hannerz, U. (1999) 'Reflections of Varieties of Culturespeak', European Journal of Cultural Studies, 2:3 pp. 393-407.

Hawkins E. (1984) Awareness of Language: an introduction, Cambridge: Cambridge University Press.

HEFCE (1995-96) Quality Assessment of French 1995-96 Subject Overview report QO 2/96 (1995-96) Quality Assessment of German and Related languages 1995-96 Subject Overview Report QO 3/96.

Herder, J. G. (1952 (1782-91)) Ideen zur Philosophie der Geschichte der Menscheit. In: Zur Philosophie der Geschichte. Eine Auswahl in zwei Bänden. Berlin: Aufbau Verlag.

Hermans, Theo (2007) The Conference of the Tongues. Manchester and Kinderhook (NY): St. Jerome Publishing.

Hofstede, G. (1994) Cultures and Organizations. London: Harper Collins Publishers.

Hofstede, G. personal website: http://www.geert-hofstede.com/

Hoggart, R. (1995) The way we live now. London: Pimlico.

Holliday, A. et al. (2004) Intercultural Communication: an Advanced Resource Book. London, New York: Routledge.

Holliday, A. (2007) Doing and Writing Qualitative Research (2nd ed.). London: Sage Publications.

Holliday, A. (2010) 'Complexity in cultural identity'. In: Language and Intercultural Communication. 10, 2.

Holquist, M. (1990) Dialogism: Bakhtin and his world. London and New York: Routledge.

Huntington, S. (1998) The Clash of Civilizations: The Remaking of the World Order. New York: Simon and Schuster.

Hymes, D. H. (1972) 'On Communicative Competence'. In J.B. Pride and J. Holmes (eds) Sociolinguistics. Harmondsworth: Penguin Books.

Hymes, D. (1967) 'Models of the interaction of language and social setting' In: Journal of Social Issues, 23, pp. 8-28.

Hymes, D. (1996) *Ethnography, linguistics, narrative inequality*: Toward under-standing of voice. London: Taylor & Francis.

Inglis, F. (1992) Relativism and Canonicality: culture and socialism *Language and Education*, 6 (2, 3 & 4), pp. 219-229.

Inglis, F. (1995) *Raymond Williams*, London and New York: Routledge, paper-back edition 1998.

Jonathan, R. (1995) Liberal Philosophy of Education: a paradigm under strain *Journal of Philosophy of Education* Vol. 29:1, pp. 75-91.

King, L. (1998) *Language Learning Futures: the way ahead*. Conference: Lan-guage Learning Futures in the University Sector, CILT and SCML, Leeds Metropolitan University.

Kramsch, C. (1993) *Context and Culture in Language Teaching*. Oxford: Oxford University Press.

Kramsch, C. (1998) *Language and Culture*. Oxford: Oxford University Press.

Kramsch, C. (2002) 'Review article: In search of the intercultural'. In *Journal of Sociolinguistics*, 6:3, pp. 275-285.

Kramsch, C. (2009) *The Multilingual Subject*. Oxford: Oxford University Press.

Kress, G. (1985) *Linguistic processes in sociocultural practice*. Victoria: Deakin University.

Kress, G. (1994) 'Against arbitrariness: the social production of the sign as a foundational issue in critical discourse analysis'. In: *Discourse and society*, Sage,Vol/2, pp. 169-191.

Kress, G. and Hodge, R. (1979) *Language and Ideology*. London: Routledge.

Kristeva, J. (1986, 1966) 'Word, Dialogue and Novel'. In Toril Moi (ed) *The Kris-teva Reader*. New York: Columbia Univeristy Press.

Kumaravadivelu, B. (2007) *Cultural Globalisation and Language Education*. New Haven and London: Yale University Press.

Lancashire University, *The intercultural language project*. Available online at: http://www.lancs.ac.uk/users/interculture/subproj4.htm [Last accessed: October, 2013].

Lantolf, J. P. (1997) Lecture on 'Second Culture Acquisition: Cognitive Consid-erations'. Institute of Education, University of London.

Law, J. (2004) *After Method: Mess in Social Science Research*. London: Routledge.

Lucy, J. (1996) The scope of linguistic relativity: an analysis and review of empirical research. In Gumperz and Levinson (eds). *Rethinking linguistic relativity*. New York: Cambridge University Press. pp. 37-69.

Luke, A. et al. (2001) 'Making community texts objects of study'. In: H. Fehring and P. Green (eds) *Critical Literacy*. Delaware: International Reading Association.

Malinowski, B. (1923) 'The Problem of Meaning in Primitive Languages'. In: C.K. Ogden and I.A. Richards (eds) *The Meaning of Meaning*. New York: Harcourt, Brace, and World Inc. pp. 296-336.

Maybin, J. (2001) 'Language, Struggle and Voice'. In: M. Wetherell et al. (eds) *Discourse Theory and Practice*. London, Thousand Oaks, New Delhi: Sage.

Meijer, M. (1996) *In tekst gevat. Inleiding tot een kritiek van representatie.* Amsterdam: Amsterdam University Press.

Michael, L. (2002) Reformulating the Sapir-Whorf Hypothesis: Discourse, Interaction, and Distributed Cognition. In: *Texas Linguistic Forum* 45, pp. 107-116. Proceedings of the Tenth Annual Symposium about Language and Society, Austin.

Morgan, C. and Cain, A. (2000) *Foreign Language and Culture Learning from a Dialogic Perspective.* Clevedon: Multilingual Matters.

Neuner, G. (1997) The role of sociocultural competence in foreign langauge teaching and learning. In: M. Byram, G. Zarate and G. Neuner (eds) *Socio-cultural competence in language learning and teaching.* Strasbourg; Council of Europe Publishing.

O'Regan, J. (2006) *The Text as a Critical Object: On Theorising Exegetic Procedure in Classroom-Based Critical Discourse Analysis.* Institute of Education, London. (Unpublished dissertation).

Pennycook, A. (1994) 'Incommensurable Discourses?'. *Applied Linguistics* Vol. 15-2, pp. 119-138.

Pennycook, A. (2001) *Critical applied linguistics: a critical introduction.* London: Lawrence Erlbaum Associates, Publishers.

Phipps, A. (2007) *Learning the Arts of Linguistic Survival.* Clevedon: Channel View Publications.

Phipps, A. and Gonzalez, M. (2004) *Modern Languages: Learning and Teaching in an Intercultural Field.* London: Sage.

Phipps, A. and Guilherme, M. (2004) *Critical Pedagogy: Political Approaches to Language and Intercultural Communication.* Clevedon: Multilingual Matters.

Pinto, D. (1990) *Interculturele communicatie: drie-stappenmethode voor het overbruggen en managen van cultuurverschillen.* Houten: Bohn Stafleu Van Loghum.

Quist, G. et al. (2006) *Intensive Dutch course.* Abingdon, New York: Routledge.

Quist, G. (2013) 'Cosmopolitan Imaginings: creativity and responsibility in the language classroom'. In: J. Fenoulhet and C. Ros i Solé (guest eds), *Language and Intercultural Communication*, 13 (3), pp. 330-342.

Rampton, B. (1995) *Crossing: language and ethnicity among adolescents.* London: Longman.

Reddy, D.S. (2009) 'The Predicaments of Ethnography in Collaboration.' In: Faubion, J.D. and Marcus, G.E. (eds) *Fieldwork is not what it used to be.* Ithaca and London: Cornell University Press.

Risager, K. (2006) *Language and Culture: Global Flows and Local Complexity.* Clevedon: Multilingual Matters.

Risager, K. (2007) *Language and Culture Pedagogy: From a national to a Transnational Paradigm.* Clevedon: Multilingual Matters.

Roberts, C. et al. (2001) *Language Learners as Ethnographers*. Clevedon: Multilingual Matters Ltd.

Robbins Committee of Higher Education (1963) *Higher Education Report of the Committee appointed by the Prime Minister under the Chairmanship of Lord Robbins 1961-1963*. London: HMSO.

Ros i Solé, C. and Fenoulhet, J. (2013) 'Introduction: Romanticising language learning: beyond instrumentalism'. In: J. Fenoulhet and C. Ros i Solé (guest eds), *Language and Intercultural Communication*, 13 (3), pp. 257-265.

Ros i Solé, C. (2013) 'Cosmopolitan speakers and the new cultural order'. In: *The Language Learning Journal, 41, 3*.

Rossum, M. and Vismans, R. (2006) 'Trading culture, teaching culture: the role of the Dutch language tutor in the acquisition of intercultural skills at beginner's level'. *Dutch Crossing. A journal of Low Countries Studies*. 30-1 pp. 143-174.

Saussure, F. (1973) Extract from 'Course in General Linguistics', reprinted in: *Readings for Applied Linguistics: The Edinburgh Course in Applied Linguistics Volume 1*, Allen, J.P.B. and Pit Corder, S (eds), Oxford: Oxford University Press, p. 11.

Scott, D. et al. (1992) *Language Teaching in Higher Education*. Coventry: University of Warwick, Centre for Educational Development, Appraisal and Research (CEDAR reports 8).

Searle, J.R. (1969) *Speech Acts*. Cambridge: Cambridge University Press.

Sercu, L. et al. (2005) *Foreign Language Teachers and Intercultural Competence*. Clevedon: Multilingual Matters.

Shafak, E. (2011) *The Happiness of Blond People: A Personal Meditation on the Dangers of Identity*. (Penguin Special). ePub eBook.

Shannon, C. and Weaver, W. (1949) *A Mathematical Model of Communication*. Urbana: University of Illinois Press.

Shetter W. (2002) *The Netherlands. The Dutch way of organising a society and its setting* (2nd ed.). Utrecht: Nederlands Centrum Buitenlanders.

Snoek, K. (2000) *Nederland leren kennen* (3rd ed.). Groningen: Noordhoff Uitgevers B.V.

Starkey, H. (1999) Foreign language teaching to adults: Implicit and explicit political education. *Oxford Review of Education*, 25 (1-2).

Starkey, H. (2010) 'Language Learning for Human Rights and Democratic Citizenship'. In J. Fenoulhet and C. Ros i Solé (eds) *Mobility and Localisation in Language Learning*. Bern: Peter Lang.

Steehouder, M. et al. (1979, 2006) *Leren communiceren*. 5e druk Groningen: Noordhoff Uitgevers.

Stougaard-Nielsen, J. (2010) 'Danishness, Cosmopolitanism and Democratic Citizenship in Danish Language-Learning Materials'. In: J. Fenoulhet and C. Ros i Solé (eds) *Mobility and Localisation in Language Learning*. Bern: Peter Lang.

Street, B.V. (1993) 'Culture is a Verb: Anthropological Aspects of language and cultural process.' In: *Language and Culture*, Graddol, D., Thompson, L., Byram, M. (eds), Clevedon: BAAL and Multilingual Matters, pp. 23-43.

Trim, J.L.M. (1997) Preface Byram, M. and Zarate, G. *Sociocultural competence in language learning and teaching.* Strasbourg: Council of Europe Publishing.

Turner, G. (1992) *British Cultural Studies: an introduction.* London and New York: Routledge, (first published in 1990 by Unwin Hyman Inc.).

Van Baalen, C. (2003) 'Crosscultureel taalonderwijs'. In: Van Baalen et al. *Cultuur in taal.* Utrecht: Nederlands Centrum Buitenlanders.

Van den Toorn-Schutte, J. (1997) *'Hoe maakt u het? De Nederlandse taal in haar culturele context.'* Baarn: Auctor.

Van Dijk, T.A. (1993) 'Principles of critical discourse analysis', *Discourse and Society,* vol. 4, pp. 249-283.

Van Ek, J.A. (1977) *The Threshold Level for Modern Language Learning in Schools (with contributions by L.G. Alexander).* Harlow: Longman [for the] Council of Europe.

Van Ek, J.A. and Trim J.L.M. (1991) *Threshold level 1990; a revised and extended version of the Threshold Level by J.A. Van Ek.* Strassbourg: Council of Europe Press.

Van Kalsbeek, A. (2003) 'Taal en cultuur of cultuur en taal? In: Van Baalen et al. *Cultuur in taal.* Utrecht: Nederlands Centrum Buitenlanders.

Verluyten, P. (2000) *Intercultural Communication in Business and Organisations.* Leuven: Acco.

Vertovec, S. (2009) *Transnationalism.* Abingdon: Routledge.

Verwoert, J. (2006) *Bas Jan Ader: In Search of the Miraculous.* Afterall Books.

Vološinov, V.N. (1973, 1996) *Marxism and the Philosophy of Language.* Cambridge, Massachusetts, London: Harvard University Press, 6th printing.

Wallace, C. (1992) 'Critical Literacy Awareness in the EFL classroom', In: Fairclough, N. (ed.) *Critical Language Awareness.* Harlow: Longman Group UK Limited, 59-93.

Wallace, C. (2003) *Critical Reading in Language Education.* Basingstoke, New York: Palgrave MacMillan.

Wells, G. (1991) 'Apprenticeship in literacy'. In: C. Walsh (ed) *Literacy as Praxis: Culture, Language and Pedagogy.* Norwood, New Jersey: Ablex.

Wenger, E. (1999) *Communities of Practice: Learning, Meaning and Identity.* Cambridge: Cambridge University Press.

Wetherell, M. (2001) 'Culture and Social Relations: Editor's Introduction.' In: Wetherell, M., Taylor, S. and Yates, S.J. (eds) *Discourse Theory and Practice.* London: Sage.

White, C., and Boucke, L. (2006) *The Undutchables: an observation of the Netherlands, its culture and its inhabitants* (5th ed.).White-Boucke Publishing.

Whorf, B.J. (1966) 'Science and Linguistics' In: J.B. Carroll (ed) *Language, Thought and Reality: selected writings of Benjamin Lee Whorf.* Cambridge Massachusetts: M.I.T. Press, 1956, second paperback printing.

Widdowson, H.G. (1979) *Explorations in Applied Linguistics.* Oxford: OUP.

Widdowson, H, (1983) 'New starts and different kinds of failures'. In: Freeman, A., Pringle, I., and Yalden, J. (eds) *Learning to Write: First Language/Second Language.* London and New York: Longman.

Wierzbicka, A. (1997) *Understanding Cultures Through Their Key Words.* New York: Oxford University Press.

Wilkins, D. 1976 *Notional syllabuses.* Oxford: OUP.

Willems, G.M. (1994) 'FL Conversational Skills in Tertiary Education: a socio-cultural and autonomous approach'. In: *Language, Culture and Curriculum,* 7 (3).

Williams, R. (1961) *The Long Revolution.* London: Chatto & Windus.

Williams, R. (1976, 1983) *Keywords - A vocabulary of culture and society.* London: Fontana Press, Harper Collins Publishers.

Worton, M. (2009) *Review of Modern Foreign Languages in higher education in England.* Higher Education Funding Council for England.

Wright, S. (1998) 'The Politicization of Culture'. In *Anthropology Today.* 14(1), pp. 7-15.

Articles

Hanssen, H.(1999) 'Huwbare mannen gezocht'. In: *Men's Health,* (2) 6, pp. 46-50

Wytzes. L. (1999) 'De man als dinosaurus'. *De Volkskrant.* 23-10-1999

Appendix: Marriageable men wanted

Translation of: 60,000 Career Women are Hunting,
Men's Health, 1999, 2(6)

They earn money like water and have everything to their heart's desire, except a man. More and more well-educated women between 35 and 54 are starting to panic because a potential father for their child has not yet turned up. They are sometimes cynical, often hard and always demanding.

Destroying men, they call it. Going out, dancing, drinking, flirting with only one aim: to humiliate the male ego. 'They' are Karin (37) and her three friends. Great, well dressed girls they are, with the gift of the gab and they have really made it. Designer clothes, roof garden, snazzy set of wheels under their cellulite-free trained buttocks, make-up from Clarins en Roc, fridge full with salmon and champagne and of course that job with challenging prospects ....they are all in their own way equally successful and ...... equally single. Well, the girls aren't missing out, you know. Dorien, 34 – top job at a bank, has had a relationship with a married bloke for some years. Jose, 36 manager of a hotel in Utrecht, has an impossible relationship with some vague painter with an alcohol problem. Suzanne, 42, art director with an expensive flat on one of the canals, seeks her pleasure in adventures with young men ('nothing older than 25, after that they are past their sell-by date'). She doesn't want to consider men of her own age. Since her great love (cliche, cliche) swopped her two years ago for a young thing, she seems to want to take revenge on every man of 35 plus. When the girls go out, she is the one who shouts 'Come, tonight we're going to destroy men!', which has become a battle cry in their little group. Provoking, flirting, bit of snogging and just when he thinks he has got it in the bag; drop him. Much more than that they don't get around to. A real relationship? No, these women don't believe in that anymore. Al least, that is what they say.

Cold shivers were running down my spine when Karin, a friend of me, told me a while ago about these escapades with her group of friends. Was this the start of a new kind of woman? Or was this just the bawdy behaviour of a few friends who in this way settle the account of a series of frustrated relationships? I recognised this 'cockteasing', and who doesn't? What man has not spent evenings with women investing a small fortune in attentiveness, humour and dinners and with zero point zero (sexual) gain? Nice game for a 19 year-old girl trying to discover the rules of sexual conduct, but do you still do that when you are 35 plus? Destroying men.... it sounded so hopelessly frustrated, so desperate, so calculated as well. During the research for this article I discovered that Karin and her friends were not the only women who were keeping themselves occupied with this 'sport'. In Nijmegen I spoke with Sybille Labrijn, a 35-year old psychologist who has carried out exhaustive research into relationship problems of the successful woman. In the past four years she conducted hundreds of therapeutic conversations with well educated women who have problems finding a partner. She published her insights in *Love is the only thing I need now* - a newly published book which unveils an honest portait of this generation of women.

Even though she never heard of the term 'destroying men', Sybille Labrijn does recognise the behaviour which the terms describes. 'Some women, especially when they have been on their own for a while or have had several failed relationships, want to armour themselves against new disappointments and being hurt again. They rather hurt others than that they have to suffer more pain in love themselves. Some hide behind an attitude of superiority and treat men with a certain air of contempt: 'We have more social skills, have a higher E.Q. (Emotional Quotient) and are in fact more dazzling than men'. During therapy I challenge them with questions such as 'What makes you think that? Does it help you to think like that?' Do you realise that by this kind of attitude you form a barrier to the possibility of having an equal relationship and is that what you want? And where does that idea come from?"

Yes, indeed. Where does that idea come from? To answer those questions we need to go back to the summer of 1986. In the States that year a statistical report was published (the Bennett-Bloom-Craig study) stating that well educated women of 35 years and older find it harder and harder to find a suitable partner. 'A woman over 40 has a higher statistical chance of dying through a terrorist attack than to marry an parner of equal standing,' Newsweek summarised the findings of the study in an oft quoted sentence which caused an uncomfortable feeling. In the Netherlands filmmaker Marijke Jongbloed (43, well-educated, living with a partner) was intrigued by this phenomenon. Armoured with her camera she went to New York, the city where it is said that for every man there are 5 single women. In her documentary *Fatal Reaction New York*, which came out in 1996, the desperately seeking successful woman became personified in the form of Laura Slutsky. With aching precision the 45 year old casting director was followed closely on her odyssey along bookshelves full of self-help books with titles such as '*If I'm so wonderful, why am I still single?*', courses in how to get a man, auctions where the highest bidder can win an evening out with a man and countless visits to psychiatrist and fitness-clubs. 'This situation is God's cruel joke,' Slutsky says at a certain moment. 'When I was twenty I had enough egg-cells, but then I didn't know myself enough to find the right man with whom to have children. And now that I am over forty and have worked hard on my mental and physical aerobics and know who I am, my biological clock has almost finished ticking - I have got only 6 egg-cells left! But the men I meet now are damaged, B-choice. That is the price I've paid. I am angry! I would warn my daughter.'

And when she unexpectedly gets a boyfriend, she confronts him in conversations with such an aggressive tone that he recoils. She then uses the shoulder of a psychiatrist to cry on. He confronts her with herself: 'Laura, you are successful. You have developed certain strategies to become successful. Confrontational behaviour and responding critically are part of that; you don't let go easily. This way a pattern of attack and defends has developed in your relationship. You attack, he defends and the other way round. You become ensnared in a constant battle. That doesn't work in friendly relationships. *Your game is power. You might win the battle, but you I'll lose the war.*'

Apart from the toe curling pleasure the film affords, Marijke Jongbloed's most important achievement is that she showed us that the single career woman is a universal phenomenon. The woman from Amsterdam also filmed well-off single women in Bombay and Singapore and a programme on Moscow is being planned. Jongbloed would have liked to direct her camera with the same surgical precision on to the arena of Dutch single women, but she didn't find a suitable woman. Even though you would imagine there is no shortage of candidates: according to the CBS our country has 60,000 women between 35 and 54 without a partner (see inset page 48).

The career-woman: instructions for use

What do you do when you get trapped in a relationship with a career woman seasoned in the top of the business world? Let's look at the way in which psychologist Sybille Labrijn analyses these women. The first thing she looks at is family history. Labrijn: 'Of course your childhood experiences do not determine everything, but through your upbringing you get a blueprint for the way you handle relationships in years to come. During the 60ies and 70ies, the era in which this generation of women has grown up, the role of the father was still quite traditional. That means: dad was often not home or had little time. Being neglected by dad invites rebellion; she ends up mistrusting and rejecting her father. And to compensate for his absence you frequently see that women will identify themselves with masculinity. Dad did not give them what was needed? Well, they'll take care of it themselves. That way they build up a strong, male ego-identity by focusing on achievements. But the male identity is nothing more than a thin protective layer, an armour against the pain caused by the rejection of their father which resulted in their feelings of self-worth being undermined'.

This 'armed Amazon', a term that Labrijn borrowed from psychologist Linda Leonard, possesses the toughness to succeed but her protective layer cuts her off from her soft side, her creativity, her ability to take on relationships on equal terms, Labrijn says in her book.

When Labrijn focuses on the way these women conduct social relationships, it appears they have an inability to show their dependent side. 'Being able to be dependent is the current taboo of the successful single woman,' Labrijn states. 'These women have told themselves not to be as dependent as their mothers. But what should they do? If they received little recognition from their fathers, they can react like: 'I don't need any recognition, I can do everything myself, I won't ask anyone for advice. I rather learn from my own mistakes then that I do something which someone else told me to do.' Look, in a good relationship you can be flexible in your attitude; sometimes you are the weaker one, sometimes the stronger one. But these what I call 'counter-dependent' women, are stuck in their attitude of 'I need to be in control, and I don't want to lean on any one'. To be contra-dependent is to be dependent on being independent. And they cannot give up that attitude of independence, not even temporarily.'

In her therapy sessions, well-educated clients are trained in alternative behaviour. Labrijn: I check with my clients what kind of behaviour they like to change. Frequently these are forms of behaviour they don't feel comfortable with. As far as the area of counter-dependency is concerned this can mean: not debating exclusively the last political developments with men; not always being quick of the mark and trying to win one over their partner. In itself that might be O.K., but not when this has become an automatic pattern of behaviour, then it's not a choice anymore and forms a barrier to intimacy. And conversely, when women are too dependent we can practise behavioural patterns such as not to worry about questions like 'what does he really think of me?', but instead to sit back and ask 'What do I actually think of him?".

It might be clear: 'an armed Amazon' is a woman who needs instructions for use. Men who fall in love with her will have to learn to 'read' her. Apart from that men need to be crystal clear themselves. Labrijn give a few practical tips: 'Be as direct as you can about what you don't like and even more importantly: be also clear about what you do want. Women are still too much the architects of the relationship. And men are inclined to withdraw if they feel a woman wants too much. Sort out together what feels right and what doesn't in the relationship, even if you haven't got ready-made answers. And stick to your own convictions. If you notice a woman is turning a conversation into a competition of who is wittiest, don't go along with it. If you initiate a more personal topic she is forced to respond to that. And when a woman is too dependent you should be true to yourself too. Don't take on any responsibilities, but pass them back to her. Be aware of your own limits and make these explicit to her. Besides, men can also be counter-dependent, too romantic, not critical enough or perhaps too critical. That influences relationships. So men get the same advice: look at yourself'.

The results of her therapeutic sessions fall occasionally on the doormat in the shape of birth or marriage announcements. 'That's really nice', Labrijn smiles. In the late 80ies she became interested in this topic because she - and a lot of her friends and colleagues - didn't seem to be able to develop lasting relationships. Two months ago she herself sent out a huge number of birth announcements to celebrate the arrival of her first son Tijmen. 'He is a real example of Men's Health,' she beams. 'My relationship has been going really well for the past five years, that is really lovely. But we had to learn, especially women of my genera-tion. We, women of 30 years and older, belong to the 'awareness' generation. This phase had to be experienced, but there was a sense of rebelling against men and there was some contempt. During the second feminist wave men were held individually responsible for all kinds of social injustice, for inequalities. That encouraged the attitude of contempt for men, and our generation does have that problem. I think now the time is right for a different attitude.

Inset:

This is how to recognise a desperada

There are places where you have to be careful to put an arm over the shoulder of a woman. Because when you take your arm away after 10 minutes or so, there's a good chance you're wearing a wedding ring. A little exaggerated of course, but the army of well-educated women looking for a Perfect Partner, contains many desperate women of 30+. And some of these will go a whole lot further than a joke with a wed-ding ring. You won't be the first one who has been 'accidently' chosen to be a father. Watch out for these desperadas. How do you recognise them? Count the points and read the result below.

- She is between 35 and 45, has a busy well-paid job and lives in a city (5)
- She doesn't have children, but she has sorted out her childcare arrangements (25)
- She can tell you all about the last episodes of ER, Friends, and Ally McBeal (8)
- She quotes from 'The Diary of Bridget Jones, 59 kilo'. In this hilarious best seller British author Helen Fielding portrays a desperate single successful woman. (10)
- She has had a difficult relationship with her father. (8)
- She has a few close friends who she sees regularly in addition she has an exten-sive social network (8)
- She likes to keep in touch with ex-boyfriends (15)
- 7 out of every 10 sentences she speaks start with one the following words: inde-pendence, space or respect (20)

- She looks down on lower educated women and she likes to tell jokes about dumb blondes (15)
- When asked to describe her ideal partner she won't stop talking for at least 15 minutes (20)
- She has read one of the following books: Alice K's Guide to the life of Caroline Knapp, Cattle market by Laura Zigman, The trouble with Single Women, Yvonne Roberts and Single Girl's Diary by Kate Morris. Each title scores 10 points.

Score

0-60   This woman has a positive attitude to life
60-120   Operate with caution!
120-180   You do like 'beschuit met muisjes' don't you?

Translation by Gerdi Quist

Index